Sources Of
American Spirituality

Bartolomé de las Casas

THE ONLY WAY

Edited by Helen Rand Parish,
Translated by Francis Patrick Sullivan, S.J.

PAULIST PRESS
New York ◊ Mahwah, N.J.

Book design by Theresa M. Sparacio.

Library of Congress Cataloging-in-Publication Data

Casas, Bartolomé de las, 1474–1566.
  [De unico vocationis. English]
  The only way: a new restored version/Bartolomé de las Casas; edited by Helen Rand Parish; translated by Francis Patrick Sullivan
      p. cm.—(Sources of American spirituality)
  Translation of: De unico vocationis.
  Includes bibliographical references and index.
  ISBN 0-8091-0367-2
  1. Evangelistic work—Early works to 1800. 2. Spirituality—Early works to 1800. I. Parish, Helen Rand. II. Sullivan, Francis, 1929–   . III. Title.
IV. Series.
BV3790.C3513   1991
266'.0089'97—dc20   91-32835
                                                                                CIP

Published by Paulist Press
997 Macarthur Boulevard
Mahwah, New Jersey 07430

Printed and bound in the United States of America

CONTENTS

GENERAL INTRODUCTION

The commemoration of the Columbian Quincentennial has riveted the attention of many on the thorny questions of justice that surrounded the European penetration of the New World. Some, like the National Council of Christian Churches, have suggested that the whole episode was so corrupt, so disastrous that the Fifth Centenary should be a time for mourning and repentance. Others have seen the event as a time to affirm the good things that the colonization wrought and to cast off effete scruples about the wrongs done by Europeans. In fact the reality of what happened five centuries ago is complex and demands our careful reevaluation.

The encounter of the Old and New Worlds had a great significance for the history of the world, as all of us have learned from the time we were old enough to read. But the encounter was more than just a major event in the history of exploration, conquest, conflict, and disenfranchisement. It was also a great event in the history of the human spirit, and that is precisely why this volume is such a timely and important contribution to a series on the history of spirituality in America.

For unlike the pundits of today, who from a distance of half a millenium have commented prodigiously on the meeting of the two worlds, Bartolomé de las Casas was there. A friend of the Columbus family, part of the second wave of Spanish colonization, Las Casas saw first hand the pristine beauty of the New World. He dreamed of a peaceful New World, one in which Spaniards and Indians could live together in harmony.

But he also saw the horror of exploitation, violence, and riot that destroyed the integrity of the native cultures and decimated the Indians. He saw how the insatiable desire for gold and financial gain ruined people, turned men into monsters, and made them capable of great evil.

He saw, he listened. And he learned that he could no longer be a good person in a bad system. He had tried doing this in Haiti and in Cuba, operating his plantations with his well-cared-for Indians. But he

1

realized that the whole situation was questionable. The preaching of the first Dominicans in Haiti, who denounced the encomienda system of forced labor, aggravated his doubts. Then came the horrors he witnessed in Cuba, where he saw a human paradise become a hell on earth in a few short months. In 1514 he awoke to his life's mission: he knew that he had to change the entire system—get rid of the encomienda, get rid of slavery, get rid of the lies about the Indians—and create a new relationship with the New World.

The drama of the spiritual history of the New World has, in Las Casas' *The Only Way,* a brilliant first act. The scintillating new translation by Francis Sullivan brings out the struggle, the anguish, and the compassion of one of the greatest advocates of human rights the hemisphere has ever known. The context for all of this is masterfully recreated by Helen Rand Parish in her Introduction and Addenda which amount to a new biography of Las Casas. Together they have attempted to get back to the original Las Casas argument, and have produced what they aptly call a "restored version." It is a unique presentation in English of a work that, by any measure, ranks among the classics of spiritual vision and strength in the history of the Americas. This book presents a clear and accessible picture of an often controverted past. We will do well to ponder that picture long and hard as we face the paradoxes and dilemmas of our past and present as Americans.

John Farina

PREFACE

Bartolomé de las Casas' *The Only Way* is a famous and influential work of New World spirituality. Yet, paradoxically, it remains unread or misunderstood. Its *author* has been famous for more than four centuries as the Defender of the Indians during the Spanish conquest. Its *ideas* have influenced mission theory and practice for centuries throughout the world—from Rome to Guatemala, to Florida, to Peru, to the Philippines, to Japan, to Paraguay, to California, and to much of present-day Latin America.[1] But *the work* itself has been relatively inaccessible. In colonial days, it circulated mostly in two short published summaries, and, occasionally, in handwritten copies of a huge, incomplete Latin treatise. One such copy has survived—a late version, recast by Las Casas himself in a messed-up form almost incomprehensible to the modern reader. This difficult text, published in our time, has led to a few serious studies.[2] But the major significance of the book has been missed because it is closely bound up with events of Las Casas' life that have just recently been discovered.

---

[1] For contemporary and posthumous influences, see the Postscript to our Introduction; for the general theme and Las Casas' own Guatemalan mission, see note 3 to this Preface.

[2] Two theses analyze the ideas: Enrique Ruiz, "Bartolomé de las Casas y la justicia en las Indias—De único . . . ," *Ciencia Tomista* 101 (1974), 351–410, and Jesús Angel Barreda, *Ideología y pastoral misionera en Bartolomé de las Casas, O.P.*, Madrid, 1981. One article attempts to fix the date: Isacio Pérez, "Sobre la fecha y el lugar de redacción del 'primer libro' de Fray Bartolomé de las Casas: 'De único . . .'," *Ciencia Tomista* 105 (1978), 125–43—see our App. I.A, sects. 1 and 2. A symposium discusses Las Casas as prophet and missiologist: Antonio Larios Ramos, "Evangelización y combate por la justicia. Colloquio de Toulouse (25–28 Oct. 1984) sobre Bartolomé de las Casas," *Communio* 18 (1985): 127–52. Introductions to the second ed. of "The Only Way" by Paulino Castañeda and Antonio García discuss the ideology and content of the work. Most comprehensive is still Lewis Hanke's Intro. to first ed. (See below, note 3 and related text.)

The full truth about Las Casas' first book, *The Only Way to Draw All People to a Living Faith* (referred to as *The Only Way*), is that it was a political as well as a religious work. Its "peaceful conversion" ideas derived originally from his most soul-searing early years: his roles both as a white shaman trying to maintain nonviolence in the bloodstained conquest of Cuba, and as a horrified provisioner watching the rapid decimation of that island at the start of the colonial gold rush. Those intense personal experiences, from 1512 to 1514, convinced Las Casas that God had called him to plead for the Indians, a spiritual crisis misinterpreted by many of his biographers.

Further, and this is totally unknown, Las Casas wrote *The Only Way* after another spiritual impasse, which he broke by two brilliant visits to the most feared Indian guerrilla chieftain in the Antilles—his second daring demonstration of the power of peaceful evangelization over warfare. Once written, *The Only Way* became the actual tool for Bartolomé de las Casas' central achievements. It was the basis, point by point, of the great papal encyclical *Sublimis Deus,* proclaiming the rationality and liberty of the Indians and the peaceful way to convert them. It was the foundation of Las Casas' greatest legislative success: Charles V's epochal New Laws for the Indies and the Indians.

When that reform was breached, Las Casas had to face the possible ruin of all his work for the Indians. In this crisis of soul, which lasted the rest of his life, *The Only Way* furnished the doctrine and the material that he would use again and again to set up barriers against the forces of reaction. It was during this dangerous final period that Las Casas himself, for strategic purposes, consciously mutilated and disfigured the work into the late version that has come down to us.

I must pause here to acknowledge my debt to those who have previously tried to make Las Casas' *The Only Way* available to the modern world. A half-century ago, in 1942, the Fondo de Cultura Económica in Mexico City brought out the first edition of *Del único modo:* a transcription by Augustín Millares Carlo of the surviving Latin manuscript, with a Spanish translation by Antenógenes Santamaría, and Lewis Hanke's classic Introduction.[3] Without their work,

---

[3] Hanke's pioneer essay (reissued as a chapter in his *La lucha por la justicia en la conquista de América,* Buenos Aires, 1949, 184–205) reviews Spanish debates on evangelization and force, Las Casas' doctrine in the treatise and his mission experiment in the Guatemalan "Land of War," other attempts at peaceful conversion, and the eventual fate of the renamed Vera Paz (True Peace) mission. Marcel Bataillon's "La Vera Paz," original article in 1951, reprinted in his *Etudes sur Bartolomé de las Casas* (Paris, 1965), 137–202, adds docs. and chronology on the mission. And André Saint-Lu's *La Vera Paz,*

this volume would not have been possible. I also want to express my gratitude to Harold E. Weidman, S.J., an accomplished Latinist and collaborator of mine on previous projects, who prepared at my request a complete literal English version of the entire Oaxaca manuscript (chapters 5, 6, and 7 of Part I). And my thanks to Clement J. McNaspy, S.J., whose literary labors on Weidman's rendition of those chapters exposed an unreadable and deadly dull classroom text—and showed me that Las Casas' spiritual masterpiece had to be restored to the form and fire that had once moved the consciences of a pope and an emperor.

Accordingly, I entrusted the difficult task of restoring and retranslating *The Only Way* to the one person best qualified to carry it out. Francis Patrick Sullivan, S.J., a poet, theologian, and translator of the Psalms, had already translated a thousand of Bartolomé de las Casas' most important and impassioned pages, and was the obvious—the only—choice. In readings from his versions of Las Casas' *Twenty Reasons* (against forced labor) and *The Decimation of the Indians* (against the atrocities of the conquest), Sullivan has deeply moved large audiences and recaptured the voice of Las Casas for our age.[4] In *The Only Way,* Sullivan focuses on the depths and nuances of Las Casas' meaning, not on the scholastic style or syntactical mannerisms of his Latin. The result is a luminous English version—with the citations banished to the footnotes—that allows Las Casas to make a clear and forceful case.

Textual Appendices explain fully how Sullivan and I established the text of the restoration. First, I assemble the documentary evidence for the shape and contents of the three versions—the first two missing, the third an oversized fragment—by citing data from manuscripts in

---

esprit evangélique et colonisation (Paris, 1968) massively expands this account with subsequent history.

A second edition of the surviving text—*De unico vocationis modo,* edited by Paulino Castañeda Delgado and Antonio García Moral—appeared in Madrid in 1990 as vol. 2 of Las Casas' *Obras completas.* An impressive technical work, it lacks the historical sweep of the Hanke–Millares Carlo volume, focusing rather on Las Casas' impeccable scholastic method and the superior clarity of his argument. (See App. III.A, sect. 2, last par.)

[4] Francis Patrick Sullivan's English translations include *Las Casas' Tracts for the Indians,* vol. 1, *For New Laws,* to be published by Sheed & Ward in 1992; and *Las Casas' Life of Columbus,* to be published by the University of California Press in 1992. He read from *Las Casas' Tracts* at the Las Casas Quincentennial Symposium, Berkeley, Jan. 21, 1985, and the LASA XIV Congress, New Orleans, March 17, 1988. Sullivan served seven years as consultant and translator of the psalms for ICEL, the International Commission on English in the Liturgy.

Madrid, Paris, and Rome, from ancient chronicles, and from internal references in the work itself. Next, Sullivan translates the two contemporary summaries of the book. And lastly, a chart shows in detail how we stripped away most (but not all) of the late additions, and partially rebuilt the missing portions with bits from Las Casas' other works, to approximate the powerful central version.

That is why we present *The Only Way* in a restored version with a biographical Introduction on "Las Casas' Spirituality: The Three Crises"—the first treatment of the topic, based on new and unpublished material from my forthcoming definitive biography and other books.[5] I had to tell the story behind *The Only Way* so that readers could understand its multiple origins, its composition and recasting for specific goals at the Spanish court, its remarkable results and final impact. The full background must wait for another volume: the economic, military, and religious forces at work in Europe; international rivalries during the era of exploration; and the rise of new American civilizations with problems that are festering even today. But in the Introduction to this book, history buffs will glimpse the larger picture —in the Preamble, in brief interludes throughout the narrative, and in a Postscript on the contemporary and posthumous influence of Las Casas' writings. The theologically inclined will want to study the Addendum on Las Casas' "Portrait of Fray Pedro de Córdoba" and the conflicting missionary spiritualities of the times; also of interest will be the Addendum on "Las Casas' Prophetic Call," which accompanies his key texts with a bibliographical note on current definitions of him as a prophet. Latin-Americanists, somewhat cognizant of Las Casas' career, will appreciate the Addendum on "Las Casas' Condemnation of African Slavery," with the familiar confession and the unfamiliar denunciation as well as a précis of past and forthcoming scholarship on an old slander. And interested scholars can turn directly to the textual Appendices to verify how we have reconstituted a coherent text of *The Only Way* after 450 years.

But the legendary General Reader, and perhaps many specialists as well, may prefer to read this book in the order in which we have

---

[5] Helen Rand Parish's definitive biography, *Las Casas: The Untold Story,* is to be published by the University of California Press in 1992. Her books on Las Casas include: with Henry R. Wagner, *The Life and Writings of Bartolomé de las Casas,* Albuquerque, 1967 (hereafter Wagner–Parish); *Las Casas as a Bishop,* Washington, 1980; and two works in press—*The Royal File* (Library of Congress); and, with paleography by Harold E. Weidman, *Las Casas en México* (Fondo de Cultura Económica)—both due to appear in late 1992. Parish directs Las Casas studies at the Graduate Theological Union, Berkeley.

arranged it: meeting first the rediscovered Las Casas himself in his spiritual crises, then hearing his authentic voice expound his doctrine of peaceful conversion and respect for native cultures. For all these readers, I now raise the curtain on what Las Casas himself always considered the greatest event in human history—the Discovery of a New World.

Helen Rand Parish
Berkeley, Palm Sunday, 1990

INTRODUCTION:
LAS CASAS' SPIRITUALITY—
THE THREE CRISES

PREAMBLE

On January 2, 1492, King Ferdinand and Queen Isabella rode out from their encampment of Santa Fe at the head of fifty thousand soldiers, the grand cardinal of Spain riding beside them. The last Moorish king, Boabdil, with only fifty horsemen, rode out from besieged Granada to meet them, dismounting by the banks of the Genil to hand Ferdinand the keys to the citadel. Then the vanguard of the Christian army passed through the city gates, the cardinal raised a silver cross and a herald hoisted the banner of Castile atop the vermilion towers—and the reconquest of Spain from the Moors was accomplished after eight centuries. It had cost Their Catholic Majesties ten years and one million silver ducats.

Three months later, on April 17, 1492, at the same camp of Santa Fe, Ferdinand and Isabella signed a contract with Christopher Columbus, naming him and his heirs admiral of the ocean sea on all the lands and continents he might discover or acquire, appointing him viceroy and governor "of all the aforesaid lands and continents" and granting him one-tenth of all precious stones, gold, silver, spices, or other articles of trade he might obtain "by purchase, barter or conquest," plus further grandiose commercial privileges. The royal promises were wildly extravagant, but no more so than Columbus' promise to open a new route to the wealth of Cathay, which had dazzled Marco Polo.

The connection between the two events was far more than symbolic. The Spanish monarchs would see the New World through a filter of war with the Moors: a complex mixture of religion, heroic discovery, gold, and the self-justified conquest of infidels, a sort of *jihad,* or Holy War.

9

The Borgia pope, Alexander VI, would see the New World through a similar filter. For a century popes had granted Christian kings the right to attack and conquer the territory of the infidels in the Holy Land and Africa. And in 1493 the Bulls of Donation gave the Catholic kings similar rights over the newly discovered lands, along with exhortations to convert the natives.

For Church and State were not separate in those days, but intertwined, with the Spanish State definitely on top. During the reconquest, and even more in the New World found for Spain by Columbus —"por Castilla y por León, nuevo mundo halló Colón"—the so-called Patronato gave the Spanish kings power to name bishops and archbishops, delimit dioceses, and collect tithes. Ecclesiastics of all ranks served in every phase of Spanish administration.

And war, cruel beyond our modern imagining, was a standard business all over Europe during the period of discovery and settlement. The sack of Rome by the mercenary troops of the Holy Roman Emperor Charles V—with the pope holed up for safety in Castel San Angelo—was a horror of unparalleled carnage, rape, looting, and destruction. (After all, the troops hadn't been paid.) So conquest, also cruel beyond our imagining, was an accepted fact all over the New World. Ferdinand, incredibly greedy and unchecked after the death of Isabella, never lost the dream of unlimited revenue from the Discovery—to be obtained by any means. Both Charles and Philip would continue to see the New World in terms of desperately needed revenue, from gold and from slavery.

And when Europeans, from Columbus on, met the natives, how would they see them? Again, through the Africa syndrome. Had not Pope Nicholas issued a categorical decree authorizing the enslavement of Africans? Didn't Francisco de Vitoria say that the African natives were better off as slaves to Christians than as free and pagan? Either Columbus himself or his brother Bartholomew or both seem to have been on the Portuguese-African slave coast, perhaps as mariners. So when the Discoverer did not find Cathay, he easily suggested a lucrative slave trade based on these gentle natives. Isabella, to her credit, said "No!" to the concept of universal, automatic slavery for these people. But then how would the conquerors be paid for the conquest? With Indian labor mining gold, Indian labor working Spanish farms—that was the only way to wealth.

So the conquerors and the first venturers saw the Indians as legitimate war prizes. These first newcomers were not settlers. They did not come to stay, but to get rich quickly, get out and go home to Spain as soon as possible. Even the Franciscan missionaries, from their revulsion at conditions in Europe—not only conditions of war, but also of depravity and irreligion—came with their minds formed by the Italian millenialist, Joachim of Floris, dreaming of converting docile natives who would happily serve the Spaniards.

So all groups saw the Indians not only through their own mental filter, but more concretely for the use they could make of them. The Spanish adventurers—whether they were the disinherited second sons of noble families, or more ordinary riffraff—saw the simple natives of the Antilles as inferior, not quite human: they didn't speak Spanish; they were not Catholic Christians; they didn't wear clothes. Even when conquistadors discovered and conquered obviously advanced civilizations, first in the Aztec and later in the Inca empires, they found new ways to call both inferior by dwelling on the supposed presence of dreadful sins—the Indians were idolaters, and what about cannibalism and sodomy (favorite charges against "barbarians").

In the century of discovery, there was one outstanding man, Bartolomé de las Casas, who saw the New World as it was: the land, the people, their initial beauty—and the resulting horror of conquest and fatal forced labor. And he made other people see it; he made other people do something about it. He never denied the marvel of the Discovery. He played an important role in Spain's colonial power structure. He saw a great Spanish civilization developing in the New World —but the Indian, the degraded remnant, was excluded. That was the bleeding underside of the tapestry. And he devoted his life to healing it.

1. A Prophetic Crisis in the New World

Bartolomé de las Casas caught the compelling vision of his whole life in vague form on a single day when he was only eight-and-a-half years old. It was Palm Sunday, the most solemn and emotionally moving day of Holy Week in his hometown of Seville. But this was Palm Sunday 1493, when the whole town was agog over the return of a crazy Genoese mariner who had just found new lands beyond the ocean sea—and there he was marching in the procession. The boy had to see it through a tightly packed crowd. The crowd witnessed such an amazing combination of elements: the confraternities in their costumes, carrying their statues and emblems, the palm branches—there was a palm branch on every balcony in town—and the solemn horror of the

hooded penitents flagellating themselves. (Then, as now, Seville celebrated Passion Sunday and Palm Sunday on the same day.) Here they
came, the prized sight of all: Christopher Columbus in black, his face
wind tanned, his eyes hooded; and with him a group of tall, naked,
bronze, lean Taino Indians; and his sailors (deloused for the occasion),
carrying brilliant red and green parrots, and Indian masks intricately
made with tiny shells, and beautiful artifacts of beaten gold plates.[6]

Little Bartolomé apparently did not get the good look he wanted,
but he had his father take him along to the inn where the Indians were
staying near the Arch of the Images in the St. Nicholas ward. The boy
saw them there—were they seven or nine?—he didn't count when he
could have. His merchant father, Pedro de las Casas, had gone to see
not the Indians but Columbus himself. Pedro, like all of Seville, was
caught up in the fever of the Discovery. And in the months that followed, several members of Bartolomé's family—his merchant father,
his uncle Francisco de Peñalosa as captain of the troops, and another
relative—all signed on to go back across the ocean sea with Columbus.
They were to go for five years as colonists in the great expedition of
some twelve hundred people on seventeen ships.[7]

Five years passed quickly for little Bartolomé who was getting his
Latin and his letters, perhaps at the cathedral school and under a distant relative, Prebendary Luis de Peñalosa.[8] For five years he waited for
the occasional letter from father to son. But mostly, the years were
spent remembering and going over the compelling vision of that day:
Holy Week, the Indians, the Discoverer, the New World beyond the
ocean sea, and the dark shadow cast on the whole vision by the flagel-
lant penitents.

In 1498 another event occurred, almost as compelling for young
Bartolomé as the first one. The merchant father, Pedro de las Casas,
came back bringing a companion for his teenage son: Juanico, a Taino
boy about Bartolomé's own age—an Indian slave given the father by

---

[6] On the crowds turning out to see Columbus as he crossed Spain, see Las Casas,
Historia de las Indias (hereafter cited as *Historia*), lib. 1, opening of cap. 78. [*N.B.* In
these notes, some of Las Casas' works are cited generically since they appear in different
editions. We prefer the superior Mexican edition of the *Historia* and the *Apologética*, but
cite them only by lib. and cap. for the benefit of those who use the handy Madrid
editions.]

[7] *Historia*, lib. 1, cap. 82, on the second voyage of Columbus. For the other family
member, see below, note 12.

[8] This is a plausible conjecture in Manuel Giménez Fernández' mostly unreliable
article on "La juventud en Sevilla de Bartolomé de las Casas," *Miscelánea de Estudios
dedicados al Doctor Fernando Ortiz* (Havana, 1956), 2:670–717.

the Discoverer himself—a boy for whose passage and rations the father had paid eight hundred maravedis.[9] What happened was the beginning of a lasting friendship between the two boys. Juanico was undoubtedly baptized at the cathedral. Young Bartolomé solemnly announced that he wanted to be a priest. And the merchant father, being lavish with the money he had made in the New World, decided to send his son to the best college, Salamanca, to study the canon law leading to the priesthood, with Juanico as his manservant. The two were together a short while at the school when the news came that Pedro de las Casas was going back to the Indies for good, and he had to take Juanico back with him. The boys parted, promising to meet again in the islands. Sure enough, the promise was fulfilled after the turn of the century, when young Bartolomé quit college and sailed across the ocean sea at the age of eighteen to help his father on the island of Hispaniola.[10]

And now on *la isla española* (the Spanish Isle), Hispaniola, that first compelling vision began to intensify for young Bartolomé, a teenager growing into early manhood. All his life he would remember the marvel of approaching the island coasts with their brilliant flowers and fragrant trees that one could smell from well offshore. And the landscapes were so different from the arid surfaces of Andalusia and even of Old Castile. His task on Hispaniola was to farm the land Columbus had given his father, with the help of nearby Indians whom Columbus had assigned. (Pedro the merchant, head of the clan, had settled in the capital, Santo Domingo.) In addition to running the plantation, young Las Casas tramped all over the island on the family provisions business, collecting supplies for the voyages of mainland discovery which set off and returned regularly from the port of Santo Domingo.[11]

The family also helped provision two military expeditions of Governor Ovando who arrived in 1502. The tragic massacre in late 1503 of the wise Queen Anacaona and leading chieftains of the island pro-

---

[9] On the entire incident, see Las Casas, *Opúsculos* (*BAE* 110) at 72a; and *Historia,* lib. 1, cap. 176, 4th par. Confirming documents are published in Vicente Rodríguez Valencia, "Isabel la Católica y la libertad de los indios de América: Devolución de los esclavos," (*Anthologica Annua,* 24–25, Rome, 1977–78), at 666–68, and 671–77, esp. on the repayment of costs to Pedro de Peñalosa [sic], by the Catholic Majesties, on May 20, 1500.

[10] The remaining information on Juanico's name, baptism, and relations with Las Casas in Spain and Hispaniola, and on young Las Casas' choice of the priesthood and early academic studies anticipates new data from unpublished documents in *Las Casas: The Untold Story.*

[11] Full details establishing that he was primarily a provisioner will be disclosed in *The Untold Story.*

voked an Indian uprising. They had been treacherously assembled for a great celebration. Young Bartolomé apparently served in the commissariat of a punitive expedition led by Captain Diego Velásquez who would become a good friend. In 1504, Bartolomé and his father and another relative certainly were provisioners in the second Higuey campaign and the capture of the remaining chieftain, Cotubanamá. For his part Bartolomé received his second Indian slave, one of the fugitives of the Anacaona massacre, and other family members were confirmed a decade later in Higuey encomiendas.

But as for young Bartolomé, he deplored all the killings, denounced them—especially that of Anacaona—and lost no opportunity to meet and make friends with Indian chieftains, even under these grisly circumstances. To be sure, the six kings and greater chiefs on Hispaniola had all died before or at the same time as Queen Anacaona, but he knew many of the surviving lesser chiefs. He was a horrified eyewitness to the atrocities of the second Higuey campaign and the capture of Cotubanamá; he evidently interceded to prevent the cruel impalement of the chieftain and stayed with his friend during a month-long journey on the provisions ship which took the captured chief back to Santo Domingo and a more "merciful" death by hanging.[12]

And as Bartolomé crisscrossed the island on his provisions work, he marveled at the fresh, exuberant landscape, at the physical beauty of the naked Indians—lean and finely tuned to their environment, living in small villages and subsisting on what the land and sea provided. He marveled at their skilled design work with shells, as beautifully done as the embroidery on a bishop's jeweled miter.[13] Of course, it was no longer all paradisal, especially around the Spaniards. He had seen some horrible conditions and heard about more: Indian men taken to the mines and worked cruelly—but not his miners, the brief time he had tried panning for gold; women left with the backbreaking labor of tilling the fields—but not his fields, and Spanish crop-eared ex-jailbirds

---

[12] See *Historia*, lib. 2, end of cap. 9, the slave; cap. 10, the Hanyguayaba expedition; and caps. 15–18, the second Higuey War. Pedro and Gabriel de Peñalosa were confirmed in almost identical Higuey grants in 1514—see *Documentos inéditos de Indias* (hereafter *DII*), 1:147. There is no evidence that Las Casas or any member of his family, except Uncle Francisco, actually bore arms. His father, as a merchant, may have sold arms. Even Uncle Francisco did not participate in these campaigns since he had already left the New World in 1499 and died a few years later fighting on the Barbary Coast. (See *The Untold Story*.)

[13] Cf. below, our restoration of *The Only Way*, "Prologue. Humanity of the Indians"; also Las Casas, *Apologética historia*, cap. 61.

lording it from litters carried by Indians—but he always walked.[14] Nevertheless, the beautiful island of Hispaniola with its forests, waterfalls, tropical flowers, and handsome semi-naked natives was a welcome contrast to the teeming filthy streets of Seville with their cutpurses, beggars, dogs, night soil, etc.

Then, in 1506, he went back to Seville himself—his five-year term was nearly up. By this time his sensitivities were so seared by the horrors of war that he now had a different motive for seeking the priesthood—to become a man of peace in the face of any violence.

And the opportunity was perfect. Christopher Columbus had died on May 21, 1506; and later in the year, the young settler Las Casas returned to Spain to rejoin Columbus' older brother Bartholomew, who was bent on securing the inheritance for the Discoverer's legitimate son, Diego. Isabella had died in 1504, and the regent Ferdinand had remarried and gone to Italy on his honeymoon. In Seville, Las Casas was ordained a deacon. He then set off for Rome in company with Bartholomew Columbus. Ferdinand had already left Italy, but for the disappointed travelers the stay in Rome proved memorable for a variety of reasons. They had arrived just before Lent in time to be shocked by the drunken revels of carnival.

But also there, in the center of Christendom, on March 3, 1507, the first Ember Day in Lent, Bartolomé de las Casas was ordained a priest (along with a group of foreign students) at the earliest possible age for a candidate, twenty-three. Then, accompanying Columbus' brother, the new priest had a private audience with the warrior pope, Julius II. It was a key experience for Las Casas, the basis of his lifelong conviction that a good way to overcome a crisis in the affairs of the Indies was by direct appeal to the pope. For Bartholomew Columbus persuaded Julius to write a glowing brief to Ferdinand, praising Columbus' Discovery of the New World, recommending Diego Columbus as the new viceroy and the second admiral of the ocean sea, and enthusing about the countless Indians to be evangelized—some of them presumably by this newly ordained priest who had come all the way to Rome from the Indies themselves.[15]

So it eventually happened. Back in Spain, young Padre Las Casas finished his studies for the degree of bachelor of canon law at Salamanca. Meanwhile Diego Columbus, through his marriage to the niece of the influential duke of Alba, was named second admiral of the ocean

---

[14] See *Historia,* lib. 2, caps. 1, 11, 13, 14 on conditions in Hispaniola at this time.

[15] These events are established by a prime discovery—the apparent register of Las Casas' ordination—and additional new material, in *The Untold Story.*

sea (though not viceroy). And they all sailed back across the Atlantic on
the same fleet—the governor of the Antilles, Diego Columbus; his new
wife, María de Toledo; the Discoverer's elder brother Bartholomew;
and, on a lesser boat, the new priest, Father Las Casas—all bound for
Hispaniola. There, in 1510, in the beautiful central valley, in the town
of Concepción de la Vega, the young cleric celebrated his new mass. It
was the first solemn high mass of a recently ordained priest ever sung in
the New World—and Las Casas' patrons, the governor and his lady,
were in attendance. Most of the settlers were on hand for the gold
smelting, and the celebrant was presented with a collection of ingots
and some of the first coins struck on the island, and thereafter assumed
the newly created post of Indian catechist.[16]

In that same year, and in that same place, the first Dominicans
(they had just landed) came to greet the governor. Their religious superior preached for the Indians a sermon so moving that Las Casas remembered it with deep emotion decades afterward. Thus began his
friendship with the man who was to be his mentor and spiritual guide.

The following year of 1511 began with pomp and circumstance
for the island colony, with the arrival of four robed magistrates to set up
a High Court, or Audiencia, that would help Diego Columbus govern
on the Spanish model. The year ended in a riot of the settlers that
rocked the colony to its foundations. On the second Sunday in Advent,
Fray Pedro de Córdoba, vicar of the Dominicans in the New World,
arranged a sensational event in the thatched cathedral church of Santo
Domingo. Antón Montesino, the best preacher among them, obeying
his superior and backed by the pledges of his tiny community, publicly
thundered damnation from the pulpit against all Spaniards who held
assigned Indians in encomienda, saying that the natives must be freed
or their holders had no hope of salvation. All the settlers reacted violently to the subversive sermon. Asked to retract what he had said,
Montesino, on orders again, only repeated it the following Sunday.
Governor Diego Columbus wrote indignantly to court and the Dominicans were threatened with expulsion and silenced by their provincial
from Spain. As for young Padre Las Casas, already on close terms with
the Dominicans, he was refused absolution when he went to confession

---

[16] On the fleet, see Enrique Otte, "La flota de Diego Colón, *Revista de Indias,* 24
(1964), 475–503; the padre probably came on one of the later ships. The famous new
mass passage in *Historia,* lib. 2, end of cap. 54, has given rise to the mistaken notion that
Las Casas was ordained in the New World though he never said any such thing. The
hitherto unknown documents on his bachelor's degree and his catechist's post are cited in
The Untold Story.

to one of the friars. But he still felt that he had been, by every standard, a good and kind encomendero, helping his Indians to prosper along with himself, and commiserating with them about other natives' sufferings under bad masters.[17] And he had been an effective priest on the island, preaching through an interpreter to the Indians and in his own eloquent voice to the Spaniards.

The subsequent year was still more decisive for Las Casas and his Dominican friends. Pedro de Córdoba, unwilling to bow to censure and silence, dispatched the eloquent Antón Montesino to court. For his part, young Padre Las Casas left his post to another catechist, his lands and Indians to another family member, and accepted an invitation to go to Cuba to work for his old friend, Diego Velásquez, who had recently been named governor of that island by Diego Columbus. Velásquez had started the conquest of Cuba with the brutal Hatuey campaign—hunting down and burning at the stake the "rebel" chief Hatuey, who had fled with his followers from Spanish mistreatment on Hispaniola. Apparently the governor realized that the "pacification" of Cuba might go better with the help of this young priest whose sermons and way with the natives he had admired. So Velásquez assigned Father Las Casas as chaplain to his commander-in-chief, Pánfilo de Narváez, with orders that they should reduce the rest of the island by *peaceful* means if possible, by force if necessary.

Padre Las Casas, in his new role as the white *behique* (priest and healer)—we would say white shaman—at once set out in advance of the troops. He took his own Indian staff from Hispaniola—interpreters he had trained, and the white-haired Camacho who was the head of the household—plus two or three reliable, unarmed Spaniards. At each village the white shaman gathered all the Indians' children so he could baptize them. He instructed the Indians to leave half the houses empty for the lodging of the oncoming Christians and to have plenty of food ready. By this means, the white shaman could see to it that no harm came to them and could prevent Spanish misconduct and needless violence to these gentle, peaceable Indians. The strategy was so successful—and such a contrast to the prior, bloody campaign—that after a

---

[17] See below, Addendum II on Pedro de Córdoba and the first Dominicans. Viceroy Diego Columbus, Pedro de Córdoba, and Bartolomé de las Casas were almost exactly the same age. For the sermons and reaction, cf. *Historia,* lib. 3, caps. 3–5; for the silencing document, cf. Manuel Serrano y Sanz, *Orígenes de la dominación española en América* 1 (*NBAE,* 25, Madrid, 1918), 349. The sermon has been made famous by Lewis Hanke as "el primer clamor por la justicia en América" (The First Cry for Justice in America), *Lucha,* title of Parte Primera, and by the statue of Antón Montesino in Santo Domingo; but it was Fray Pedro's initiative.

few months Padre Las Casas needed only to send ahead a messenger with a piece of paper on a forked stick, and oral instructions, to have the people comply. For almost two years the campaign was bloodless, with the Indians turning out to gape at these strange visitors and their huge, four-footed beasts, the horses. It was bloodless, that is, until the army neared the large town of Caonao where two thousand unarmed men, women, and children were sitting in a meadow waiting to see the Spaniards. Tragically, Narváez' advancing column stopped at a nearby stream to water the horses. The stream ran over large boulders which inspired the Spaniards to whet all of their swords. When shortly thereafter they came upon the waiting Indians, a wanton massacre broke out. Las Casas was nearby at a large *bohío* (longhouse) with four or five hundred Indians, when he heard the terrible sound of swords and slaughter and saw the river turn to blood. Some berserk Spaniards rushed into the longhouse with swords ready, and Las Casas ordered them out and promised the natives protection. But other Spaniards pushed him out of the way and went at the slaughter.

Forty years later he gave agonizing descriptions of the event. He had baptized a dying man already disemboweled. He had seen another Indian with the whole side of his body cut off, and he wondered if he could have put it back on and healed him with turtle grease, as he had healed so many. And he described the tongue-lashing he gave Narváez who sat like a statue on his horse, watching a carnage he could have stopped with a single word.

After the massacre, the Indians had fled—as they always did after bloodshed—leaving the Spaniards without provisions. In time, an Indian emissary returned—the white shaman had already noted the subsistence economy of these natives: they could not be sheltered elsewhere; each group had to get its own food. He again communicated his assurances of future protection, and, after a long wait, 180 natives returned to their houses—to the great joy of Narváez and the Spaniards who put up their swords for the remainder of the two-year march.

Once the "reduction" of the island had been accomplished, Governor Velásquez rewarded Padre Las Casas with a grant of land and Indians to till it—a grant he held jointly with a fellow provisioner, the pious Pedro de la Rentería, an old friend from Hispaniola, once Velásquez' chief magistrate. Up to this point, Padre Las Casas had seen Cuba as an unspoiled tropical paradise and still believed that the Spaniards could, like himself, live peacefully beside the Indians with benefit to both. So as they began their partnership, Rentería occupied himself with the (unpaid) office of catechist, while the more experienced provisioner, Las Casas, was in charge of their joint venture.[18]

Within a half-year, however, Cuba, once a tropical paradise, became before his eyes a hell on earth. Las Casas, the dedicated farmer, watched the fields abandoned and the native economy destroyed—both men and women dragged off to be worked to death, digging, panning for gold, with the younger women taken to the cities to serve the pleasures and households of the Spaniards. Soon no one was left in the deserted villages except children and old people. Padre Las Casas walked through mostly empty places, listening to famished voices groaning the single Spanish word, "Hambre!" "Hambre!"—in other words, "Food!" "Food!" At the mines, he estimated that seven thousand children starved to death because their parents had taken them there and could not feed them—many of them, he personally had baptized. He also saw whole families, reunited at year's end, commit suicide by taking poison or hanging themselves from trees. All this was much swifter and much worse than what he had witnessed on Hispaniola. Here he saw the teeming native peoples in their innocence, and a destruction of them that was sudden and terrible.[19] The reasons were obvious: the rivers were richer in gold, the people gentler; the absentee encomiendas, which belonged to the king and to his officials in Spain, were deathtraps, since they had to be kept up to full complement; and the get-rich-and-get-out Spaniards had signed up for only five years—they wanted to make a pile and go home to Spain. There was no law to control anyone. And the Indians on Cuba were being used up so fast that the Spaniards began to raid the Bahamas, kidnapping and branding the natives so as to bring them as *naborias* and slaves back to Cuba to be used up even faster.[20]

---

[18] See *Historia*, lib. 3, cap. 25, the Hatuey campaign; and caps. 28–32.

[19] The devastation of Cuba was an eye-opening experience that Las Casas describes and refers to again and again in his writings. See the first version in *Historia*, lib. 3, end of cap. 78, as translated at the beginning of Addendum I.A below. Later versions appear in his Memorial of Abuses, see note 24 below. Also in the Cuba section of the *Brevísima relación*, see his *Opúsculos, cartas y memoriales* (hereafter *Opúsculos* [*BAE*, vol. 110], doc. 14, 142; and *Entre los remedios*, Eleventh Reason, *Opúsculos*, doc. 11, at 103b–104a, 105b–106a, 105b–107a.

[20] In 1508 Ferdinand decreed that all Indians on "useless' (non-gold-bearing) islands could be branded and forcibly removed to replace the dwindling labor supply on gold-bearing islands. If any native protested or resisted the branding or removal, he/she was rebranded on the face as a slave who could be sold publicly, otherwise he was a

Realization of the horror grew inside him until the approach of Pentecost 1514. By then, Rentería was away buying grain and hogs in Jamaica, and Father Las Casas was doing double duty as preacher to the Indians and itinerant chaplain for the Spaniards on an island where there was only one other priest. And on this feast day he was to celebrate mass at the governor's main settlement.

He had to choose his sermon text for the big event, Pentecost Sunday, one of the four times of the year when these settlers (who used the term Christian as synonymous with Spaniard) went to confession and received the Eucharist. It was his duty as a priest to lay the moral truth of their lives in front of them. How could he tell them to be good encomenderos? In search of the best text, he came across a powerful passage in Ecclesiasticus 34:

> Unclean is the offering sacrificed by an oppressor. [Such] mockeries of the unjust are not pleasing [to God]. The Lord is pleased only by those who keep to the way of truth and justice. The Most High does not accept the gifts of unjust people, He does not look well upon their offerings. Their sins will not be expiated by repeat sacrifices. The one whose sacrifice come from the goods of the poor is like one who kills his neighbor. The one who sheds blood and the one who defrauds the laborer are kin and kind.

At that moment (he wrote later) the blinders fell from his eyes and he saw that *everything* the Spaniards had done in the Indies from the beginning—all that brutal exploitation and decimation of innocent Indians, with no heed for their welfare or their conversion—was completely wrong and mortal sin besides. At that moment also, Bartolomé de las Casas had the shattering experience which connected him with all the chastising prophets of the ancient Hebrew tradition. He saw social injustice not as ordinary people see it, but with a totality and a burning intensity that would never leave him and that transformed the rest of his life. Now he understood that he had been wrong, and that the first Dominicans had been right, and in the days that followed he proceeded to verify it in his books—law, scripture, whatever he had. (He was a scholar all his life and carried books wherever he went.) There was no other answer, the whole encomienda system was damnable; it was not a question of personal morality but of racial and social jus-

---

naboria who could only be owned privately. In practice, however, *naborias* were also privately sold.

tice.[21] From then on he groped painfully for his new course. He had to preach against the encomienda as the Dominicans had, so he would have to give up his own encomienda. He would have to renounce into the hands of Velásquez the Indians under his own protection, knowing they would be assigned to another master who would most likely work them to death. When he told this to his old friend Velásquez, it was an irrevocable decision, yet he asked the governor not to make it public until the return of his pious partner, Pedro de la Rentería. But Rentería agreed to the resolution, so on the Feast of the Assumption Las Casas made his decision public and told a shocked congregation that damnation awaited those who held, and those who distributed, Indians.[22] Las Casas continued thereafter to preach subversive sermons against the encomienda. Four Dominicans from Hispaniola came over and preached with him, but no encomendero was converted.

Again he sought guidance in his scriptural sources, in the stories of ancient Hebrew prophets denouncing social injustice. He found the answer, and it can be well stated in the old Quaker phrase: "Speak truth to power!" Surely, if the king knew about conditions, His Majesty would remedy the situation. Of course—as with the Hebrew prophets —Las Casas might suffer for it, but he must tell the king in the most convincing manner. So he drew up a full account of the shocking devastation he himself had witnessed. More importantly, like the ancient prophets, he realized that a break with existing institutions was not enough. Out of his long, successful, and optimistic experience with the Indians on Hispaniola and Cuba, he prepared a landmark proposal of new ideas to save the Indians and change the nature of the Spanish venture.[23]

---

[21] The Cuban narrative continues in *Historia*, lib. 3, the first part of cap. 79, trans. in Addendum I.A below. Cf. Abraham Heschel's prologue to his *The Prophets* (New York, 1962), where he describes the classic call of the Hebrew prophet; the description fits Las Casas' experience. For the modern scholars who define Las Casas as a prophet, see Introductory Note to Addendum I. Las Casas himself briefly summarized his prophetic call in a speech given before Charles I, translated in Addendum I.B. In his will, two years before his death, he affirmed that God chose him to plead for the Indians and that he had carried out this task for about fifty years—see the trans. in Addendum I.C.

[22] The story concludes in *Historia*, lib. 3, end of cap. 79, translated in the closing portion of Addendum I.A.

[23] There is nothing Utopian about his plan. It is the first proposal for acculturation in the New World. The points were: (1) Rest first, to stop the native mortality rate; (2) Peasant colonists instead of soldiers and slavers; (3) For Hispaniola, peasant/Indian cooperatives to improve farming and increase yield; (4) For Cuba, safe Indian towns with exploiters excluded, and run by their own chiefs with Spanish priests for churches and hospitals, and an overall Spanish administrator for each island to guide the new Indian

Now came the dangerous part, the actual leaving. If the settlers realized where he was bound, they would try to stop him. To allay suspicion in Cuba, and to be heard favorably in Spain, he took two precautionary steps. He drew up a sworn and notarized document on his services to the crown for three-and-one-half years on the island of Cuba; and he gave out that he was going to Paris to get his doctorate.[24]

Returning to Hispaniola with the Dominicans who had helped him, he consulted with his mentor, Fray Pedro de Córdoba, who had seen the truth first, had it daringly preached from the pulpit, and instead of accepting silence, had arranged to have the matter pursued in Spain before the king himself. In 1512, the same year that Las Casas went to Cuba, Pedro de Córdoba had sent Fray Antón Montesino to court to present a memorial of New World conditions to Ferdinand. Even the hardhearted king had been appalled, so he convoked at Burgos the first reform junta—which, unfortunately, legalized the encomienda, and issued a series of regulations for better treatment of the Indians at the mines, but with a cynical preamble about correcting the Indians' "vice of idleness." A disappointed Pedro de Córdoba had gone back to Spain himself the following year but only succeeded in obtaining a few amendments. In the impassioned young priest, Las Casas, the Dominican vicar saw the person to whom he could entrust the cause of liberating the Indians from the encomienda. He warned him, however, "You and I will not achieve our goal while Ferdinand lives."

Nevertheless, the occasion was propitious. His patron, Diego Columbus, had just returned to court to bolster his own position with Ferdinand against complaints on the islands. And Fray Pedro named Fray Antón Montesino to accompany and help Padre Las Casas in Spain.[25] When they reached Seville, Fray Antón introduced the young priest to the Dominican archbishop and friend of Columbus, Fray Diego de Deza, the authority over all diocesan priests in the New World. The archbishop not only endorsed Las Casas' mission but gave him a letter of introduction to the king. So in 1515, with strong support

---

economy. The dispossessed Spanish encomenderos would become stockholders in these towns, contributing to them and sharing in the profits. See the detailed analysis in Wagner–Parish, 20–22.

[24] For the events, see *Historia,* lib. 3, caps. 80–81; also cf. Wagner–Parish, Catalogue, no. 1, for his *Información* of services; and nos. 2 and 5, the Memorials on Abuses and Reforms.

[25] See *Historia,* lib. 3, caps. 6-18—the main primary source on the Junta of Burgos, the proclamation of the laws, a critique of their contents, and the follow-up activities by Pedro de Córdoba. On Las Casas' meeting with Fray Pedro and return to Spain with Antón Montesino, see *Historia,* lib. 3, cap. 83.

from both Church and State, Bartolomé de las Casas literally embarked on his life mission: to tell the truth to the king. Little did he dream that he was going to spend the rest of his days, fifty mortal years, doing just that.

At the end of that first year, Las Casas confronted Ferdinand on his deathbed with such a sickening tale of atrocities committed in the New World that he won the promise of an audience for reform. It never took place. Instead, Ferdinand died. As regent of Spain after Isabella's death, he had ordered an era of unbridled exploitation in the Indies— insisting on forced labor, decreeing virtual slavery for the Indians of the Lesser Antilles, demanding the highest yield possible from the gold mines.

But Ferdinand was dead and Las Casas had his opportunity. Now he could present his exposé and plans for institutional reform to a new administration: the aging regent, Cardinal Cisneros, who was to rule Spain and the Indies (with a figurehead coregent, Adrian of Utrecht) until the coming of the new Hapsburg king, Charles I, Isabella's grandson. Las Casas already knew Cisneros through the Columbus family, and now the second admiral personally presented Las Casas' two Memorials on Abuses and Reforms to the cardinal. And the priest from the Indies did manage to get a couple of reform projects enacted. The regent Cisneros actually handed Las Casas' scheme for free Indian towns to a reform commission of three Hieronymite friars, though the cardinal never trusted Las Casas personally because of his close association with the Columbus family. (It was Cisneros who had ordered Christopher Columbus sent back from the New World in chains in 1499; Las Casas did not know this, and few scholars know it today.) These Hieronymites were apparently chosen because of their fame as managers of huge estates worked by serflike peasants. And they were soon reached and influenced by agents of the colonists at court. So they disregarded the young priest who had been given a purely nominal appointment as "Protector of the Indians," and sailed without him. Upon arrival in Hispaniola, they conducted a loaded interrogatory, pronouncing the free town plan unworkable because the Indians lacked capacity. When the "Protector" arrived and denounced the kidnapping and sale in Santo Domingo of Indians captured on the Bahamas and the Spanish Main (the north coast of South America), they complained to the regent who ordered the troublesome priest sent back, in chains if necessary.[26]

---

[26] The account above includes unknown information about Diego Columbus and Cardinal Cisneros that will be presented in *The Untold Story*. See Wagner-Parish, chaps.

Fortunately, Las Casas returned to court on his own before the censure, and after seeing Cisneros on *his* deathbed, resumed efforts at the court of the young Charles, with some help from the Flemish courtiers. At first things went well. He rewrote the community scheme to make the Indians free vassals paying tribute to the crown (in order to take them away from subjection to the Spaniards). And his rewritten peasant-emigration project was actually adopted. A law was enacted for royal maintenance of the peasants, and he was officially put in charge of recruitment. But the venture was soon resisted by grandees who did not want to lose their farm laborers; and it was sabotaged by the disloyalty of an aide appointed to help him. Finally it was killed by the partial withdrawal of royal subsidy.

So the padre changed course and devoted himself to a major effort based on a plan he had originally devised for his mentor, Pedro de Córdoba, plus a new suggestion just received from Fray Pedro. The young Dominican vicar, discouraged at the hopelessness of any missionary effort on the islands given the brutal conditions, had sent his friars to the mainland where they encountered slave raids beginning on a large scale. His attempts to have the slaving forbidden and a responsible layman placed on the Main to supervise barter at trading stations proved fruitless. So he wrote to Las Casas at court, begging him to seek total exclusion of Spaniards from a smaller stretch of land where he and his friars might then attempt a peaceful conversion of the Indians. When the padre first presented the proposal—it assumed no revenue for the king—he ran into opposition from the powerful bishop of Burgos (Ferdinand's tool) who had paid the king money, and, consequently, was once again in charge of Spain's administration of the Indies. Bishop Fonseca openly laughed at the prospect of granting land that would bring no revenue to the king; thereupon the padre revised the original mainland plan to include a series of trading posts with forts, bishops, peaceful colonists, and friars to convert the Indians and make them free, tribute-paying vassals of the king. No encomiendas.

But this effort came to naught. Now, with the collapse of the peasant plan, Las Casas revised the mainland plan, plus Fray Pedro's exclusion idea, into a request for an extensive land grant on the Spanish Main where he himself could found model agricultural colonies, super-

---

2 and 3 for a concise account from the published primary sources. Manuel Giménez Fernández' massive volume on this interval, *Bartolomé de las Casas, I: Delegado de Cisneros para la reformación de las Indias, 1516–1517* (Seville, 1953) adds valuable archival material, despite distorted premises and a major omission—cf. Wagner–Parish, xvi.

vise barter with the natives, and guarantee profits for the crown. Spanish trading armadas (i.e., slavers) would be excluded, and Dominican and Franciscan missionary ventures could proceed unthreatened.[27]

The padre's proposal raised a year-long storm at court. His foes—the bishop of Burgos, heading a new Council of the Indies, and the colonial agents—concocted offers for the same land and attacked Las Casas' competence and character. His friends—Diego Columbus and the Flemings—set up a convocation from other councils to hear him occasionally. And best of all, there was a solemn session before young King Charles, at which "Micer Bartolomé" held forth on the sufferings of the Indians under conquest and forced labor as well as on their full human capacity. And he declared that Christianity approached all nations—not to conquer or oppress—but to receive them in, without costing them their liberty, their lands, their lives.

Las Casas' plan was finally approved due to the influence of Adrian of Utrecht, cardinal and future pope, formerly coregent of Spain with Cisneros, and tutor and advisor to young King Charles who had just been elected Holy Roman Emperor. Adrian had been kept apprised by Las Casas of all Indian matters during the whole time. And in the last days before Charles' departure, the Flemish cardinal, now governor of Spain and the Indies, declared in a learned discourse that "the Indians of the New World should be brought to the knowledge of God and the bosom of Holy Mother Church through peace and love and the evangelical way, according to the form established by Christ and not by war and servitude"—a tacit condemnation of the "Mohammedan" approach of the Spaniards in the early years. As a result, it was decreed that the Indians were free people and Bartolomé Las Casas should be in charge of their conversion by the friars in that part of Tierra Firme as he had asked.

Charles signed Las Casas' grant on May 19, 1519. But by this time the padre's concession had been so drastically reduced that he could hardly hope to recruit his expected "50 associates." Besides, the ven-

---

[27] Wagner–Parish, chap. 4, relates Las Casas' first efforts at the Flemish court. For Fray Pedro's letter and the new plan, see *Historia,* lib. 3, last par. of cap. 104; the revised mainland plan is doc. 5 of *Opúsculos* [*BAE,* vol. 110]. Demetrio Ramos' "El P. Córdoba y las Casas en el plan de conquista pacífica de Tierra Firme," *Boletín Americanista* 1 (1959), 175–210, supplies the story of the Pearl Coast missions, but attributes Las Casas' remedies to Fray Pedro. Enrique Otte, "Los Jerónimos y el tráfico humano en el Caribe," *Anuario de Estudios Américanos* 32 (1975), 187–204, documents the involvement of colonial officials in the slave trade, but misreads the Hieronymites' good intentions. A recently found complaint by Pedro de Córdoba (see note 29 below) paints an eyewitness picture of their inaction and dissimulation.

ture was fatally compromised: there was *no* exclusion of Spanish (slave) ships. It took another nine months for his papers and preparations—during this final delay, Las Casas acquired the degree of licentiate in canon law from the University of Valladolid.[28]

Still hopeful, he sailed in 1521 with a group of hastily assembled peasants, only to receive devastating news when his ship stopped at Puerto Rico. In the territory of his grant, coastal Indians, outraged by repeated slaving and atrocities, had wiped out the Dominican outpost of Chiribichí. Las Casas never knew that nearby Dominican friars had issued slaving licenses, but only that the government had sent a punitive expedition to punish the Indians for the "massacre," and to take slaves. Worse still, as he later learned, his peasant colonists were delighted with the tragic news. And though he left them in Puerto Rico to await him, they all deserted him to go into the lucrative slave trade themselves.

A dejected Las Casas finally reached Hispaniola with nothing left but his complaints, a small staff, some trade goods purchased with borrowed money, a leaking boat that was promptly condemned, and his hard-won but flawed royal grant. At this juncture, Diego Columbus, now returned to the island as viceroy, made one more offer of help. In Spain, the second admiral had been willing to back the model colony with his own funds. Now, though he said he could not call off the armada, he got the magistrates of the High Court (who governed the Antilles with him) to put up capital for a "Company" to provide Las Casas with another ship for founding his colony. The priest had barely settled his staff at a tiny outpost on the Main near the Franciscan mission at Cumaná, when he went back to Santo Domingo to protest the rampant slaving in the vicinity.

News of the inevitable tragedy reached him on Hispaniola. The nearby Indians, angered and suspicious at the appearance of a Spaniard with a cannibal questionnaire (the standard pretext for slave raiding) as well as by the ferocity of the Spanish reprisals, had decided that the remaining friars and the tiny staff were fronts for slavers, and they attacked the outpost, killing a lay brother and several servants and burning the place to the ground. The remainder escaped by boat and

---

[28] Wagner–Parish chap. 5, "A Tierra Firme Grant," condenses the court battle from contemporary sources and *Historia,* lib. 3, caps. 130–33 and 138–41. The semi-junta and Adrian's oration are presented in the subsequent caps. 148–49 and the third par. of cap. 155; Las Casas' speech is translated in Addendum I below. Las Casas' second academic degree is established and dated, from unpublished docs., in the *The Untold Story.*

brought the news. With this apparent destruction of all his work for the past six years, Bartolomé de las Casas went into a profound depression that would change the future direction of all his efforts.[29]

2. A Christian Crisis in the New World

Now in 1521, as at Pentecost 1514, Bartolomé de las Casas had to wrestle with himself. He was beaten, dispirited. He could only seek refuge with his friends, the Dominicans, who had sheltered him during his open quarrel with the Hieronymites about not freeing the Hispaniola Indians and permitting the decimation of the Lucayos. What had gone so wrong? Why had all his work of six years, begun so optimistically, ended in death and ashes? The prophet was supposed to confront the person in authority, and he had: Governor Velásquez who gave him the encomienda, Diego Columbus who had originally complained against the first Dominican sermons and Pedro de Córdoba, Ferdinand on his deathbed, Cardinal Cisneros, the young King Charles I. . . .

Had he compromised with worldliness in the desperate effort to carry out his plan? He had not sought gain or glory for himself. When he heard that a friendly councilor had criticized him for seeking privileges for his associates and for promising revenues for the king, he had defended himself in the strongest terms:

> If you saw Our Lord Jesus Christ scourged and mocked, would you not try to rescue him? And if you couldn't do it for free, wouldn't you buy him? I left behind in the Indies Our Lord Jesus Christ being scourged and crucified, not once, but thousands of times in what the Spaniards are doing to the Indians, abusing and destroying them before they can be converted. They wouldn't let me—or the friars— do it for free. So I offered to buy Christ back with promises of revenue for the king.

No, the venture was not worldly. . . . Then the truth came to him. At the very end he *had* compromised with worldliness, he *had* compro-

---

[29] See Wagner–Parish, chap. 6, the Cumaná fiasco, summarizing published official docs. and Las Casas' own account in *Historia*, lib. 3, caps. 156–59. Manuel Giménez Fernández' oversized study *Bartolomé de las Casas, II: Capellán de S.M. Carlos I, poblador de Cumaná, 1517–1523* (Seville, 1960) adds archival material to this interval, but with further serious distortions. For the complicity of certain Dominican friars see below, note 38 on Fray Tomás Ortiz; also Vicente Rubio, "Una carta inédita de Fray Pedro de Córdoba, O.P.," *Communio* 1 (Seville, 1980), the transcript at 421–25. *N.B.* This is a letter to Antón Montesino, not the one to Las Casas discussed in the text above. There were doubtless other letters from Fray Pedro to Las Casas and the Montesino brothers, Antón and Reginaldo, at court.

mised with power in his desperate, final attempt to save something of the venture in that bad contract with the "Company." After all, those men were the judges of the High Court that had permitted the capturing and selling of Indians, and they were motivated by hopes of gain. He had even let them put in that if he found cannibals he would declare it so the Spaniards could enslave them—as if he would ever do such a thing! Had God punished him for that? Should he listen to that fervid Fray Domingo de Betanzos who said that he had done enough for the Indians for now, and should think of the welfare of his own soul and choose religious life?[30]

In 1522, at the age of thirty-eight, Bartolomé de las Casas entered the Dominican Order under the impression—which later proved false —that he had betrayed his vocation, that God had chastised him for allying himself with power in the person of Diego Columbus, especially in that final mercenary "Company." If he had only been able to consult with Pedro de Córdoba who was mortally ill when Las Casas returned to the island. But his mentor died just before Las Casas sailed on that fatal trip to found his colony.[31] It was a saddened man who received the habit in the House of Studies, Santo Domingo, in 1522.

For the next twelve years, as a Dominican friar under obedience, Fray Bartolomé "to all outward appearances," slept. To put it candidly, he was stuck with a rash vow taken in depression and his superiors evidently knew it. During the year of his novitiate, letters for him came from his friends in Spain, urging him to return to court where the climate was still favorable to reform. His superiors carefully hid all these communications until after his first profession. But nothing could turn him away from his vocation to the Indians and the Indies— even though for the next four years he was kept busy all day and part of the night in that House of Studies, doing the courses in scripture, patristics, and theology that were obligatory for all new Dominicans. The only study he was excused from was elementary canon law, because he

---

[30] For the verbatim text of the famous passage in which Las Casas identifies Christ crucified with the Indians, see *Historia,* lib. 3, end of cap. 38. For his getting the news of the Cumaná massacre and his soul-searching, end of cap. 159. And his entering the Dominican Order, end of cap. 160. As for the ambiguous Betanzos, he always placed the ascetic life first and was generally averse to missionary work with the Indians. But Las Casas apparently was not aware of it at this time. See below, text preceding note 37 on Betanzos' later defamation of the Indians; also note 39 and Introductory Note to Addendum II, on the conflicting currents among Dominicans in the Indies.

[31] On the correct date of Pedro de Córdoba's death, see Isacio Pérez, *Cronología documentada de los viajes, estancias y actuaciones de Fray Bartolomé de las Casas* (Bayamón, Puerto Rico, 1984), 297–99.

already had a licentiate in that discipline. But by good fortune his studies included the works of St. Thomas Aquinas, especially the *Summa Theologiae,* and not just the *Summa,* but also the new best-seller of the 1520s, the great Cajetan *Commentary.* He took this interlude of studies as an opportunity to measure the accumulated wisdom of the Old World against the reality of the New World in all its beauty, and the horror that it had been reduced to by the Spaniards. Every book he read in Spanish or in Latin contained some argument or citation which supported him in his conclusion—every commentator on the law, passages of Scripture, and Cajetan on St. Thomas.[32]

During his four years of study he led the austere life of those reformed Dominicans whom he had admired from early on. When Pedro de Córdoba got his full complement of twelve friars, he and they unanimously adopted rules even more rigorous than those they had followed in Spain. They ate native foods. They decided not to beg for bread, wine, or oil provided they were healthy. They fasted for seven months of the year instead of just the seven weeks of Lent. The purpose was to set an example to the Spaniards who openly defied the fasts, the abstinences required by the Church.[33]

Even after Fray Bartolomé had finished the full four-year course and made his solemn profession, his new superiors would not send him back to Spain. Quite clearly he was a big catch for them. His Cumaná fiasco was the talk of the island (it would later be written about maliciously by Oviedo and Gómara, contemporary historians). And he still did have very influential friends in the Old World. Among the letters of encouragement was one from Pope Adrian himself, sending a papal brief with a plenary indulgence for his Cumaná expeditionists! And in 1525 came word that another junta had been held in Spain and the granting of encomiendas had been forbidden (temporarily) in newly conquered Mexico. His early efforts were beginning to bear fruit, but that only made the danger of losing him all the greater.

So in 1526, his superiors, instead of sending him back to court as Pedro de Córdoba surely would have done, sent him as prior to an outpost, Puerto de Plata, on the north coast of Haiti, to found a new Dominican house. Ever obedient, ever observant, ever close to the earth, Fray Bartolomé began to build a stone monastery and planted a

---

[32] The Cajetan *Commentary* appeared in 1518 and is still the standard. On Las Casas finding all the confirming authorities, see below Addendum I.A, sect. 2, last par.

[33] For these customs see below, Addendum II.A, sect. 1. Daniel Ulloa, *Los predicadores divididos* (Mexico, 1977), caps. 1 and 2, traces the Dominican reform movement and its relation to the Dominicans in the New World.

kitchen garden. The following year, out of frustration and a need to pre-serve the Indian side of the story, he began a crucial work which would occupy him intermittently for the rest of his days: writing from first-hand knowledge and primary documents the *History of the Indies*.[34]

Two years later, a pair of other Dominicans, the veteran Antón Montesino and Tomás de Berlanga, were sent back to court carrying impassioned memorials by Fray Bartolomé, while he was left behind. Nonetheless, Las Casas' memorials, even presented by other hands, had their usual powerful effect. Cardinal Loaysa, president of the Council of the Indies, had been removed as imperial confessor and exiled to Rome. And the emperor Charles convoked a special reform junta under Cardinal Tavera, president of the Council of Castile, which came out strongly for the abolition of forced labor and of Indian slav-ery. The encomienda was not abolished, but a new institution—the corregimiento or town of free Indians under the crown, based on Las Casas' modified proposal—was permanently introduced as an alterna-tive to the system of forced labor. The second recommendation was actually enacted in 1530, in the famous antislavery law which contem-porary chroniclers correctly attributed to Las Casas, without knowing he achieved it in absentia. And peasants kept coming over under the statute that he had drafted—well provisioned with seeds, farm imple-ments, and supplies. His early efforts had not failed but succeeded![35]

However, Las Casas, as prior in Puerto de Plata and thereby freed from close supervision, did not stop at memorials to the faraway court —no matter how successful. From his own pulpit he thundered against the slave trade and the settlers rushing off to the conquest of Peru—to no avail. He was accused of withholding deathbed viaticum from an encomendero, ordered back to Santo Domingo, and officially silenced by a government order forbidding him to preach for two years.[36]

Then, in 1534, came the worst blow of all. The disturbed and disturbing Domingo de Betanzos had gone to Rome in an effort to set up Mexico as a separate Dominican Province. In Rome he had written

---

[34] See Wagner–Parish, 72, 1st par.

[35] For Las Casas' dominant influence at the Junta de Tavera, see *Las Casas en México*, cap. 3, note 29. Zavala, *La encomienda indiana* (Mexico, 1973), cap. 2, at 55–58, describes the implantation of the corregimiento in Mexico. For the antislavery ordinance of 1530, see Richard Konetzke, *Colección de Documentos para la Historia de la Formación Social de Hispanoamérica* (Madrid, 1953), vol. 1, doc. 68, 134–36. (For Loaysa's temporary demotion, see *Las Casas en México*, cap. 1, note 9, 1st par.)

[36] *The Untold Story* relates the full incident from the complaint of the *Audiencia*, Las Casas' letter of 1534 defending himself (*Opúsculos* [*BAE*, 110], doc. 8), and a later report by a Mercedarian friar who was in town at the time.

a shocking defamation of the Indians, declaring them incapable of receiving the faith, attacking the Franciscan conversions, and saying that God had condemned the Indians to extinction for their bestial sins—and all laws to protect them were pointless, and all efforts to convert them were useless! And Cardinal Loaysa, back in power after his short "exile" in Rome, immediately used the Betanzos document as a pretext to revoke the antislavery ordinance, and on his own issued a new decree allowing the resumption of slaving. When notice of these events reached the New World, all the friends of the Indians were stirred into action. In Mexico City, Bishop Fuenleal, who had come from Santo Domingo and was serving as the reformist president of the second Mexican Audiencia, wrote his own protest and organized a letter-writing campaign, among all the friars, against the new slaving decree and against Betanzos who had obviously lost his mind.[37]

Meanwhile in the Dominican monastery of Santo Domingo, Fray Bartolomé de las Casas, the real author of the antislavery law, was the most shocked of all by the revocation of the law and the baseless defamation of the Indians by Fray Domingo de Betanzos, the man who had persuaded him to ask for the Dominican habit. This represented the collapse of the best protection he had achieved to date for the Indians, though he had done it all at a distance without going back to court. Now his lifework was threatened again, more than it had been by the Cumaná massacre. And here he was, under censure, removed from his priorate, silenced, unable to preach, unable to go back to court, unable to do anything but write.

Had it been a mistake to follow Betanzos' advice and become a Dominican and thus submit himself to a vow of obedience? What could he do now from a distance with his pen alone? Letters and memorials could not avail. Had he betrayed his calling once again, this time by trusting a religious structure that could contain opposite kinds of Dominicans—the ones who had first shown him the way and encouraged him, and the ones who were now defaming the Indians? For there were others besides Betanzos. Reformers at court had written to him about Tomás Ortiz, the former vicar of the Cubagua friars, who had used the Chiribichí massacre as a pretext to defame the Indians before the council and provoke a slaving ordinance.[38] And the Betanzos/Ortiz

---

[37] The entire episode is told for the first time from primary sources in *Las Casas en México,* cap. 1: see note 10 on the letter writing campaign; and for the Betanzos defamation and the reaction, read the complete section, i.e., text preceding notes 9 and 10.

[38] The Ortiz defamation is quoted in Hanke, *Lucha,* 97–98, from Pedro Mártir de Anglería. Las Casas corrects Pedro Mártir's version of the Chiribichí massacre in his

faction had brought over like-minded friars.[39] They were a total contra-diction to the late Fray Pedro de Córdoba. Fray Pedro had fought tirelessly against colonial authorities for the welfare of the Indians. He had fought for the chance to work at the conversion of the Indians away from the Spanish-imposed horrors—and had given his life in the process. It was this man who had originally blessed Las Casas when he went back to Spain as a young priest to plead the cause of the Indians, and had assured him that God had called him to this mission.

What kind of a situation had Fray Bartolomé gotten himself into? What did God want of him now? He had always said that one is never given a task without the means to do it. He knew what his task was—to be back at court in this emergency, defending the rights of the Indians. But he had taken a vow of obedience as a friar and he could not even ask; his superiors had to send him. Then where were the means?[40]

Just at this juncture, something providential occurred. A wild piece of news burst upon the capital city of Santo Domingo—the end of the Enriquillo War. . . .

Enriquillo, Chief Little Henry, was a famous rebel. Son of an In-dian chief and raised by the Franciscans, he had fled to the hills after his Spanish encomendero raped his Christian wife on their wedding day, and the authorities beat and jailed Little Henry who dared to complain. For fifteen years as a guerrilla chief, he had been safe in his mountain fastness, Bahoruco, in the interior of the island where more and more rebel Indians and runaway African slaves flocked to join him. A con-

---

Apologética historia, cap. 246. Otte, in *Las perlas del Caribe,* 188–193, fully documents the unspeakable atrocities of the slavers which put the Pearl Coast on the warpath and ultimately led to the massacre; and a recently discovered letter of Fray Pedro de Córdoba tells of a slave ship going along the coast of the Spanish Main with, he fears, a slaving license from Dominican friars. (See Rubio, "Una carta inédita," 422.) In fact, the Ortiz defamation is a cannibal declaration, the standard pretext to help slavers; it seems to have been written *before* the Chiribichí massacre, but was presented at court a few years *afterward* and led to the issuance of a slaving authorization for that coast. See Francisco López de Gómara, *Hispania Victrix* (*BAE,* vol. 22), 290.

[39] The first half of Ulloa's *Los predicadores divididos* is concerned with contradic-tory Dominican currents in the New World and the triumph of observance over mission in New Spain. (See Introductory Note to Addendum II below.) Ulloa's indispensable work nonetheless lacks some damning information about the Betanzos' faction. See *Las Casas en México,* Appendix 3, and note 14 for the prior of the convent of Santo Do-mingo de México chaining his own provincial, and preaching publicly before Cortés that the Indians were slaves by nature and even Montezuma could rightly have been branded [in the face].

[40] We know almost exactly what Fray Bartolomé was thinking from a letter he wrote shortly after this point, and from another letter a year later—see *Opúsculos* [*BAE,* vol. 110], doc. 8 at 59a and doc. 9 at 68b.

summate strategist, Enriquillo had led Spanish war parties—eager to capture him—on futile chases through the mountains until their sandals were worn out. Then, as they nursed their bleeding feet, Enriquillo's people crept up behind them, seized their weapons, and ordered them back to town. Finally, after the island was beggared by the 'Enriquillo tax' to run the war, the Spanish government had sent a large armada under Captain Hernando de Barrionuevo to put an end to the Enriquillo rebellion. But the High Court warned Barrionuevo: they were deadly afraid that if he attacked and lost, and lose he would, Enriquillo would then capture enough weapons to take over the whole island. Barrionuevo called off the attack, allowed himself to be led in alone by Indian guards to see Enriquillo, and quickly signed a peace treaty. This was the startling news that ran through the capital and reached the monastery. . . .[41]

Revived by the report, Fray Bartolomé went at once to his superiors and pleaded with them. This was an opportunity for him to do what God wanted of him. Because of his long acquaintance with Indian chieftains, they should send him secretly, with only one companion, to visit Enriquillo and cement the precarious peace. Of course it was dangerous. Of course he could lose his life. But God had spared him from the Cumaná massacre. Maybe he could do something worthwhile with his spared life. His superiors were not to worry if they did not hear from him again.

The permission was given. The two friars set out on foot and nothing was heard from them for a month. And then there was a new sensation, a new wild story repeated all over Santo Domingo, this time starting in the monastery: "Bartolomé de las Casas and his companion friar had spent an entire month in Enriquillo's hidden camp, baptizing the babies, marrying the couples, saying mass, hearing confessions." As in his youth, Fray Bartolomé had made friends with the chieftain—something no one else had done in all these fifteen years. He had even brought Enriquillo and his guards briefly out of the mountains for a banquet with the Spaniards in a nearby town. And he reported to the authorities that he had left the peace confirmed stronger than the Pillars of Hercules. The members of the High Court were at first startled, then grateful that he had saved the island. So they begged Fray Bartolomé to bring Enriquillo in person to the capital to formalize good relations. This he did, and a grand reception and exchange of gifts

---

[41] Wagner–Parish, chap. 3, section on "The Enriquillo Story" at 74–77. The fear was justified; the historian Oviedo, no indiophile, compared Enriquillo to Alexander the Great.

took place. Next, they asked if he could prevail upon Enriquillo to come out of the mountains and settle on assigned lands with all his people. Again Las Casas complied. This was something Barrionuevo, with his force of arms, could never accomplish.[42]

But what Fray Bartolomé had achieved for himself and his prophetic calling was even greater. When he returned home to the monastery and added the biography of Enriquillo to the manuscript of his *History of the Indies,* he had found the missing element to his own vocation! The twelve years of "enforced sleep" were over, and they had not been wasted—he had been forced to become effective by writing in absentia. And write he did—with the Enriquillo experience as his inspiration.

Now, in 1534, at the monastery of Santo Domingo, working at top speed, he wrote out the initial draft of his first finished book, *The Only Way to Draw All People to a Living Faith.* He had found 'The Way' at last—the way of Christ. He could do it himself as a missionary friar. Two friars alone had accomplished more in one month than the soldiers and armies of the "Enriquillo War" had in fifteen years. This was the only way to bring the Indians peacefully into right relationship with the Spaniards, the only way to bring them the gift of the faith. Christ Himself had given the commandment to go and preach to all people, and He had instituted the way for those who would bear His good news. Go poor among the poor; go without power, without purse, without provisions; go with charity and respect for those encountered —speaking peace first, then truth, then goodness, staying if invited, departing if not wanted. Here was the perfect answer to Fray Domingo de Betanzos' defamation that the Indians were incapable of the faith and doomed to extinction for their past sins, and to his claim that all efforts to convert them were in vain, and to his knowledge by prophetic vision that all laws to help them were useless. For Las Casas, this was blasphemy! Just the opposite was true, he wrote. Our Lord had said to preach to *all peoples.* Therefore it followed that all peoples had capacity and, to correct Betanzos' own argument on predestination, the "elect" chosen for salvation were among all peoples—and that included the Indians. Furthermore, the Indians had special capacities which Las

---

[42] The rest of the story through the first visit and the reaction of the authorities is documented in Wagner–Parish, "The Enriquillo story," 76–78. For the finale, see *Las Casas en México,* opening of chap. 3, correcting the confusion of a contemporary chronicler. *The Untold Story* documents the tragic end of Enriquillo. The chieftain was given lands and the title of Don, but fortunately died before the arrival of a secret order to break the peace, arrest him, and send him back to Spain.

Casas could attest to in countless ways from his own experience and observation dating from near 1500.

Even more, Las Casas could demonstrate that the wrong way was everything the Spaniards had done until now: war, greed, oppression, forced labor, brutality—everything that had made the name of Christian hateful. So everything that the Spaniards held in the Indies had been stolen. Consequently, everything that the Spaniards held in the Indies must be given back. The New World could be won for Spain and Christendom—he still believed in the relationship—by those with a gentle mission. And he himself would be one of those gentle missioners —like Pedro de Córdoba, the real influence on his Dominican life.[43]

Las Casas wrote this mentor of his into his text as the prototype of the ideal missionary. He would always live off the memory of that young first vicar of the Hispaniola Dominicans: only twenty-eight when he came to the Indies and thirty-eight when he died, he was of a noble family, physically tall and handsome, gifted with graciousness— body and soul—at peace with himself, and formed in the great intellectual and reformed convent of San Esteban at Salamanca, proficient in the arts, philosophy, and theology. He would have been summa cum laude if he had not induced intense, prolonged headaches from his severe practices of penance.[44] Above all, it was Fray Pedro de Córdoba's work on Hispaniola that had brought Las Casas himself to his own first awakening, his own first entry into work for the Indians, and his true vocation as their defender.

So it had not been a mistake to become a Dominican. Not only had Bartolomé de las Casas finished his own first book, but he had decided on his future course of action. He sent a copy of his tract to a former associate at court, along with a lengthy letter about Betanzos and the revocation. Next he consulted with his superiors, and especially with Fray Tomás de Berlanga who had returned from Spain as bishop of Panama and was now bound for Peru on a special assignment. And with everyone's approval, Las Casas arranged to embark on his own career as a missionary by leading a small band of Dominicans to Peru.

Fate ruled otherwise. Berlanga was detained by fevers in Panama; and Las Casas and his party were becalmed on their voyage to Peru and nearly perished. When the wind did rise, it was northerly, and they decided to transfer to a northbound coastal vessel which deposited

---

[43] The foregoing paragraphs are a summary of *The Only Way* in its first, or Hispaniola version. See below, App. I.A.

[44] See below, Addendum II, "Las Casas' Portrait of Pedro de Córdoba."

them, shaken but alive, in Nicaragua. From there, the observant Las Casas made his way to Dominican mainland headquarters in Mexico City, where he was welcomed by President Fuenleal and the friars who had protested the defamation. And he was especially welcomed by the provincial superiors of the new Province of Santiago de México, who begged him to join their number. While he waited for his official transfer from the Santa Cruz Province of Hispaniola, he returned with his friars to Nicaragua, which was under his old province, and began to teach the Indians and to preach his new ideas about *The Only Way.*

But Nicaragua was a lawless backwater where Indians were openly mistreated. Settlers flogged the natives for wasting time to learn about Christianity from Las Casas and his friars! In despair he sent a long report to Spain—about how the Spaniards had devastated the land for a decade, and had shipped more than fifty thousand Indians as slaves to Panama and Peru—and he begged for a royal order. As a last try, he denounced a planned armed foray into the interior—only to be pulled down from the pulpit by order of the governor's wife. The situation was too dangerous, so Fray Bartolomé prudently removed his friars once more to Mexico City.[45]

Again, fortuitously, Bartolomé de Las Casas reached the capital in 1536, in time to participate in the ecclesiastical conference of that year. Meetings of bishops and friars enacted missionary principles that incorporated the tenets of Las Casas' *The Only Way,* which were personally backed by the bishop of Mexico and another prominent Franciscan, Fray Jacobo de Tastera, who had written the most powerful letter against Betanzos. However, the dissident Franciscans, outvoted in the controversy over their mass baptism of adult Indians, decided to send an envoy to Rome. For their part, the observant Dominicans and Augustinians and the bishops of New Spain all decided to send to the pope the former Dominican prior, Bernardino Minaya, with an impressive batch of documents: letters of introduction, the resolutions of the conference, and supporting tracts including *The Only Way.* And Fray Ja-

---

[45] The move was prudent; Governor Contreras' men later murdered their own bishop, a Dominican friend of Las Casas. In *The Untold Story,* Las Casas' Nicaraguan interlude is well documented from primary sources, including the belated royal order authorizing a peaceful conversion experiment. Confusion has existed from 17th-century chroniclers to 20th-century scholars on the dates and events of Las Casas' first two visits to Mexico City—see note 46 below.

cobo, the most pro-Indian Franciscan, set off for Yucatan to attempt peaceful conversion.[46]

As for Fray Bartolomé himself, since the transfer had come and he was formally adopted by the Mexican province, he was officially sent south again as their vicar for Guatemala. There, in 1537, he at last embarked on a missionary venture of his own to put *The Only Way* into practice. He made his famous contract with Governor Maldonado for the peaceful conversion of the unconquered "Land of War," Tuzulutlán, where the Indians had three times turned back would-be conquistadors. The terms were these: for five years Spaniards were forbidden to enter the territory, and all Indians whom the friars peacefully converted should be forever free Indians living in crown towns with no threat of encomienda. The enterprise was well under way with the aid of friendly Indian merchants, when in 1538 he and his friars were called back to a provincial chapter in the capital.[47]

In Mexico City that year, Fray Bartolomé de las Casas realized his most cherished dream since entering the Dominican Order. At last, the Mexican province was sending him back to court as missions procurator to recruit friars for New Spain. He stayed over in or near the viceregal capital to prepare—and it was almost a dress rehearsal for his return to the political arena as well. Mexico-Tenochtitlán was now the capital of New Spain; and a viceroy had replaced President Fuenleal the previous year. What had once been Montezuma's capital was now a Spanish metropolis built on its ruins and with its very stones. Spanish horses and carts filled the causeways across the surrounding lake; Spanish soldiers and townspeople crowded the streets and canals. The Indians were just pack-bearers, servants, and shop apprentices, who lived in a crowded "native quarter"; most of them—after having built the new city with incredible loss of life—had been relocated to the countryside to labor on Spanish estates.

---

[46] For these new discoveries, see *Las Casas en México:* cap. 2 "Reuniones en la ciudad virreinal, 1536"; and the concluding section of cap. 3, i.e., notes 38–41 and corresp. text.

[47] The basic, near-contemporary account of this episode by Antonio de Remesal, *Historia de la Provincia de San Vicente de Chyapa y Guatemala de la Orden de Sancto Domingo* (Madrid, 1619/1620, hereafter Remesal), lib. 3, caps. 10–11, 15–18, attributes later events to this promising start. Marcel Bataillon's critical article, "La Vera Paz," rectified the chronology from documents, but created a new, severe anachronism. (Cf. *Las Casas as a Bishop,* note 20 and corresp. text). André Saint-Lu's expanded work, *La Vera Paz,* at 65–105, adds new documents about Las Casas' initial work in the Land of War, but retains the anachronism. A corrected account will be presented in *The Untold Story.*

On this extended stay in this Hispanicized city, Las Casas' new friends, friars and officials, gave him important additional material for his *History of the Indies* and his memorials. They all told a familiar story of gruesome early years under the brutal first governor, president of the first High Court, and his army of conquistadors-turned-loose: countless Indians dying in the mines; the entire regions of Pánuco and Jalisco devastated by slaving; Indian slaves resold so often that their faces were completely covered with brands and looked like scrawled-over paper; massacres and horrors in every conquest of Central and South America; and slow tortures and ghastly executions of Indian leaders in order to extort more treasure.[48]

Nevertheless, there was hope for change. Viceroy Mendoza seemed an upright man, and a promising packet of papers had come from Rome earlier in the year. Fray Bernardino Minaya had obtained three papal decrees corresponding to the resolutions of the 1536 junta and was sending printed and handwritten copies to the friends of the Indians. Best of the three was the encyclical *Sublimis Deus* issued by Paul III on June 2, 1537, enunciating by fiat all the principles of *The Only Way*, not just for the Indians of the New World, but for all peoples to be discovered in the future! It was a Magna Carta for the Indians, which Las Casas translated into Spanish so the friars could circulate it.[49] But bad news came later in the year from Spain: all Minaya's papers had been confiscated and copies of the decrees were ordered sent back from the New World. Nevertheless, the bull regulating adult baptism of Indians as well as their fasts and feasts was neither recalled, nor revoked; instead an order came to implement it. So Fray Bartolomé stayed on for the ensuing ecclesiastical conference in the capital at the beginning of the next year.

Again, 1539 was a time of good and bad for Las Casas. In Febru-

---

[48] Some of these friends from his two visits to Mexico City would become Las Casas' staunchest allies back at court: President Fuenleal would be a member of the great reform junta; and Judge Salmerón and the Franciscan Jacobo de Tastera would support Fray Bartolomé's petitions with their own demands for reform. (See *The Royal File*, Introduction, text at notes 37* and 38*; also heading of doc. 1; doc. 2B and note 12; and doc. 7 and note 41.) On his friends, see Lino Gómez Canedo, "Bartolomé de las Casas y sus amigos franciscanos," in *Libro Jubilar de Emetrio S. Santovenia* (Havana, 1957), 75–84; and *Las Casas en México*, note 59. And for his gathering historical material in Mexico City, see Wagner–Parish, 202 and note 21.

[49] See *Las Casas en México:* cap. 1 "Roma—tres decretos para una crisis"; also cap. 3, the section following note 32, for a-point-by-point comparison of the tract and the encyclical. *Sublimis Deus* is translated below in the text of *The Only Way*, Part I, last section.

ary, he had the satisfaction of having the viceroy and High Court ratify his contract for the peaceful conversion of the "Land of War," and hearing it proclaimed publicly. But the meetings of 1539 were only a shaky success. The bishops decreed the implementation of the papal regulations, and after a stormy protest, the Franciscans reluctantly promised to comply. Yet only a few months later, Fray Toríbio Motolinia and a companion boasted defiantly that they had baptized fourteen thousand adult Indians in five days.[50]

But at length, after these ups and downs of good and bad, Bartolomé de las Casas was finally able to settle for a few months in the Dominican monastery of Oaxaca to get ready for his return to court after an absence of more than twenty years. Following his earlier pattern, but drawing on his expanded *History,* he completed an extensive memorial of atrocities—not just on the islands this time, but also in the conquest of Mexico and Peru and the rest of the mainland, a very full account of *The Decimation of the Indians.* (An abridged version, which he would later publish himself, still ranks as perhaps the most concentrated horror story of all time.) Along with that account, he drew up a new set of reform institutions and laws: *Sixteen Remedies for the Plagues [of the Encomienda and Slavery] that are Destroying the Indies* —targeting abuses from every region.

Finally, with mounting satisfaction, Las Casas composed an expanded version of his first book—*How the Kings of Spain Must Care for the Indies! viz.,* by *The Only Way of Calling All People to a Living Faith*—with a dedication aimed at the emperor, and powerful additions. Especially important was the new papal encyclical *Sublimis Deus* confirming his doctrine, and the implementing brief directing Cardinal Tavera to announce automatic excommunication of all who harmed the Indians or deprived them of their liberty or property. Likewise included was an enlarged section on Indian capacity, with data arranged according to Aristotle's eight requisites, but not naming the philosopher (as in Fray Jacobo de Tastera's strong letter). Also, from the monastery library, there came more citations from Scripture, Church Fathers, Roman and canon law, like those in Cardinal Adrian's learned speech on peaceful conversion that had swayed the councils. Above all, the dedication pointedly told Charles V that the papal Bull of Donation was *for the conversion of the Indians,* which His

---

[50] Again see *Las Casas en México:* cap. 4, penultimate section, i.e. following note 49, on the 1539 meeting; notes 52, 54, and 55, with corresp. text, for the proclamation of the contract and the relative failure of the meetings; also note 55 and corresp. text for Motolinía's disobedience.

Majesty must accomplish in the peaceful way Christ had commanded and not by the horrors of conquest and exploitation.[51]

His preparations done, Fray Bartolomé de las Casas stopped briefly in Guatemala to give his blessing to the friars who were continuing his peaceful conversion experiment in the "Land of War," and sailed back to Spain in 1540. As before in 1515, he was returning with allies: his Dominican assistant, Fray Rodrigo de Ladrada; the Franciscan missions procurator, Fray Jacobo de Tastera, whose peaceful conversion experiment had failed owing to the intrusion of Spanish slavers; and also a dark-skinned Indian companion.[52]

At court, Bartolomé de las Casas achieved the greatest legislative triumph of his career, the New Laws of 1542–1543—"The Laws and Ordinances Newly Made for the Good Government of the Indies and the Preservation of the Indians." Up until that event, he had found himself trapped in existing power structures, both civil and ecclesiastical—forced to compromise with the civil, forced to obey the ecclesiastical. On this climactic try to help the Indians, he was able to go beyond both. First he accomplished successfully his duties as missions procurator. Then, through the personal intervention of the emperor, he was ordered to remain at court and attend to more important matters.[53] He personally instigated the naming of an imperial legislative commission, he lobbied for the choice of its members, and he himself drafted many of the reform laws. Further, he denounced the corruption of the Council of the Indies, a denunciation which resulted in the public removal of the corrupt councilors and the appointment of new, reformist ones. In fact, he was personally responsible for the private downfall of the once all-powerful Cardinal Loaysa, and his replacement by the reformist

---

[51] For the Oaxaca interlude, see *Las Casas en México*, cap. 4, last section, i.e., following note 56. The revocation of "Pastorale officium," is related in the same cap. 4, first section.

[52] The details of his return and the unpublished document about his hitherto unknown Indian companion are given in *The Untold Story*.

[53] See *The Untold Story* for a full account of Fray Jacobo de Tastera carrying Las Casas' letter and a summary of *The Decimation of the Indies* to the emperor, and the provincial ordering Las Casas and Fray Rodrigo to stay on in Spain. For the letter, see Wagner–Parish, 104 last line to 105, and 106–7, especially note 38. His missionary work is reflected in a multitude of royal orders to benefit the Land of War and his recruitment of friars for the New World—see Saint-Lu, *La Vera Paz*, Catalogue, nos. 73–89, orders issued in 1540; 93, 95, 97, 98, orders issued in 1541.

Cardinal Tavera as president of the great junta that actually framed the New Laws.[54]

Las Casas' technique in achieving these goals was powerful and dramatic. For hours without interruption he held the councilors motionless with a complete reading of the *Decimation* (the memorial on atrocities), while his two aides, the friar and the Indian, displayed piles of notarized proofs to back what he was describing.[55] No less powerful was his impassioned presentation of *Twenty Reasons Against the Encomienda*—and the first reason was that the papal Bull of Donation could only be a grant for conversion.[56]

When at last the laws were voted on by the commission, and approved by the emperor, Bartolomé de las Casas was offered the best bishopric in the Indies, the wealthy See of Cuzco. He declined it. But when he was urged to accept the impoverished diocese of Chiapa—it contained his own "Land of War" experiment, now renamed the "Land of True Peace"—the temptation was irresistible. His friends impressed on him that by accepting the miter, he would automatically be free from the vow of obedience, and could then use the ecclesiastical arm to enforce the New Laws.[57] Finally persuaded, Las Casas was consecrated as bishop in the Church of San Pablo of Seville on March 31, 1544.

3. An Apostolic Crisis in the New World

It was with hope against hope that Bishop Bartolomé de las Casas went back to the New World. He knew that he was going into a dangerous situation: the "abolition" of the encomienda had been leaked to the colonists. The troublemakers had not been deported as he had advised. He had not been given the juridical powers he needed. But he brought with him the largest missionary contingent ever assembled, forty-five Dominican friars, and a lay staff of five. He *had* won the New

---

[54] For Loaysa's downfall, see *Las Casas as a Bishop,* xiiiab, note 11; for his replacement by Tavera, see *The Royal File,* Introduction, text corresp. to note 39*, and note 19 explaining "Addendum to doc. 2."

[55] See Wagner-Parish, 108–9 citing Alonso de Santa Cruz's eyewitness account. And cf. *Las Casas en México,* Appendix 16D, opening of par. [8]. on the stacks of probanzas. The scene is reconstructed in *The Untold Story.*

[56] Cf. *Opúsculos* [*BAE* 110], "Primera Razon," 70a–72a.

[57] See *Las Casas as a Bishop,* Introduction, first section, "How Las Casas became a Bishop," xi–xiv, citing all the primary sources, both chroniclers and documents.

Laws and reformed the council, and now he expected to use his new episcopal power to enforce those laws and to run a model diocese.[58] Both expectations proved vain. In Chiapa, Las Casas' unruly clergy and flock defied his authority, rioted when he refused absolution to slaveholders, and actually drew swords on him, though he faced them down. When he went for help to the new High Court of Central America, the president proved hopelessly corrupt; and the judges, far from giving him the needed aid of the secular arm, refused to implement the New Laws. He threatened them with anathema to no effect. And then the New Laws themselves began to fall apart.

Emperor Charles V, on October 20, 1545, afraid of the civil wars in Peru, and persuaded by a handsome bribe from the colonists revoked the key ordinance—the law of inheritance, which would have wiped out encomiendas on the death of the encomendero, and set the Indians free in crown towns. Three years earlier, Charles *had* listened to Las Casas and the great junta, but now he was in hock to his bankers. He had dreamed of creating a peaceful Europe united by dynastic alliances, but all he had achieved were endless wars. He had to have the gold of the Indies.[59]

The tragic news of this latest revocation reached Bishop Las Casas at Oaxaca, while he was en route to Mexico City for a meeting of the bishops of New Spain. Again, as after the Cumaná massacre in 1522, and as with the revocation of the antislavery law in 1534, and as with the blocking of the papal decrees in 1539, Bartolomé de las Casas found himself facing the ruin of his whole defense of the Indians.[60] But he had a plan. He entered Mexico City on foot with only a tiny entourage. The authorities had feared a riot among the Spaniards because, as the author of the New Laws, Las Casas was "the most hated man in the Indies." But there was no riot. The whole town turned out peacefully to

---

[58] As a bishop, Las Casas was an authentic figure of the Catholic pre-Reformation, planning to run his diocese according to the precepts of a Dominican friend, Carranza de Miranda, precepts later adopted by Trent. Fray Bartolomé had earlier presented at court Bishop Zumárraga's petition on reforming the diocesan clergy—see Bataillon, "Zumárraga, reformador del clero seglar: una carta inédita . . ." *Historia méxicana* 3 (1953): 1–10. Bishop-elect Las Casas had obtained a brief permitting him to have his chapter live with him in community. And he would conduct a visitation of his diocese, notably the Tuzulutlán mission, and issue an Easter proclamation—all actions of a reforming bishop. See Francesca Cantù, "Per un rinovammento della coscenza pastorale del cinquecento: il vescovo Bartolomé de las Casas . . ." *Annuario del Istituto Storico Italiano per l'età moderna e contemporanea* 25–26 (1973–74), Rome, 1976.

[59] See Ramón Carande, *Carlos V y sus banqueros,* 2 vols., Madrid, 1965, 1967.

[60] For the events of his bishopric to this point, see Wagner–Parish, chaps. 11–13, and chap. 14, first section.

see him. Indians knelt as he passed. Ordinary people lined the streets and one was heard to cry out, "There goes the sainted bishop, the father of the Indians."[61]

The "sainted bishop" promptly brought the authorities to heel. In a curt note, he told the viceroy and the Audiencia that he could not call on them and pay his respects, since they were all in a state of automatic excommunication because they had ordered the hand cut off of a priest in Oaxaca. Of course, the specific case was not the point; if there was guilt, the Church authorities could discipline the offender. But the secular arm had not the power to silence the ecclesiastical voice of conscience, i.e., Las Casas himself—that was the point. Viceroy Mendoza and the eight judges, properly humiliated, had to troop down to the cathedral where the provisor gave them a penance.[62]

Next the "sainted bishop" brought the ecclesiastical authorities to heel. His fellow bishops were deeply ashamed that they had failed to stand up for their right to make conscience judgments. At his urging, they wrote a strong memorandum to the emperor, asking him to enforce the statutes on ecclesiastical immunities.[63]

Bishop Las Casas went even farther at the ecclesiastical conference of 1546. He promoted a series of resolutions defending the Indians. Encomenderos who had not installed priests or catechists—almost none had—must make restitution to the Indians out of the tribute they had collected. Conversion of the Indians should be paid for by the crown. Indians should be completely exempt from tithes and from being preached to about buying Bulls of Indulgence. Apart from these main ones, there were other resolutions dealing with special protection for the Indians.[64]

He got all this approved by the conference, even though the viceroy had ruled out of order his opening speech denouncing Indian slavery and abusive personal services under the continuing encomienda.[65] But Bishop Las Casas had not yet finished with Viceroy Mendoza.

---

[61] The scene, from Remesal, is reconstructed in *Las Casas en México,* opening of cap. 5. Cf. Pérez, *Viajes y estancias,* 695, for an enumeration of his companions.

[62] See *Las Casas en México,* cap. 5, end of first section, citing Remesal's account and a confirming letter by Zumárraga which also relates the penance.

[63] See *Las Casas en México,* note 81 and corresp. text, on the bishops' action; and note 66 on Zumárraga's regret. Also cf. below, note 68 and corresp. text on the old bishop correcting his own fault.

[64] See *Las Casas en México,* cap. 6, "Logros lascasianos en las juntas de 1546," for a complete reconstruction of ten resolutions voted by this conference.

[65] For eyewitness information from Bishop Marroquín of Guatemala and Inspector General Sandoval, cf. *Las Casas en México,* note 75 and corresp. text.

Stung by the viceroy's prohibition of discussing these topics at the conference, he brought Mendoza himself to heel in a daring sermon in the cathedral. Choosing a subversive Old Testament text, Las Casas openly accused the colonists of wanting false prophets who would tell them only what they wished to hear; then he launched into an impassioned sermon warning them not to mistreat or enslave the Indians. The viceroy, already under investigation for his enslavement of Indian prisoners in the Mixtón War, got the message and agreed to let Bishop Las Casas convoke a separate junta of friars and confessors. Right away it denounced Indian slavery and abusive personal services under the encomienda—exactly the subjects they had not let him bring up.[66]

But now in Mexico City, at the age of sixty-two, in the monastery of Santo Domingo, Bartolomé de las Casas faced the greatest crisis of his entire career. Here in the capital, he had just been putting ecclesiastical patches on the ruin of the New Laws. What could he really do? Twelve years earlier, at that other revocation (of the antislavery law), he had friends and allies. In New Spain, Audiencia President Fuenleal and the friars had written letters home saying Betanzos was out of his mind and the revocation was an outrage. In Spain itself, Doctor Bernal, new on the Council of the Indies, had received a copy of *The Only Way,* and had helped Minaya go to Rome. And in Rome, Minaya—armed with letters from the New World and the Old and Las Casas' book—had found other allies, doctors and cardinals and the pope himself.[67] This time Bishop Las Casas had *no one* to support him. They had all caved in. With the backing of the provincials of the three Orders, Mexican envoys had gone to Flanders to ask the emperor for the revocation. Even his friend Zumárraga had betrayed his principles and taken the wrong side.

And on the recent affront to the power of the Church, the rest of the bishops had played dead and let the civil powers do what they pleased. But at least, after Las Casas explained canon law to Zumárraga, the old bishop got some of his courage back. For on the Feast of Sts. Peter and Paul, Bishop Zumárraga had thundered at the

---

[66] Remesal's full account, lib. 7, cap. 17, nos. 2–3, is confirmed by Las Casas himself in his *Tratado sobre los indios que se han hecho esclavos* (Against Enslavement of Indians), third corollary, giving the conclusions of the friars' junta. Cf. *Opúsculos* [*BAE,* vol. 110], 289a, and the trans. of Latin passages in Las Casas' *Tratados* (Mexico, 1965), 2:1325.

[67] On Dr. Bernal's help and Minaya's Roman allies, see *Las Casas en México:* cap. 1, first section after the opening scene, and penultimate section; also Appendices 5–7 and 16A.

[68] For the Mexican campaign against the law of inheritance, see Hanke, *Lucha,* 231–41, and especially notes 72–74; and cf. Wagner–Parish, 159–61 for a concise ac-

viceroy about respecting ecclesiastical authority.[68] So now, what could Las Casas, one bishop, do all alone—with nothing to support him but God's commandment to look after the welfare of the Indians?

But that was his plan: he *was* a bishop! Therefore he had received the apostolic mission, the one Our Lord had given to Peter and the rest when He told them to preach with love and gentleness a true and living faith. And a bishop must not be a mercenary serving his own comfort and the powers of the earth. A bishop must be a true shepherd protecting his flock from all oppressors. He must, if need be, defy the powers of the earth even at the risk of his life.[69]

Las Casas had been in danger before, but so far he had escaped: from massacre at Cumaná; from Nicaragua where he had enraged the governor, whose thugs later murdered their own bishop; from Chiapa where encomenderos burst in on him with drawn swords. But those times he had not chosen the danger. It was different now. He must follow a new course that would lay his life on the line. He must tell the truth to the prince, and the prince might execute him for it.

For Bartolomé de las Casas had made up his mind *to commit high treason.* He called in a notary and drafted two documents under his episcopal seal. One appointed a vicar general with authority to place his entire diocese under interdict if required; the other appointed confessors and directed them to use, in the strictest secrecy, an enclosed "Twelve Rules for Confessors," especially at the deathbed of encomenderos. These rules were designed to force compliance with all the New Laws, including the law of inheritance just revoked. But his rules went even farther. He insisted that everything had been stolen from the Indians because the conquest and the encomienda were illegal and immoral. Therefore the Spaniards were obligated to make total restitution, as circumstances would permit—he had spelled this out in the last section of *The Only Way.* But if this was the truth, then it followed that the king, who must rule for the good of his subjects, had no right to authorize conquests and grant encomiendas which would doom the Indians to death and the Spaniards to hell. Challenging that right was high treason and Las Casas knew it.

So without delay, he composed a forthright tract in Latin, virtually threatening the regent, Prince Philip, with excommunication if he

---

count. Zumárraga's sermon is reconstructed from his own report in *Las Casas en México,* cap. 5, note 70, and the entire corresp. section.

[69] See *Tratado sobre los indios que se han hecho esclavos,* second corollary, in *Opúsculos (BAE* 110) 281b–289a—cf. the trans. of Latin passages in his *Tratados* (Mexico, 1965), 2:1314–25. See also *Las Casas en México,* Appendix 30, first draft of this Latin Corrolarium with Spanish trans. following.

dared lay a finger on a cleric (Bishop Las Casas) even for the crime of high treason! What he really had in mind is clear from the anecdote he cites of Bishop Ambrose excommunicating the emperor Theodosius for a massacre committed by the imperial troops in a far-off province. By this example he was telling Philip that an individual can revoke human laws but a person cannot revoke divine ones, that conscience has a duty to speak truth to power, and if someone tries to kill conscience that person kills his own soul.[70]

Next, Bishop Las Casas set about preparing for his last return to Spain. After the tragedy of the revocation, he knew that his place had to be permanently at court, defending what was left of the New Laws, and watching over all the rights of the Indians. The next battleground would certainly be the antislavery laws. So he finished and revised two horror stories about slavery that he would present to the council—a bulky new one about the Indians blown to bits or enslaved by Viceroy Mendoza in the Mixtón War, and a revision of the antislavery tract he had left with the council when he sailed as a bishop in 1544. To this tract he added corollaries defining and announcing his own future course, and what he expected of Philip and Charles. It was the duty of kings to create a just society in which the Indians could be converted, therefore the king must free all the slaves. It was the duty of Indies' bishops to plead before king and council, even at the risk of their lives, to obtain the freedom of the Indians—that meant demanding liberation of the slaves and the substitution of tribute for forced labor under the encomienda.[71]

Back in Spain, Bishop Las Casas faced the expected charge of high treason and the added charge of heresy for denying the pope's power in the Bull of Donation—and also a scheme concocted in his absence to revoke the antislavery laws. The charges and the scheme all came from the same source. . . .

The chief tool of the colonial agents at court had been the renowned translator of Aristotle, Juan Ginés de Sepúlveda. He had been persuaded by Cardinal Loaysa, out of power as a result of Las Casas'

---

[70] See *Las Casas en México,* cap. 7, "Un arma secreta y un reto real," first three sections, for the scene of the notary and Las Casas writing "¡La exención o la damnación!" *N.B.* He does not cite the example of Henry kneeling in the snow at Canossa, but rather the example of Bishop Ambrose, at the door of the Milan cathedral, refusing entrance to the Emperor Theodosius.

[71] For these final activities, see *Las Casas en México,* cap. 7, last section. For the three corollaries, i.e., the duty of kings, the duty of bishops, the conclusions of the friars' junta, see *Opúsculos* (*BAE* 110), doc. 28, the Spanish passages on 279a–290a. Cf. supra notes 69 and 69 for the trans. of Latin passages in second and third corollaries.

denunciations, to write a tract defending the conquest as a just war—for if a war is just, one can legally enslave the captives. To do this, Sepúlveda had produced a new and terrible defamation of the Indians. They were, he declared, clearly inferior to the Spaniards. They were barbarians, incompetent and servile by nature according to Aristotle's definition of barbarian, and they should be ruled by superior beings—Spaniards—and conquest was therefore a holy war necessary to Christianize them.

In quick succession, Bishop Las Casas had the publication of Sepúlveda's book blocked as unsound doctrine, skillfully defended himself against Sepúlveda's charges, and presented his treatises against Indian slavery to the Council of the Indies. Then, at his request and on the council's recommendation, the emperor convoked a junta on conquests and slavery, where Las Casas faced Sepúlveda head-on in his last great public defense of the Indians.

For five days solid, Bartolomé de las Casas read aloud an enormous tract denouncing Sepúlveda and all other defamers of the Indians as misled tools, and marshaled his best arguments—again from *The Only Way*—to show that the Indians were *not* inferior and conquest was *not* a Christian means of conversion. Once more he succeeded. The revocation drive fizzled—even a hasty mini-junta on perpetual encomiendas collapsed. Conquests were officially halted; Indian slavery was abolished once more (for the third time); the remaining New Laws were saved and strengthened.[72]

The danger was past for now, so Las Casas could arrange his permanent residence at court. He resigned his diocese; he could not function there because of the resistance. But as an absentee bishop he had done his duty to Chiapa—freeing the slaves, enforcing the New Laws, removing the corrupt Audiencia president, and naming his successor-bishop. Then he made over his episcopal pension from the Indies, and other sums, to the Dominican College of San Gregorio at Valladolid for living quarters, because the council of the Indies normally met in that city.[73]

---

[72] See the short summary of known events in Wagner–Parish, chap. 15, "Casas versus Sepúlveda." *The Untold Story* uses new and neglected documents from *The Royal File* to reveal Las Casas' further activities at court and his *success* (long questioned) in blocking further conquests. For the mini-junta on perpetuity, see Wagner–Parish, 211–12; and Pérez, *Viajes y estancias,* 796–98, the junta members (but only the first seven listed were members, the rest were speakers). Also see *Las Casas en México,* cap. 8, "Las Nuevas Leyes renovadas."

[73] For his contract with San Gregorio, see Wagner–Parish, 184 and note 2; for the Chiapa resistance and his work as an absentee bishop, see *Las Casas as a Bishop,* Introduction, third section, on "Las Casas' episcopal achievements."

But first he had to publish short versions of his major memorials from his great battles to win and then save the New Laws. He did not want to argue the issues all over again before Philip. Also he had to take care of recruiting, financing, and sending more expeditions of missionaries. Both tasks took him to Seville, the book capital of Spain, and the river port from which everyone had to leave for the Indies. These intermittent chores kept him there for most of 1552. But he was glad to be staying again at the Dominican monastery of San Pablo, where he could get at the library of the late Hernando Columbus (the Discoverer's illegitimate second son), which he had barely seen when he sailed as a bishop in 1544. It contained all sorts of books and papers relating to the Discovery, especially the priceless (though partly abridged) copy of the "Log of the First Voyage," Don Hernando's manuscript of the life of his father, Christopher, the Discoverer's own books, etc. And he even had access to the Columbus family archives, in a chapel of the local Carthusian monastery. This was a historian's dream.[74]

So in 1552, Bartolomé de las Casas began a systematic rewriting of his *History of the Indies,* copying documents, scanning books, making a plan. He would add, from Don Hernando and the library, all ancient antecedents to the Discovery: cosmography, legends, earlier voyages. And then would come the stepping stones of the Atlantic Islands—especially the Canaries and West Africa, since both were part of his own family history from way back and right up to Uncle Francisco, who had left Hispaniola in 1496 to serve with Alfonso de Lugo on Grand Canary, and died in 1502 on an African foray. And he knew that the Discoverer's brother Bartholomew, and probably Christopher himself, had been on some Guinea excursions. . . .[75]

But as Las Casas searched out the Columbus material in Gomez' book on Guinea and in other Portuguese histories, his soul was sud-

---

[74] Las Casas' holograph *transcription* of the partly abridged Log is today the only surviving text of this precious document. All copies of the original Log have disappeared. Las Casas did NOT abridge the Log, as is carelessly asserted. He always meticulously copied documents, and his use of this abridged version demonstrates that the abridgment was not by himself—compare Antonio Rumeu de Armas, *Hernando Colón, historiador del descubrimiento de América* (1973), at 127–33. What Fray Bartolomé apparently copied was an abridgment made for the Columbus heirs' lawsuit against the crown. *The Untold Story* solves the mystery with pre-trial data and information from recent critical studies (1989): Consuelo Varela's on Las Casas' copy of the First and Third Voyage Logs, and Rumeu's on the newly discovered *Libro copiador* of nine Columbus letters to the Catholic Monarchs (see Bibliography).

[75] See Manuel Giménez Fernández, "Bartolomé de las Casas en 1552," Introduction to Las Casas' *Tratados,* vol. 1, at lvii–lxxxvi, on Las Casas' tasks in Seville.

denly filled with horror. Once again, as in 1514, the blinders fell from his eyes. These historians were as callous as Oviedo and the other defamers who wanted to enslave the Indians. How could he have failed to realize the truth! How could he have believed the lie that African slaves were taken in just war! With mounting passion, Bartolomé de las Casas wrote his Canaries/African prelude to the Discovery. In language from *The Only Way* and his own prophetic call, he denounced this infamy—the enslavement of blacks who had never seen or harmed the Christians—which was as much contrary to the will of God as the enslavement of the Indians.

He had not known this when he began his reform efforts at court —he examined himself unsparingly. In those early days all the reformers had urged bringing over African slaves to stem the disappearance of the island Indians who were being totally used up under brutal mistreatment. African slaves in Spain had not come from the slave trade, but from the wars with the Moors, and no one saw anything wrong about it. Such slaves were retainers, like members of the family; some had expertise in gold mining and metallurgy and in other technologies, surpassing the Europeans; they were bigger and stronger than the Spaniards. He himself had *at first* ("primero") made the same suggestion and repeated it at intervals for quite some time. But this was just like when he gave up his own encomienda: *it didn't matter how good the relations were, the whole system was wrong.* And he hoped God would forgive him for not having denounced African slavery sooner. . . .[76]

During this interval, Fray Rodrigo had seen to the printing of the eight tracts Las Casas had wanted. And at the beginning of 1553, they saw off the last group of Dominicans, with the friars carrying copies of the books for distribution in the Indies where they changed minds. He himself carried copies back to San Gregorio for distribution in Spain where they strengthened his position.[77]

Now Bartolomé de Las Casas could take up his new post as "Representative of All the Indians" to the Spanish crown, with the council of the Indies reserving two hours a day to hear him. He was receiving correspondence from all over the Indies, from officials, from friars,

---

[76] See Addendum 3, "Las Casas' Condemnation of African Slavery," translated from *Historia,* lib. 1, cap. 24, and lib. 3, caps. 102 and 129.

[77] See Wagner–Parish, Catalogue, nos. 18, 19, 23, 41, 43, 44, 48, 49, for the publication of these works; also the narrative section on "Eight Famous Tracts," at 186–87. For the impact of the tracts in Mexico City, see *Las Casas en México,* "Conclusión," note 120 and corresp. text.

even from penniless conquistadors, and he dealt with the matters they presented. He had three rooms in the college for himself and his assistants, Fray Rodrigo and the dark-skinned giant, Juanillo. He had students to work for him, doing legal research and copying his treatises, for he was writing as never before—including daily petitions and polemical books. Above all, he was composing a massive new *Defense of the Indian Civilizations,* according to Aristotelian categories, to put a stop to all future defamations. He had promised to do this at the end of his big treatise against Sepúlveda. So he took the Indian capacity material from his big *History,* from the opening chapters of *The Only Way,* and from reports of friars in the Indies—and he added comparisons to ancient cultures, from books in the college library. Also he stuffed the central part of *The Only Way* with quotes from Aristotle and Aquinas and the apocryphal Abdyas of Babylon for use in the theology and philosophy classes.[78]

But in 1555, without warning, something happened which plunged the retired bishop of Chiapa into the great final battle of his life. Charles abdicated. And Philip, still in England, inherited Spain, the Indies, and the crushing burden of his father's debts. He saw no way out of those debts but to borrow and beg and tax and pawn and confiscate and sell on every side. The Peruvian encomenderos chose the moment to descend on him with an irresistible offer of eight million gold ducats to buy perpetual rights to their Indians. As soon as Las Casas heard of the scheme, he acted. He knew that if it succeeded there would be no protection of any kind for the Indians, no crown to watch over them, no universal protector, and ultimately no Indians. He had to reach the conscience of the future king. So he wrote to his informant —and old friend and ally, the Dominican Carranza, who was right on the spot in England as confessor to Queen Mary. He sent Carranza not a letter but a booklet ("libellus") denouncing the horrors of the encomienda, the mortal sin of giving away one's vassals, and the need for the king to think what kind of candle he would carry on the day of judgment. Carranza showed it to Philip and got him to convoke a junta of twelve. But ten voted for the sale, and one of the pro-sale people actually started a fist-fight with Carranza over the booklet of the bishop of Chiapa. As Carranza wrote to Las Casas, Philip was more adamant

---

[78] See Wagner–Parish, section on "Petitioner and correspondent," 190–94; also in chap. 17, "Historian of the Indies," section on "Octogenarian" (*sic:* he was actually in his seventies), 204–7 for his books and papers at this time. The 'stuffing' of *The Only Way* is charted in App. III.B below.

than ever about selling the Indians. The monarch had a conscience but his need for money had wiped it out.[79]

In this emergency, Las Casas devised a new strategy. He personally wrote to Philip, telling him not to sell the encomiendas because he, Las Casas, was putting together a better offer. Nothing stopped Philip. Over the protests of all his councils he barged ahead and named a perpetuity commission which actually went to Peru to prepare for the sale. But, meanwhile, Las Casas came up with the audacious counteroffer, arranged by his Dominican allies in Peru and Mexico, who had worked out the details and sent him power of attorney.

Then Las Casas and the Dominican provincial, fresh from Peru, went before the Council of the Indies and sprang the offer: the Peruvian chieftains were ready to buy the freedom of their country! The chiefs alleged that the encomenderos did not have the eight million promised ducats, but whatever sum they did have, the Indians would raise the ante by a hundred thousand to obtain their freedom and restore the rule of the Inca (who had fled inland with his followers and established his hidden capital on the far side of the Andes). A similar offer to buy their own freedom came in from the Mexican chieftains, put together by a protégé of Las Casas who had succeeded to the bishopric of Vera Paz ("The Land of True Peace").[80] At almost the same time, Philip's attempt to sell the Peruvian Indians came to naught. The perpetuity commission members had created a swamp of corruption and were caught in it themselves; two of them were sent home to face charges and jail for bribery.[81]

The battle against perpetuity had been won for the moment, but Philip turned vengeful. Carranza had returned from London and been made cardinal archbishop of Toledo and primate of Spain—only to be arrested by the Inquisition as a heretic! Las Casas was called as a wit-

---

[79] See Wagner–Parish: chap. 18. "Peru and Perpetuity," section on "His appeal to Carranza de Miranda," 213–16; and Catalogue, no. 57. See also Luciano Pereña's Estudio Preliminar to Las Casas' *De regia potestate* (*Corpus Hispanorum de Pace,* vol. 8, Madrid, 1969): esp. xc–xcvi on Fray Bartolomé's appeal to Carranza; and xlviii–xlix on the Junta de Londres, based on José Ignacio Tellechea, "Bartolomé de las Casas y Bartolomé Carranza," in *Scriptorium Victoriense* 6 (1959):11.

[80] Only *The Untold Story* tells the Mexican counter-offer. For the Peruvian events, see Wagner–Parish, chap. 18, "Peru and Perpetuity," section on "The counter-offer," 216–20 and Catalogue, no. 63; also Pereña's Estudio Preliminar to *De regia potestate,* esp. ci–cix.

[81] On the sordid end of the perpetuity commission, see *The Royal File,* Introduction, note 25* and corresp. text. Also Marvin Goldwert, "La lucha por la perpetuidad de las encomiendas en el Perú virreinal," *Revista histórica* 23 (Peru, 1957–58): 220–22.

ness, courageously defended his friend, and demanded to know how
they could have arrested a bishop. They said they had a papal brief. He
asked if it was only for Carranza's arrest, or did it cover bishops in
general. They wouldn't tell him, but he knew, and he was not intimi-
dated. The Spanish Inquisition was nothing but an arm of Philip's
secular power, so Las Casas kept right on and composed a treatise on
his boldest theme, *The Limits of Royal Power,* challenging the king's
right to sell his vassals in perpetuity. This doctrine was based on *The
Only Way* where he described Christ's kingdom of compassion and
peace as a model for earthly rulers who must govern for the good of
their people. The Inquisitors seized the manuscript limiting royal
power, and harassed him openly, though they didn't dare interrogate him.[82]

Still Las Casas was not afraid. At the age of eighty he pursued the
battle against perpetuity with the greatest effort of his entire career. His
last two books, *Who Owns the Treasures in the Inca Tombs?* and its
shorter sequel, *Twelve Doubts about the Conquest of Peru,* made an
offer of fabulous wealth—annual tribute of gold and precious stones
buried in the tombs of past Inca rulers, tombs known only to a few—in
return for Indian self-rule. This offer would obsess Philip and then his
new Peruvian viceroy for the next five years. For despite their topical
titles, both works were comprehensive in scope, and merited the desig-
nation with which he offered them to Philip—"my greatest gift to Your
Majesty, my last will and testament, and its codicil."[83]

In these last books, Las Casas spelled out in full detail his final plan
for the restoration of the Indies. He argued that the whole Spanish
enterprise had followed such a wrong course that total restitution, total
restoration were required. That meant freedom for the Indians and
restoration of native rulers and native rule. For Spain had only a "po-
tential" title to the Indies, and it would not become an "actual" title
unless ratified by the free consent of the Indians themselves. He wanted

---

[82] Bishops were exempt from the jurisdiction of the Inquisition until Fray Ber-
naldo de Fresneda (Carranza's chief opponent) went to Rome in 1559 and secured the
brief "Cum sicuti nuper." On Las Casas and the Inquisition, see Wagner–Parish, 187–90;
also *Las Casas en México,* cap. 8, second section and note 107. For the actual tract seized
in manuscript, see Isacio Pérez, *Inventario documentado de los escritos de Las Casas*
(Bayamon, Puerto Rico, 1981), nos. 287 and 314. Las Casas' Inquisition troubles were all
caused by Sepúlveda; in addition to the known denunciation to the Spanish Inquisition,
The Untold Story reveals an unknown denunciation to the *Roman* Inquisition!

[83] See Wagner–Parish, chap. 19, "Last Testament," section on Treasures and
Doubts, a bequest and codicil, 231–36. For the text of *Doce Dudas,* see *Opúsculos (BAE,*
vol. 110), doc. 50; for the larger work, see note 84 below.

these free native kingdoms to become a kind of commonwealth under the king of Spain, on the model of the Turkish empire, where the separate kingdoms paid a precious jewel as annual tribute. The sovereign ruler in Spain could defend the commonwealth from incursions by Portuguese or British pirates. But, essentially, native civilizations would be fully respected and fully restored.[84]

Gone were all his early concepts of superior European technology to be taught to the Indians. Gone was the concept of protective legislation to correct abuses. Gone was the concept of these Indians as pagans to be converted at all costs. Rather, the gift of faith must be offered as Christ had commanded, with gentleness, with love, and with full respect. He was sure the faith would be accepted by the Indians *if so offered after restoration.* But if conquest and oppression—and all the horrors of the encomienda and slavery and mining—were the price of evangelization, then it would be better for Spain to leave the Indies alone, and trust that God had better plans for their peaceful conversion at the eleventh hour of the world.[85]

There is a persistent tradition which has reached us in garbled form that Las Casas almost did persuade the king to give Peru back to the Inca.[86] In fact, his restoration schemes for Middle and South America were dropped because of the death of the main proponent.

In Madrid, at the age of eighty-two, Bartolomé de las Casas died, still fighting for the rights of the Indians.[87] As he lay on his deathbed in the monastery of Atocha in Madrid, coworkers across town read aloud to the council his last petition asking the monarch for a junta magna to

---

[84] Angel Losada's edition of Las Casas' *Los tesoros del Perú* (Madrid, 1958), lacks the crucial cap. 36 which is printed in Las Casas' *De regia potestate,* Appendix 11. The tomb treasures, says Las Casas, belong to the Indians, who can use them freely for an annual tribute to the king. Peruvian Viceroy Toledo spent years trying to prove Inca monarchy illegitimate, a device to claim all the wealth of the hidden tombs as legitimate booty for the Spanish monarchs.

[85] This doctrine is put strongly in Las Casas' *Twenty Reasons Against the Encomienda,* 20th Reason, near the end, see *Opúsculos (BAE* 110), doc. 11, 118a. Preaching the faith to the Inca, *after* he came out of the mountains, was suggested in the counter-offer.

[86] The garbled tradition is in the Parecer de Yucay—see *Documentos inéditos de España* (hereafter *DIE*) 13 (Madrid, 1848): 425–69. See the discussion in cap. 2.b of Gustavo Gutiérrez' *Dios o el oro en las Indias* (Lima, 1989). For the underlying motive of Viceroy Toledo, and his relative who wrote the Parecer, see above, note 84, and below, note 94 and corresp. text.

[87] See Helen Rand Parish with Harold E. Weidman, "The Correct Birthdate of Bartolomé de las Casas" in *Hispanic American Historical Review* 56 (1976), at 401, last par.

reform the Indies. And a trusted messenger carried his last letter addressed to the new Dominican pope, Pius V, begging His Holiness to condemn conquest as a means of conversion. And in his last will, Las Casas warned that Spain would lose her empire if she did not awaken to the destruction of the Indies. And in his last petition he declared that the Indians of the New World, because of what they had suffered at the hands of the Spaniards, had the right to make just war against Spain, and "this right will last until the day of judgment." And in his last words he professed that he had kept faith, for fifty years of untiring labor, with the charge that God had laid upon him to plead for the restoration of the Indians to their original lands, liberty and freedom.[88]

POSTSCRIPT

The work in the following pages is the Oaxaca version of *The Only Way.* Las Casas wrote it at the climactic central point of his life—just before he went back to court for the second time and obtained the New Laws. Nevertheless this text reveals his full spiritual doctrine. And the reader has the original structure. It begins with his first vision of the New World, land and people in their beauty and capacity as if before the Spaniards came. Both spoke to him of God's creation, of Adam and Eve before the Fall. In his *History of the Indies* he repeatedly describes the earthly paradise. We have restored this lost opening briefly from his other writings. The large central portion lays out the true way of evangelizing these fine peoples, according to the Lord. The work then lays out the false way of war, brutality, and conquest. We stripped the central section of later accretions and rearranged a few sections for logical continuity. Finally, we have separated out the conclusion and called it "restoration" rather than "restitution" because that conforms to Las Casas' overall thinking that the world of the Indians had to be restored to them insofar as it was possible.[89] An increment to his doctrine occurs in his last two works, *Who Owns the Treasures in the Inca Tombs?* and *Twelve Doubts about the Conquest of Peru,* where he argues openly for total restoration, the Spanish settlers pulling out entirely if they could not reform their ways. The providence of God would take care of

---

[88] For Las Casas' last petition and last letter, see *Opúsculos* (*BAE*, 110), docs. 51 and 53; the par. from his will is in doc. 52. The deathbed scene is described by Gabriel de Cepeda, *Historia de la milagrosa y venerabiel imagen de Nuestra Señora de Atocha, patrona de Madrid* (Madrid, 1670), 260.

[89] See below, App. III.B, "Our Restoration: Methodology, Chart."

Indian conversion, even at the eleventh hour of the world. This final proposal is not utopian, but original political thought, far in advance of his time, about a commonwealth of free nations paying tribute to and protected by the emperor. But the goal is the same: the restoration of land and liberty to the Indians, i.e., the restoration of God's creation which conquest and exploitation had degraded and ruined.

So powerful was the doctrine argued in these manuscript works—and in the eight tracts he himself had "printed in type" in 1552—that they have had a remarkable influence from his lifetime to ours. Three years after it was written, the *first version* of *The Only Way* and the antislavery ordinance of 1530 were carried to Rome by Fray Bernardino de Minaya—who then brought back the resulting papal encyclical *Sublimis Deus* and its implementing brief. Going and coming, Minaya almost certainly stopped to visit Fray Francisco de Vitoria at the University of Salamanca, with sensational consequences: Vitoria's three pronouncements on the American Indians. In 1537–38, using information only Minaya could have given him, Vitoria attacked the cannibal questionnaire and the requisition, the two standard pretexts for justifying conquest and enslavement of the Indians. He did so by inserting a section, ostensibly on cannibalism, in his prepared lecture on "Temperance"; but the section was later suppressed. Then in early 1539, he delivered his most famous public lecture, "De Indis" ("On the Indies"), on the announced theme of what was the legitimate way to convert the Indians, using the same scriptural text and theme as *The Only Way*. But the same year, in a follow-up lecture, "De bello justo," he backed down from his previous position, under pressure, but could not stave off a royal order from the emperor forbidding further discussion of the topic at Salamanca. Nevertheless, in 1541, at the request of Bartolomé de las Casas, the crown asked Vitoria for a pronouncement on forced and adult baptism in the New World—and Vitoria, joined by the Salamanca theologians, issued a document that went beyond the question and insisted that conversion of the Indians could only take place in a just society. So Vitoria had joined the Córdoba/Las Casas school.[90]

Therefore the much admired school of Salamanca, starting with Vitoria, stems originally from Las Casas—and so does the great flowering of Spanish canonists who treated Spain's title to the Indies for the

---

[90] For Las Casas' influence and Vitoria's first three pronouncements, see *Las Casas en México,* notes 47–49 and corresp. section; also note 60 for Las Casas' role in Vitoria's final pronouncement. In his *Apologia adversus Sepúlvedam,* 375–76, Las Casas himself refers to Vitoria's backing down.

rest of the century. Las Casas' academic expansion of *The Only Way* and his other "heavy" late works were read and studied in the lecture halls of the great Spanish universities during his lifetime and educated a whole generation of students and professors. For from 1560 on, all the great canonists discarded the early doctrine that the Bull of Donation authorized the *conquest* of the Indies by Spain; instead they followed the doctrine, first enunciated by Las Casas and told by him to Charles V, that the papal donation was for *conversion* and not for *exploitation*.[91]

In the next centuries, *The Only Way*, in manuscript form, was so widely circulated in the New World that a summary of the work occupied an entire chapter in a steady seller of the times—the *Itinerario para parochos de Indios* (*Handbook for Parish Priests of Indians*) that went through at least seven editions (in Madrid, Lyons, and Antwerp) from 1668 to 1771. How well known the work became in missionary circles can be judged from an unpublished proposal of a Mexican Franciscan that the missions of Alta California should be established "according to the ideas of Las Casas in *The Only Way*."[92]

And Bartolomé de las Casas' final masterpiece on the tomb treasures in Peru had an unexpectedly powerful impact on Church and State just two years after his death—both events connected with the dispatch of Francisco de Toledo as the new viceroy of Peru in 1568. In Rome, Francis Borgia (the Jesuit general) urged Pope Pius V to issue directives for the missions in Peru to which Borgia was sending the first group of Jesuits. The request recalled Las Casas' last injunction to this Dominican pope. Accordingly Pius named a commission of four cardinals, handed them Las Casas' last two works, and told them to confer with Francis Borgia. The result was a set of papal exhortations on good treatment for the Indians, drafted by Borgia, that read as if they had been written by Las Casas.[93]

---

[91] See Kenneth Pennington, "Bartolomé de las Casas and the Tradition of Medieval Law," *Church History*, 39 (1970), 147–61, esp. 154–55 and note 27 on the changed opinion of Spanish canonists in the late 16th century. Pennington, of course, could not know that Las Casas' late works influenced the change. For Las Casas' earlier enunciation and use of his doctrine, see above, notes 51 and 56 and corresp. texts, and below App. I.A, sect. 1, last par.; and I.B, sect. 2, central par.

[92] See below App. II.B, the extract from the *Itinerario*.

[93] Borgia's role is established from a newly discovered manuscript in Ernest J. Burrus, S.J., "Pius V and Francis Borgia: Their Efforts on behalf of the American Indians," *Archivum Historicum Societatis Jesu*, 41:207–26. For Las Casas' influence, see *Las Casas as a Bishop*, note 74. This amazing episode is fully related for the first time in *The Untold Story*.

In Madrid also, Philip received new pleas for reform, remembered Las Casas' last petition for a great junta, and actually did constitute the junta magna which came out flatly *against* perpetual encomiendas, and *for* the maintenance of all the protective measures promoted by Las Casas—they would remain in effect for the remaining colonial centuries. With his instructions for governing Peru, Viceroy Toledo also seems to have received from the king copies of Las Casas' last two treatises, *The Treasures in the Inca Tombs* and *The Twelve Doubts,* for the viceroy would spend years trying to refute the legitimacy of Inca rule and thereby establish the king of Spain's right to those treasures.[94]

The influence of the eight printed tracts, though less specific, was even more widespread through the subsequent centuries. Printed copies, printed translations, manuscript copies, and fresh editions all coincided with reform movements in many lands. Indeed, the arrival of the eight tracts in Mexico City apparently inspired the Augustinian, Fray Alonso de la Vera Cruz, to discuss Spain's dominion over the Indies in his opening lectures at the newly founded University of Mexico; and further, the tracts provoked a new conference which repudiated the revocation of the law of inheritance and condemned the encomienda.[95]

Also in the sixteenth century, *The Decimation of the Indies* became popular in translation in Protestant northern Europe which had suffered from the sword of the Catholic duke of Alba. And one edition became permanently world famous because of its grisly woodcut illustrations.[96] In the seventeenth century, the *Rules for Confessors* was most influential in the colonies, judging from the many instances of voluntary restitution by conquistadors and encomenderos, especially in Peru.[97] Copies in print and in manuscript form found their way into Italian libraries. "Italian writers [of the seventeenth century] repeatedly invoked the name of Las Casas and his principle of self-determination

---

[94] Stafford Poole's forthcoming study on the Junta Magna shows the continuance of these reform measures. Viceroy Toledo's attack on Las Casas and the Incas has been studied by Lewis Hanke in *Lucha,* last chapter; also see Gustavo Gutiérrez, as cited above in note 86.

[95] For concise bibliographical studies of these many editions, see the Hanke–Giménez Fernández *Bartolomé de las Casas: Bibliografía crítica* (Santiago de Chile, 1954), under the separate tracts; and for additional details see Pérez' *Inventario documentado,* on the separate items. For the impact of the 1552 tracts in Mexico City, see *Las Casas en México,* Conclusión, note 120 and corresp. text.

[96] See Pérez, *Inventario documentado,* no. 126 on the *Brevissima* (*The Decimation of the Indians*), esp. note 9, and in particular p. 325 on the engravings.

[97] Cf. Guillermo Lohmann Villena, "La restitución por conquistadores y encomenderos: un aspecto de la incidencia lascasiana en el Perú," in *Anuario de estudios Américanos* 23 (Seville, 1966): 21–89.

to attack Spanish policies in Italy," and "beginning in 1616 a stream of Italian editions of Las Casas [tracts] issued from Venice."[98] The French Enlightenment in the eighteenth century embraced Las Casas' doctrine; and Las Casas was hailed as a precursor of the American and French Revolutions.[99] In the nineteenth century, Spanish-American leaders and intellectuals during the Wars of Independence, including Bolivar himself, were frequently Lascasian, quoting ideas by the Defender of the Indians.[100]

In the first half of the twentieth century, Las Casas' ideas were embodied in documents of the United Nations, and the Indian Claims Act of the United States.[101] And in the second half, Las Casas' influence can be found not only in liberation theology, but also in official pronouncements of the Latin-American bishops in conferences at Medellín and Puebla.[102]

Why has *The Only Way* and its doctrine, why have Las Casas' other works—written four hundred years ago and in such terrible circumstances—remained so influential through the centuries, and why is he still so demanding on conscience today? Because Las Casas learned that you cannot preach the first commandment unless you live the second—you cannot preach the love of God unless you live the love of neighbor.[103] *The Only Way,* as restored here, allows the reader to hear him expound that doctrine as he lived it and used it in the defense of the Indians. There is no more important work of spirituality in and for the New World.

---

[98] See Benjamin Keen, "Approaches to Las Casas, 1535–1970," Introduction to *Bartolomé de las Casas in History* (DeKalb, IL, 1971), 16–17, first par. and notes 43 and 44. Also Miguel Batllori, "Las ideas de las Casas en la Italia del siglo XVII: Turin y Venecia como centros de difusión," in *Estudios sobre Fray Bartolomé de las Casas* (Seville, 1974), 303–17.

[99] See Angel Losada, "La doctrina de Las Casas y su impacto en la Illustración francesa: Voltaire, Rousseau . . . ," in *En el Quinto Centenario de Bartolomé de las Casas,* 169–81. Also Keen, "Approaches to Las Casas," 23.

[100] Keen, "Approaches to Las Casas," at 23–29.

[101] Las Casas' principles are to be found in the UN Charter and Human Rights Declarations. The US Indian Claims Act of 1948 provides financial restitution for land taken from the Indians, but they must litigate in order to obtain it.

[102] Gustavo Gutiérrez, who first defined A Theology of Liberation in 1971, is a distinguished Lascasista, and has just published the first of his projected three volumes on the theology of Las Casas, *Dios o el oro en las Indias.* See also Enrique Dussel, "Lascasian Perspectives from Medellín and Puebla," unpublished paper given at the Quincentennial Symposium, "Las Casas Lives Today," Berkeley, Jan. 22, 1985.

[103] See Marie Augusta Neal, *The Just Demands of the Poor: Essays in Socio-theology* (New York, 1987), esp. first two and last two chapters, for the application of this doctrine to the modern world.

BARTOLOMÉ DE LAS CASAS—

THE ONLY WAY

*TO DRAW ALL PEOPLE
TO A LIVING FAITH*

In the following pages, the reader can see that Las Casas' doctrine is mainline Christianity. That is the import of all his proof-texts and of our extensive annotation of them. He uses crucial scriptural passages, commentaries on them by the greatest Church Fathers, principles of ancient and medieval philosophy, key tenets of Roman and canon law. And he uses authoritative decrees of the Church right up to his own time. Therefore this work has a polemical tone. However, the reader should remember that Las Casas drew his doctrine from the agony and compassion he experienced over the fate of the Indians, then found it confirmed in all these sources.

ABBREVIATIONS, STANDARD EDITIONS

Las Casas' bulkier citations are banished to the bottom of the page, as his own footnotes. [We verify them in brackets, using these abbreviations and standard editions.]

BIBLE:	Las Casas' Vulgate had chapter but not verse; we supply verse.
PATRISTICS:	Las Casas cites individual Fathers for ideas; we verify Latin or Greek Fathers in Migne, *PL* or *PG*. (Las Casas uses *Catena Aurea* for several Fathers on specific gospel verses.)
PL	Migne, Jacques-Paul. *Patrologiae Cursus Completus.* Series Latina, 221 vols. Paris, 1844–55.
PG	Migne, Jacques-Paul. *Patrologiae Cursus Completus.* Series Graeca, 161 vols. Paris, 1857–66.
LAW:	Las Casas cites Roman and canon laws by names and titles. We convert to short

forms and numbers, and verify in modern critical editions.

Krueger

Corpus Iuris Civilis. Rev. and ed. by Paul Krueger; ed. Theodore Mommsen, and Rudolph Schoell. Berlin, 1928, 15th ed.

Friedberg

Corpus Iuris Canonici. Ed. by Emil Friedberg. 2 vols. Leipzig, 1879–81.

PHILOSOPHY AND THEOLOGY:

We refer Las Casas' citations of Aristotle to McKeon's English version. We refer his citations of Thomas Aquinas to the Leonine edition—except for *Catena Aurea* which we cite from the Parma edition.

Aristotle

The Basic Works of Aristotle. Trans. by Richard P. McKeon. New York: Random House, 1941.

Aquinas

Thomas Aquinas. *Opera Omnia.* Ed. commissioned by Leo XIII. Rome: Tipografia Poliglota, S.C. de Propaganda Fide, 1882–1988–.

Thomas Aquinas. *Opera Omnia.* 2nd ed. Parma: Pietro Ficcadori, 1852–1873.

PROLOGUE: HUMANITY OF THE INDIANS

It was due to the will and work of Christ, the head of the Church, that God's chosen should be called, should be culled from every race, every tribe, every language, every corner of the world. Thus, no race, no nation on this entire globe would be left totally untouched by the free gift of divine grace. Some among them, be they few or many, are to be taken into eternal life. We must hold this to be true also of our Indian nations. [They are as called as we.] . . .[1]

The reason is, they are all human beings. Their minds are very quick, alive, capable, clear. This mind comes to them primarily from the will of God who wished to make them so. Then, secondarily, it comes from the fostering influence of the heavens, from the kind conditions of the places God gave them to live in, the fair and clement weather.[2] For most of the Indies have land that is dry, land that is open, spacious, level, pleasant, fertile, and in fine locations. The hills, valleys, mountains, plains are uncluttered; they are free of stagnant pools; they are blanketed with aromatic plants, medicinal herbs of all kinds, and commonplace charmers spread everywhere so all the fields are smiling. Every morning they breathe a scent which lasts until noonday, a scent that delights and strengthens a traveler's soul. They are a consolation. Both mountains and trees are lofty throughout the region, at least be-

---

NOTA BENE

The first four chapters are missing from the only known manuscript of *De unico modo*, probably cut off by Las Casas himself. They are reconstructed very briefly here from the fragmentary summary at the start of Chapter Five, and a contemporary summary—see App. II.A; also Chart at end of App. III.B, sect. 2. Ed.'s notes on reconstruction and proof-texts are in brackets. Nonbracketed notes are by Las Casas.

[1] [*De unico modo* (hereafter *DUM*) MS, par. 1.]
[2] [*Apologética historia sumaria,* cap. 263, from first half of par. 1. Corresponds to *DUM* MS, beginning of par. 2.]

tween the two tropics, the stretch of forty-five degrees to either side of the equator, to use nautical terms. They are huge, imposing. And it is a fact that often, for a man to be able to gauge their size, he has to throw his head back the way he must when he wants to look at the pitch of the sky. There is an experience which surely indicates the temperate nature of the region, its even, gentle, wholesome, delightful climate. When ships come from Spain and begin to raise the first islands or any of the coast of Tierra Firme, people aboard ship sense a marvelous fragrance, fresh smells coming offshore. It is as if rose flowers were right there present to them. . . .[3]

Next, this condition of mind comes to them from the fine state of their bodies and sense organs, the inward, the outward, from sound and healthy nourishment, from the excellent sanitary conditions of the land, the habitations, the air of each place, from the people's temperance and moderation in food and drink, from the state of their sensual passions—calm, quiet, controlled—from the lack of upset and anxiety —their habitual state—about those worldly affairs which elicit the passions of the soul—pleasure, love, anger, grief—and even after being disturbed, for the things that passions do and the effects they cause. . . .[4]

Then too there exist extraordinary kingdoms among our Indians who live in the regions west and south from us. There are large groupings of human beings who live according to a political and a social order. There are large cities, there are kings, judges, laws, all within civilizations where commerce occurs, buying and selling and lending and all the other dealings proper to the law of nations. That is to say, their republics are properly set up, they are seriously run according to a fine body of law, there is religion, there are institutions. And our Indians cultivate friendship and they live in lifegiving ways in large cities. They manage their affairs in them with goodness and equity, affairs of peace as well as war. They run their governments according to laws that are often superior to our own. . . .[5]

---

[3] [*Apologética historia sumaria,* cap. 21, par. 6, except last sentence, joined to par. 10—corresponds to next fragment of *DUM* MS, par. 2. *N.B.* caps. 23, 24, and 29 of the *Apologética,* on the heavens and climate influencing Indian character and capacity answer Bernardo de Mesa's claim that Indians were servile by nature due to the climate and the islands. Cf. *Historia de las Indias,* lib. 3, beg. of cap. 9, Mesa's 2nd prop.; and beg. of cap. 11, Las Casas' indignant comment.]

[4] [*Apologética historia sumaria,* cap. 263, remainder of par. 1. Corresponds to *DUM* MS, remainder of par. 2.]

[5] [*Apologia vs. Sepulvedam,* ff. 22v–23, omitting Sepúlveda's contempt. A preliminary par., for all that follows.]

The quality of their minds is seen finally in superb artifacts, finely, beautifully fashioned, fashioned by hand. They are so skilled in the practical arts that their reputation should place them well ahead of the rest of the known world, and rightly so. The practical things these people make are striking for their art and elegance, utensils that are charmingly done, feather work, lace work. Mind does this. The practical arts result from a basic power of mind—a power we define as knowledge of how to do things the right way, a planning power that guides the various decisions the artisan makes so he acts in an ordered and economical fashion and does not err as he thinks his way along. . . .

And in the liberal and allied arts, to date, these people offer no less an indication of sound intelligence. They make objects that are high art and with a genius that awes everyone. The genius of an artist shows in the art work. It is as the poet says: "The work applauds its maker." Prosper remarks in one of his *Epigrams:* "It must be so, that an author shows in the fine things he has written. They sing praise to their maker."

The Indians are highly skilled also in the arts we educate ourselves to, the Indians we have taught thus far: grammar, logic. And they charm the ear of an audience with every kind of music, remarkable beauty. Their handwriting is skillful and lovely, such that one cannot tell often if the letters are handwritten or printed. . . . I have seen all this with my own eyes, touched it with my own hands, heard it with my own ears, over the long time I passed among those peoples. . . .[6]

Due to all these influences—the broad/celestial, the narrow/ terrestrial, the essential/accidental—the Indians come to be endowed, first by force of nature, next by force of personal achievement and experience, with the three kinds of self-rule required: (1) personal, by which one knows how to rule oneself, (2) domestic, by which one knows how to rule a household, and (3) political, knowledge of how to set up and rule a city.

Their political rule presupposes fully developed personal and domestic elements, i.e., farmers, artisans, soldiery, wealthy people; religion, temples, priests, sacrifices; judges and agents of justice; governors; customs; and throughout, everything touched by qualities of mind and will . . . their society is the equal of that of many nations in the world renowned for being politically astute. They surpass many another. They are inferior to none. Those they equal are the Greeks and Romans. And in a good many customs they outdo, they surpass

---

[6] [Both pars. above open with sents. from *DUM* MS, par. 3. Rest is from *Apologia vs. S*, ff. 23v–24, minus Sepúlveda's contempt, and ff. 24–24v, minus bad historians.]

the Greeks and Romans. They surpass the English, the French, and
some groups in our native Spain. In the possession of good customs, in
the lack of bad ones, they are superior to so many other peoples that
these latter do not merit comparison to our Indians.

All of this stands clearly proven and explained. Our comparisons
show that in the entire world, in the old days of paganism, there were
countless peoples who were much less rational in their use of mind
than our Indians, peoples who had customs far more horrible, vices far
more depraved. That conclusion is enough to confound those who
have so rashly, perhaps unforgivably, defamed our Indians, to make
those defamers ashamed in and for themselves, to make them admit
their error. . . . And all those who know of them should consider them
false witnesses. The more so because, as we have seen through comparison and contrast, the Indians are and were ahead of others—many,
many others—more ordered in their use of mind, more ordered in
their use of will, with less of the taint of malice and malignancy.

Since all these Indian peoples, excepting none in the vast world of
that hemisphere, universally have good and natural intelligence, have
ready wills, they thus can be drawn to and taught a complete and sound
morality, and more so to our Christian belief, even though some peoples in some places have not yet developed political maturity, an ordered body politic, the kind we said many possessed. And some have
certain corrupt customs. But these are curable finally with human effort, and more so, better so, with the preaching of the gospel.[7]

It is clear as clear can be that the nations of our Indies fall into [a
special category of infidels]. They have and hold their realms, their
lands, by natural law and by the law of nations. They owe allegiance to
no one higher than themselves, outside themselves, neither de jure nor
de facto. We find them in possession of their countries, with plenty of
princes over plenty of principalities having great numbers of people,
people who serve and obey their lords and masters, while the latter
exercise full authority over their people without hindrance, exercise
full power in large and in small, so no one would have the legitimate
right to seize their power, or their realms, so distant from our own, so
far from harming us or our Church or our Catholic faith or any
member thereof. They are of the fourth kind of infidels [faraway non-
hostile pagans], no one can doubt it.

---

[7] [*Apologética historia sumaria,* cap. 263, pars. 2, 3, and first half of 4. This is Las
Casas' own later summary of Indian capacity; but note that the final part of par. 4
forcefully repeats the basic doctrine of *The Only Way.* See App. I.B, sect. 1, penultimate
par.]

Cajetan spoke of this fourth kind of infidel more clearly and distinctly than of the other three when commenting on Thomas Aquinas, *Summa Theologiae,* Secunda Secundae, q. 66, art. 8, especially when he said as follows:

> There are some pagans who ... have never been under Christian rule, who live in lands never reached by the name of Christ. Their rulers, though they are pagans, are legitimate authorities, whether they govern in a monarchy or a republic. They are not to be deprived of their authority because of their pagan belonging. Such authority is a matter of positive law. Divine law deals with pagan belief. Divine law does not invalidate positive law. I know of no law abrogating their temporal possessions. No king, no emperor, not the Roman Church itself, can make war on them for the purpose of occupying their territory or subjecting them to temporal rule. There is no just cause for such a war. The reason: Jesus Christ, the King of Kings (to whom all power is given in heaven and on earth) did not send armed soldiery to take possession of the earth but holy men, preachers, sent sheep among wolves.

Further on [Cajetan] says:

> So we would sin mortally if we sought to spread the faith of Christ by way of war. We would not be the legitimate rulers of the conquered, we would have committed a mighty theft, we would be held to restitution for being unjust aggressors in an unjust occupation.[8]

So let us turn now to explaining the way, the natural, overall, single and settled way of calling God's chosen, God's elect, to the faith of Christ, of inviting them into the Christian way of life.[9]

---

[8] [*Doce dudas,* Second Principle, 3rd par. from end, here followed by 4th par. from the end, but minus the repetitious sent. after Cajetan's Latin passage—*Opúsculos,* i.e., *BAE* 110: 490ab, 490a. *N.B.* Although *Doce dudas* was put together in 1564, Las Casas wrote this Principle, on the 4 kinds of infidels (487b–490a), in 1539—c.f. *Las Casas en México,* note 39, also last par. of note 58. Both contemporary summaries of *The Only Way* include the 4 kinds of infidels—see below, Introductory Note to App. II.]

PART ONE: TRUE EVANGELIZATION

The Only Way: Winning the Mind and Will

One way, one way only, of teaching a living faith, to everyone, everywhere, always, was set by Divine Providence: the way that wins the mind with reasons, that wins the will with gentleness, with invitation. It has to fit all people on earth, no distinction made for sect, for error, even for evil.

Many proofs support this thesis: proofs from reason, from the practice of the patriarchs, from the once-and-for-all way of preaching willed by Christ, from the practice of the apostles and the procedures they ordered, from the teachings of Church Doctors, the ancient Church customs, the long list of Church decrees.

First from reason, a crucial proof. One, only one way is characteristic of Divine Wisdom in its care for creatures, in its leading of them to fulfill their natural purposes—a gentle, coaxing, gracious way. Among creatures, the rational one is the higher, of more worth than the rest. The rest are not made in the image of God. Divine Providence cares for the rational creature in a special way, for itself. It cares for others for the sake of the rational creature. So Divine Wisdom leads the rational creature, the human, to fulfill its natural purpose in a gentle, coaxing, gracious way. But it is a teaching of the faith that people be called to, be led to a living faith under the universal command as it is stated in Matthew 28:19–20: "Go teach all nations, baptizing them in the name of the Father, and of the Son, and of the Holy Spirit, teaching them to obey all that I have commanded you." And Paul to the Romans (10:17): "Faith comes from hearing, hearing from the word of Christ." Therefore the way of teaching people has to be a gentle, coaxing, gracious way. It wins the mind with reasons, it wins the will with graciousness. So, one way, one way only, of teaching a living faith, to everyone, everywhere, always, was set by Divine Providence, a way that wins the mind with reasons, that wins the will with gentleness, with invitation.

The major premise is clear: Divine Wisdom cares for all its creatures, not just by leading them to fulfill their natural purposes, but also by endowing them with inner powers, with potentialities which are at the source of performance, so they would be able to act on their own initiative as well. Thus actions invited by God are actions native to creatures, consonant with them; they flow easily. Creatures possess the sources of response within themselves. For that reason their responses are natural and easy, the way gravity affects a stone, so it tends to fall naturally, easily.

In a certain sense, creatures are not just led to fulfill their purposes, they do so of themselves, as if the movement originates within. For this reason Wisdom 8:1 says that Divine Wisdom "reaches the whole of creation with its power." That is, it runs all things perfectly. As the gloss puts it: "It provides for everything smoothly."[10]

So each creature moves toward what Divine Wisdom wants for it by means of a nature divinity gives it, according to the leaning built into nature. It is the goodness in God from which all natures flow . . . so every creature has in it a power to want goodness due to the imprint of its Creator upon it.[11] Goodness means fulfillment because each thing's activity is normed by its goal, the activity being one perfection, the fulfillment being a second. We call something good and virtuous when it acts harmoniously with itself, and thus with the goal set for it by God, in God's own way. And so, in creation, there is a certain circularity: goodness going out, goodness coming back.[12]

BY THE WAY OF CHRIST

Divine Wisdom, Divine Providence are behind the way, the form Christ fashioned and prescribed in preaching and teaching His gospel, His belief, to all and sundry, everywhere, every time, from His ascension into heaven until the day of judgment. But that way, that form, wins the mind with reasons, wins the will with gentleness, with invita-

---

[10] [Nicholas of Lyra, *Postilla Super Totam Bibliam,* Strasburg, 1492, III:Rr-5a, s.n.]

[11] Cf. Dionysius, "De divinis nominibus," 4 [*PL,* 122:1128–1137, esp. 1131. The Latin text also contains a reference to Augustine, *De civitate dei,* lib. 21, cap. 22 (*PL,* 41:735) which is not apt and seems to be a copyist's error.].

[12] St. Thomas treats this subject quite extensively in *Summa Theologiae.* See Ia IIae: q. 6, art. 1, corp. [*Opera,* 6:55–56]; and q. 110, art. 2, corp. [*Opera,* 7:312]. Also IIa IIae, q. 23, art. 2 [*Opera,* 8:165.]; and q. 165, art. 1 [*Opera,* 10:339]; and many other places.

tion. So Divine Wisdom, Divine Providence are behind this way of teaching people a living faith, winning their minds, winning their wills, etc.

Both the conclusion and major premise are clear because Christ, the Son of God, is the Wisdom of His Father, is true God, one God with His Father and Holy Spirit. There is one Godhood in these three Persons, so there is one Wisdom, one Providence. When the Son is active, Father and Holy Spirit are active. The activity of the Son is the activity of God. Hilary says, in *On The Trinity,* bk. 7: Sound faith asserts that the actions of the Trinity that reach outward are of all three together, not separately.[13] So Divine Providence fashioned and prescribed what Christ fashioned and prescribed when He was mortal in His flesh.

The minor is proven by the form Christ gave to His apostles and disciples the two times He sent them out preaching. First, Matthew 10 and Luke 9, the time He called the apostles together then sent them out to preach to the Jews. Likewise in Luke 10, He sent a separate seventy-two to the same people. They were to be preached to first. Christ was sent to them primarily, it was willed by God that way: "The word of God had to be preached to you first, . . ." (Acts 13:46). "So the Jews would have no excuse for not accepting Him, saying He had sent the apostles to the pagans," as [Jerome] comments on the text.[14] Christ said to the apostles: "Go and preach, say that the Kingdom of heaven is near" (Matthew 10:7). For sinning makes us earthly; virtue makes us heavenly; God rules in the heavenly. For this we say, the Kingdom of God is within you, etc.

And Christ further said:

> Heal the sick, raise the dead, cleanse the lepers, cast out demons. You received without pay, give without pay. Take no gold, nor silver, nor copper in your belts, no bag for your journey . . . no staff. . . . In whatever town or village you enter, find out who is worthy in it and stay with him until you depart. As you enter the house, salute it saying, Peace to this house! (Matthew 10:7–12 passim).

And in Luke 10:5 it says,

> First say, Peace to this house. And if the house is worthy, let your peace come upon it, but if it is not worthy, let your peace return to you.

---

[13] [Here Las Casas is giving the gist of lib. 7—Cf. *PL,* 10:198–278, esp. 204.]

[14] [*Catena Aurea*—S. Thomas, *Opera,* Parma, 11:130a. This was the basic compilation of patristic comments on the four Gospels, text by text.]

And in Matthew 10:13–16

> If anyone will not receive you or listen to your words, shake off the
> dust from your feet as you leave that house or town. Truly I say to
> you, it shall be more tolerable on the day of judgment for the land of
> Sodom and Gomorrah than for that town. Behold I send you out as
> sheep in the midst of wolves [or as Luke says, as sheep among
> wolves, meaning the same]. So be wise as serpents and simple as
> doves. . . . People will deliver you up to councils and synagogues. . . .

We can add a germane saying from Matthew 11:29–30:

> Come to me all you who labor and are sorely burdened and I will
> refresh you. Take my yoke upon you and learn of me, for I am meek
> and humble of heart, and you shall find rest for your souls. My yoke
> is easy, my burden light.

It all means: learn from me that you also may be meek and humble
of heart.

This is the way, the form of preaching Christ's law, of drawing
people to a living faith, to Christianity. It is what Christ Himself, Son of
God, Wisdom of the Father, fashioned and prescribed for His apostles,
His disciples, and their successors, the method He first used and they
kept to with consummate tact in their approach to everyone.

Now to see that this way, this form of preaching a living faith wins
the mind with reasons, wins the will gently, by attraction, by graciousness. First off, because Christ, when He said preach that the kingdom of
God is near, meant preach repentance for the remission of sins. That
was the theme of His sermon in Matthew 4:17: "Jesus began to preach
and say, Repent, the Kingdom of Heaven is near." Also in Mark 6:12
the description is of apostles setting out preaching that people should
repent, so that by repentance they would be brought near to the kingdom of heaven.

It is clear that preaching the kingdom of heaven or the kingdom of
God can mean several things: (a) Christ Himself was the kingdom of
God, as in Matthew 12:28: "If by the power of God I exorcise demons,
surely the Kingdom of God is among you"—i.e., Christ, the bringer of
that kingdom. He proved He was the Christ by exorcising demons with
the power of God. And so, accept Christ here, accept the kingdom here,
according to Nicholas of Lyra.[15] That was the preaching of the apostles

---

[15] [Cf. Nicholas of Lyra, *Postilla super totam Bibliam IV* Strasburg, 1492, fol. d
4–6, s.n.]

at the will of Christ for that time, announcing Christ's arrival to the Jews, again according to Nicholas.

Or (b): The kingdom of heaven—and this is the better opinion— was what Christ really commanded the apostles to announce, eternal happiness, eternal life, as stated in Matthew: "Unless your justice is more than that of the Scribes and Pharisees, you will not enter the Kingdom of Heaven" (5:20). No one ever before heard this beatitude announced by any prophet. Chrysostom speaks of the Matthean passage in Homily 32:

> You see the extraordinary role of the apostles—they are required to announce nothing crass, nothing our senses can control, nothing akin to what Moses and the Prophets taught, but something new, something unique no predecessor ever taught—they promised the goods of this earth! The apostles taught the Kingdom of Heaven and its total bliss.[16]

Or (c): The kingdom of heaven was the gospel, the era of the New Testament, as Matthew 13:52 says: "Every scribe learned in the Kingdom of Heaven is like the father of a family. . . ." A scribe, someone learned in the kingdom of heaven, equals someone learned in the gospel, in the New Testament, etc.

The apostles had to give reasons to explain the kingdom of heaven, whichever way it is to be understood. So their hearers could understand their words and grasp their teaching and be brought to repentance. [The apostles had to give reasons] so that people's minds could be brought to clarity, so they could judge that it was good and useful to yield to the words and teachings of the apostles.

It is not likely that they just uttered the bare words 'kingdom' and 'repentance.' It is more likely that as they preached eternal life they preached also the means to acquire it. So they said all sin must be surrendered, no sinner could locate in eternal life: "Do not sin. Those who do not fornicate, adore idols, commit adultery, . . . will possess the Kingdom of God" (1 Corinthians 6:9). So, since a sin-free time is acceptable to God and in it people can gain eternal life, then people should avoid all sin. Christ said as much in Luke 4:19, that the Spirit of God had sent Him to preach a holy year acceptable to God.

So the apostles preached it—Paul's preaching is proof: "Behold, now is an acceptable time, now is a time of grace. Offending no one in any way, . . ." (2 Corinthians 6:2–3). Avoid all sin was His teaching,

---

[16] [*PG,* 57:381.]

because it was a time of grace. The other apostles preached the same, they all preached with the same Spirit (1 Corinthians 12). They announced the kingdom of heaven to people, that people must reach it, so they preached that people must avoid all that could keep them from reaching it. And so Paul said: "Every athlete exercises self-control in all things. They do it to receive a perishable wreath, but we an imperishable, . . ." (1 Corinthians 9:25). People had to give up a lot to gain that wreath. As Ephesians 4:22 says it: "Put aside your old behavior. . . . Let the thief no longer steal. . . ."

The passage shows that the apostles preached a program of good morals. They used reasons to win the minds of their hearers, to exercise those minds. It is useless to preach to people the kingdom of God, of heaven, to preach repentance and eternal life without giving people both map and directions to get there. The apostles preached a whole program, they offered persuasive explanations. It was true of Christ preaching. Matthew 4:17 speaks of Him saying: "Do penance!" as if it was His only message. Yet we know He said a great deal about moral conduct.

And Paul says, in 1 Corinthians 2:2: "For I decided to know nothing among you except Jesus Christ and Him crucified." That means I preached only the death of Christ to you. Yet it is clear he preached on moral matters a great deal, on the source of death, on the profit of the moral life, etc.

So Christ used one expression with His apostles: the kingdom of God is near. When someone is required to do something, he is required to take all the steps necessary to accomplish the job. Christ ordered that the kingdom of heaven be proclaimed. So He ordered preached all that pertained to that kingdom. There is a clearer indication in Luke 9. Christ told his apostles to preach the kingdom of God.

We have listed above all the reasons for winning the mind. The point is self-evident. So the way, the form Christ gave His apostles and disciples for preaching His message, the way He willed, was to win the mind.

Next, that this way wins the will with gentleness, draws it, invites it, is clear also. It is so precious it makes people greet one another first, in the cities and towns and households they enter, before any other ritual. People are accustomed in their first words to each other, especially to strangers, to use a polite greeting, so that the start of speech between them is a good wish. If anyone does not greet others politely, people think him an ill-mannered clod. So a greeting is a necessity, almost, between people, the customary start of a relationship. It is why Christ ordered His apostles to be first in greeting others. It is more generous to offer a respect before receiving one. Paul says in Romans 12:10: "Outdo one another in showing honor." He means people should try to show their respect before respect is shown to them. And Chrysostom comments on this passage of Matthew in Homily 32: "Because you are teachers, do not therefore think you should stay aloof until people pay their respects to you. Pay your respects to them first!"[17]

Christ commanded a special greeting, used the words, "Peace to this house!" It was a strong custom among Hebrews and Syrians to use this greeting, as Jerome implies, commenting on Matthew.[18] The apostles worked among Hebrews and Syrians. Or it was that no other greeting seemed to embrace more blessings than wishing someone peace. All greetings are prayers for blessings, but more are enveloped in this particular one because peace is the tranquility of order, as Augustine says in *The City of God,* bk. 19, chap. 13.[19] Where the tranquility of order prevails, blessings abound. Peace is a state of calm and quiet and of multiple friendships according to Isidore in his *Etymologies.* Everyone is made for happiness. Where the tranquility of order prevails, everyone is happy since nothing upsets the order. If tranquility exists, people want the quiet life; they work for it. Should something block it, they must pursue it. They will have it, and not a counterfeit. Peace is a supreme good, there is nothing more beautiful than it in society. Nothing more precious, nothing more enjoyable or useful has ever been heard of or hoped for or held. As it says in a certain *Extravagante* under the heading "On Burials In Common" [*sic*][20]: "We know from evidence we collected that only in a time of peace is there true worship of the Author of peace." There are some sayings about this: "Peace makes the word 'peace' also a sign of love. It is a gentle word that teaches all there is to love. Peace is pure salvation. Whoever despises peace will never possess the One for whom peace is the vision of heaven."

So, what Denys the Great says is plausible: "It is natural for everything to want peace. A peaceful king who acts peaceably produces subjects who will be chaste, controlled, civilized." So says the introduction to the *Decretals.*[21]

---

[17] [*Catena Aurea*—S. Thomas, *Opera,* Parma, 11:132b.]

[18] [*Catena Aurea*—S. Thomas, *Opera,* Parma, 11:132b.]

[19] [Cf. *PL,* 41:640.]

[20] *Clementines,* lib. 3, tit. 7, cap. 2. [Friedberg, 2:1162. We have corrected Las Casas' citation from memory to the canon he is really quoting.]

[21] [See Friedberg 2, page 2, Gregory's foreword, for the second sentence in Las Casas' citation. Las Casas is citing the original passage from memory.]

Remigius says,

> The Lord taught His disciples to say peace when they arrived some-
> where, to choose a house or a host by a greeting of peace, as if the
> Lord said in so many words: "Greet everyone with peace." So those
> who accepted would be worthy hosts, those who did not, unworthy.
> Though a host may be chosen by his public reputation, still he must
> be greeted with peace, so the preachers may be invited in because of
> their own dignity and not force themselves on him for another
> reason.[22]

Christ ordered His apostles to find a worthy host for the sake of the
apostles' good name. For if they stayed with suspect, criminal types,
they would be suspected themselves of criminality. Because all creatures love their like and live with them (Ecclesiasticus 13, 19). Likeness
is the source of love, says Aristotle in 8 *Ethics,* chapters 1–3. Those who
live with good people are thought to be good. "With the pure, you will
be pure" (Psalm 18:26). The preachers who are holy "must be well
thought of by outsiders" (1 Timothy 3:7). Jerome says as much: "A
host must be chosen on what people think of him i.e., his neighbors, so
the reputation of the preacher is not sullied."[23]

The Lord wanted His preachers to be good and to look good,
lovers of peace, messengers of peace, to quote Isaiah 52:7: "How beautiful upon the mountains are the feet of him who brings the good tidings
of peace." The kind the Lord made, "peace by the blood of His
cross, . . ." (Colossians 1:20). He broadcast peace, as Ephesians 2:17
says: "And He came and brought good tidings of peace to you who
were far off, and good tidings to those who were near." No wonder He
ordered good tidings to be preached.

The apostles preached peace first—a value so wanted, so palat-
able, so loved and lovable by those people who lived in city, town, and
household that it's clear they could only attract such people! And
render them gracious and kind enough to welcome the apostles and
shelter them generously and warmly and listen to their teaching
willingly.

It was very winning to see the apostles poor, humble, kind—not
after gold, not after silver, not after coin, not after stuff of any kind, not
the least thing earthly or passing, not even asking for the meal they
needed unless from people willing to provide it.

---

[22] [*Catena Aurea*—S. Thomas, *Opera,* Parma, 11:133a.]

[23] [*Catena Aurea*—S. Thomas, *Opera,* Parma, 11:132.b.]

For St. Thomas, commenting on Matthew, the apostles were allowed not just any house for their room and board, but only that of someone found willing and worthy. The Lord expressly said: "Whatever city you enter, whatever town, ask who is a worthy person there, and stay with him until you leave" (Matthew 10:11). That means, do not hop from house to house.

Jerome [and other Fathers] give the reasons for this injunction: (1) So as not to embarrass the hosts—they might appear to be slighted. It is also unseemly, a sign of ingratitude, for guests to embarrass, to insult hosts, who have treated them with welcome and warmth. (2) So as not to seem superficial to people. It is not fitting for preachers of Christian persuasion. For Christ wanted them to be serious and steady men, so they could gain greater reverence and authority, and as a result their teaching would be worth more to their hearers, and result in a richer harvest. (3) To escape the reputation of being a voracious glutton. Some people might think the apostles changed lodgings so they could enjoy a richer fare with other hosts. That would be reminiscent of the Pharisees blaming Christ for eating with publicans, saying He did so out of voracity.[24]

For the apostles to heal the sick at no cost, to raise the dead, to cleanse lepers, to rid tormented bodies of demons, was a winning way indeed; it gained the good will of people, it was influential on them. There is nothing more gratifying for people everywhere than to receive great favors or great gifts from others, but not if afterward they are made to render more than thanks and they are unwilling. It is apparent that the rare, the wonderful gifts the apostles gave, miraculous gifts, to their hosts, their hearers, created a climate of love and affection—gifts like infants, able to make a crowd willing, apt, and open to a teaching, to hear it, to accept, to believe it.

If people were forced to pay a price for miraculous cures, for gifts of life, they would be deeply depressed. But no price was asked. The opposite occurred. The people loved the apostles happily, they were quick and eager to hear with rapt attention what the apostles taught and to accept it.

> Christ told His men to heal the sick in the various towns, so that the miracles would draw people to the message they preached. Remember what He said: "And say to the people, The Kingdom of God has touched you . . ." If you cure first, and preach after, your

---

[24] Commenting on Matthew 11 and Luke 17 [Las Casas is summarizing citations by Jerome, Chrysostom, Ambrose, Cyril, and Theophilact in *Catena Aurea*—S. Thomas, *Opera,* Parma, 11:132b, 12:100b, 12:370a.].

words will come easily. People will believe that the Kingdom has touched *you*. (Thus Theophilact on Luke 10.)[25]

Their generosity proved the apostles to be holy men. They gave gratis their gifts of goodness to people oppressed by terrible conditions and incurable diseases. They could have amassed great wealth, have piled up riches if they wanted to. Instead they despised wealth as they would night-soil.

Conclusion: It was a winning way indeed to heal the sick, to raise the dead, etc.; a way to affect, to draw the will of the watcher without force to love the apostles, to listen gladly to what they taught, etc. So then the way, the form Christ fashioned for preaching the gospel not only wins the mind with reasons, but wins the will also, gently, attractively, with motives. It was a winning way indeed, and it worked well for getting good will and a hearing from people when the apostles preached the goods of eternal life, goods beyond nature, beyond expectation, beyond imagination. Nothing more charming or gratifying was ever concocted. It was the greatest good that could be preached to people, nothing more powerful than it for attracting them, so they would move as if by gravity to hear and heed the teachings of the apostles. They were to understand that after the work, the worries, the woes of this life in time, those who had faith would last in eternity forever in happiness and calm.

It is now clear that the way Christ wanted for preaching the gospel, and willed for His apostles and their successors, was to win the mind with reasons and win the will with motives, gently, graciously.

After the Lord taught His apostles and disciples the form and fashion for their behavior toward the city, the town, the household that took them in, willingly, even graciously, He then gave them a norm they should act on toward those who were resistant. "Whoever is unreceptive, who does not listen to your words, leave the house, the town, shake its dust off your feet. I tell you solemnly it will go easier for Sodom and Gomorrah on judgment day than for that town" (Matthew 10:14).

What is clear is that Christ gave His apostles permission and power to preach the gospel to those willing to hear it, and that only! Not power to punish the unwilling by any force, pressure, or harshness. He granted no power to apostle or preacher of the faith to force the unwilling to listen, no power to punish even those who drove the apostles out of town. He decreed punishment in eternity, not in time. "Whoever is

---

[25] [*PG*, 123:835. Also *Catena Aurea*—S. Thomas, *Opera*, Parma, 12:117.]

unreceptive, and does not listen to your words, leave the place." He did not say, "Confront them! Preach to them willy nilly! If they persist tenaciously in trying to drive you out, do not hesitate to use human punishment!" He said: "Shake the dust off your feet. I tell you solemnly it will go easier for Sodom and Gomorrah on judgment day than for that town." As if He said flatly: "I reserve the punishment for such rejection to myself. I do not grant it to you!"

Thus Christ set no earthly sentence on those in this world who refused to accept the faith, so their refusal would not be punished, at least not punished by human beings, for being unbelievers. Christ set an otherworldly sentence, as stated in Mark 16:16: "The non-believer shall be damned." And Matthew 11:21, and Luke 10:13: "He then began to reprove the towns in which so many wonders had been worked." They had had no change of heart—they had not believed.

A bad end to you Corozain, to you Bethsaida! If the wonders that have been worked in you had been worked in Tyre and Sidon, they would long ago have done penance in sackcloth and ashes. I must tell you, Tyre and Sidon will be forgiven on the day of judgment, not you. As for you Capharnaum . . . if in Sodom . . . I must tell you the land of Sodom will be forgiven on the day of judgment, not you.

So this is the pattern: Christ did not give human beings the power to inflict earthly punishment on those who refused to listen to the faith being preached or on those who refused to welcome or want the preachers of that faith—it was an eternal punishment payable in the life hereafter. He reserved to Himself the punishment of both types.

St. Thomas confirms this view in his tract *Against the Enemies of Religion,* ch. 15, 4th argument, explaining the command, "Shake the dust. . . ." He says

To objection four, we must say that the Lord ordered His apostles to shake the dust from their feet as a symbol for those who refused to accept them. And it says in Mark 6: "Shake the dust off your feet as a symbol against them." The gloss on the text of Luke 10: "Shake the dust . . ." says: "To symbolize the fruitlessness of the human effort undertaken on their behalf." And this symbol points to the divine judgment.[26]

So Matthew 10 sums it up: "I must tell you, it will go easier for the land of Sodom and Gomorrah on judgment day than for that town." From

---

[26] [S. Thomas, *Opera,* 41:145.]

these citations we learn that the Lord ordered us as disciples to leave a place if not welcome. Its people will be judged for their sinfulness at the last, the faithless people spoken of in 1 Corinthians 5:13: "God will judge those outside the faith. Those who are within the fold, the faithful, lie under the judgment of the Church." So if someone wants to be received into the company of the faithful, then injures that company unjustly, the man ought not to be left to God to judge, but ought to be submitted to the Church for judgment.

What could be clearer, what more cogent, I ask you, to prove Christ gave no power to any human being to bring force or punishment to bear on any pagan whatever or anyone unwilling to hear the faith preached or to welcome the preachers into their territory? The punishment for such rejection falls to the divine judgment after this life, not to the human one here. And so that no doubt of this will linger in anyone's mind, we should note here what Christ did to confirm this truth. On His way up to Jerusalem, when He had to stop at a Samaritan town, He sent James and John ahead to prepare a lodging and acquire the necessaries there. The Samaritans refused the lodging. The apostles were enraged at the unfriendliness, at the rejection. They said: "Lord, do you want us to pray a fire down on them from heaven to destroy them?" The Lord turned to them with this reproach: "You do not know what Spirit you belong to. The Son of Man did not come to damn souls but to save them" (Luke 9:55–56). The Spirit of Christ is a gentle Spirit, as the passage from Isaiah 61:1 says: "The Spirit of God is upon me. Therefore he has consecrated me, he has sent me to preach the good news to gentle people." And chapter 42: "Behold my servant, I will cherish him." Next: "I sent my Spirit upon him." Next: "He will not break the half-broken reed, nor snuff out the smoking wick."

Christ wanted them to possess this Spirit, to be good disciples, in the likeness of a good master, which is why He added the words: "The Son of Man came to save souls, not damn them." It was not the arrival of justice but mercy, as John 3:17 says: "God did not send his Son to judge the world, God wanted to save the world through Him." For that purpose He accepted to be called Jesus, as Matthew 1:11 says: "You will call His name Jesus for He will save His people from their sins."

Theophilact says: "Christ, teaching a law more lofty than the life of Elias, reproached His disciples, led them away from violent ideas when He taught them to bear peaceably those who inflicted harm on them."[27] And Cyril:

---

[27] [*PG*, 123:830.]

Though the Lord with foreknowledge knew His disciples would not
be welcomed by the Samaritans, even so he ordered them ahead
because it was His way of doing all He could for their improvement.
They were the future teachers of the world. They were to traverse
city and town to preach the Gospel truth. They would sometime
meet up with people reluctant to hear the holy word—i.e., offering
Jesus no lodging. He taught the disciples that when preaching the
Gospel they must be totally patient, totally gentle, not hostile or
irritable by coming down harshly on those who sinned against them.
The disciples were not there yet. They were not without zealotry.
They wanted to bring fire from heaven down on the Samaritans.[28]

There was a great gain in being so gentle. Some few days later the
conversion of the Samaritans, worked by the Lord through the Samaritan woman, showed it clearly. Next in the story comes: "And they went
to another town." He showed a behavior pattern to His disciples, according to Bonaventure on Luke. They should leave people rather than
quarrel with them. Christ gave the pattern to His disciples in Matthew
10:14: "If they persecute you in one town, leave it for another. . . ."

The conclusion is clear from Christ's normative behavior. What
Christ does teaches us, because the Father gave Him to us as a witness,
a leader, a teacher, as the prophecy in Isaiah 55:4 puts it: "Look, he
said, I gave Him as a witness to the people, as a leader, as a teacher to
the Gentiles." And Matthew 13:17: "This is my beloved Son in whom I
am well pleased. Hear Him." That means obey Him, imitate Him. He
teaches not just by words but by deeds as well what one must do to
imitate Him. There must be no evil inflicted in any way, no force, no
punition on pagans who have never had the faith, if they do not want to
listen to it or to welcome its preachers. There is a consequence immediately evident: Those who do the opposite usurp divine judgment. They
are forthwith in violation of divine law.

In my treatment of the preceding material you see forcibly confirmed in a thousand ways—excuse the hyperbole—the form Christ
fixed for preaching the gospel truth, for inviting, for drawing people to
a living faith, fixed for His apostles and for those called to fill their
places. It is remarkably kind, gentle, peaceable, sensible, faultless, edi-
fying, lovable. It is suffused with compassion, patience, forgiveness,
charm, with charity abounding in benefits freely given to those who
hear preached the name of Christ. We say this of the form Christ set the
first time He sent His holy apostles and disciples out, as if into training,

---

[28] [*Catena Aurea*—S. Thomas, *Opera,* Parma, 12:111.]

so they could be schooled and readied slowly for the future struggle with the entire world by preaching first to the Jews.

After His resurrection He sent His disciples to win over the whole world, on a second, definitive mission. He added little about the form of preaching. He reiterated, reemphasized what He said at the first sending, what He had insisted on strongly. The second sending was as the first: "Go, He said, teach all people, baptize them in the name of the Father and the Son and the Holy Spirit, teach them to keep all the commandments I gave you" (Matthew 28:19–20). Then Mark: "Go everywhere in the world, preach the Gospel to everyone [i.e., to people of every nation]. Whoever believes and is baptized will be saved. Whoever does not believe shall be condemned." Finally the Evangelist writes: "They went out and preached everywhere, with the Lord's help, with the Lord backing their preaching by miracles that followed" (16:15, 20).

Luke is briefer than the others when he writes about the form of preaching the gospel: "For so it was prophesied, so ought Christ to have died, to have risen from the dead on the third day, so ought repentance to be preached in His name, and forgiveness of sins, to everyone, beginning with Jerusalem. You are witnesses of what happened" (Luke 24:46–48). In Acts 10:42–43, Luke speaks again somewhat about form and tells us to preach and bear witness: "Because it is Christ Himself who is made judge by God of all living, all dead. Every prophet testified to this: All those who believe in Him gain forgiveness of sins in His name." He ordered baptism to accompany repentance. In baptism, repentance occurs through confession, the putting aside of old evils, of unbelief. Forgiveness of sin goes with all this, says Theophilact.[29] The margin gloss on the text says pardon had to be offered to those who crucified Christ, to help the ministers who were going to preach repentance and forgiveness beginning from Jerusalem.

> Not because the words of God were entrusted to them and because theirs was the adoption as sons of God, the worth that went with it, the legacy, the law, but rather because people enmeshed in varieties of confusion and criminality would be spurred to a hope of forgiveness by this overwhelming sign of divine grace.[30]

The interlinear gloss says: "What has to be preached has to be preached in more than the one people of Israel, than the one part of the world."

---

[29] [*Catena Aurea*—S. Thomas, *Opera,* Parma, 12:254a.]

[30] [*Catena Aurea*—S. Thomas, *Opera,* Parma, 12:254a. Citation is from Bede.]

The previous instruction was: Do not go among the Gentiles.[31] So the preaching of the apostles was rejected first in Judea. The present instruction says, according to Theophilact: "Preach the Gospel to everyone, believer, unbeliever alike!" And the interlinear gloss on the words, "They exorcised demons [Mark 6:13]," says: "by gracious encouragement removing malice from people's hearts." And Bede says: "The one who said before His passion, 'Do not go to other races!' after His resurrection said, 'Go, teach every race!' "[32] Severus also says: "One and the same power which created every life redeems every life."[33]

The Lord laid a triple duty on the apostles when He sent them to preach to the entire world. The first, to preach the faith. The second, nourishing believers with sacraments. The third, teaching believers nourished by sacraments to keep the commandments of God and live a good life. The first is found in: "Go, teach all races." The second in: "Baptize them in the name of the Father and of the Son and of the Holy Spirit." The third in: "Teaching them to keep all I have commanded you."

And speaking of the triple duty, it is fairly clear from earlier statements what an effort the apostles and disciples of Christ exerted on the first and second missions, what care, what concern, what burning zeal, what charity. Fairly clear what the preachers also were required to do, who took their places out of a duty given them to fulfill. It is quite clear in Mark 6:12–13: "[The apostles] went out preaching that people should do penance. They exorcised many demons, they anointed many sick people and cured them." And in Luke 9:6: "They set out and went through the towns preaching and healing everywhere." And in Mark 16:20: "They went and preached everywhere, the Lord helping them, backing their words with miracles later." Finally, it is quite clear in the Acts of the Apostles, St. Luke's testimony, in what Paul writes in his Epistles, and in what Chrysostom says in a signal and striking way commenting on Matthew in Homilies 33 and 34, and further in Homily 7 on 1 Corinthians, chapter 2, in these and in many other places in his works.[34]

The evidence shows that Christ set a form for preaching the gospel that was one and the same—before His resurrection and after it—to win the mind with reasons, to win the will with motives, to attract it, because the form is peaceful, gentle, kind, full of the taste of charity. To

---

[31] [Nicholas of Lyra, *Postilla IV*, Strasburg, 1492, h 10b]
[32] [*Catena Aurea*—S. Thomas, *Opera*, Parma, 11:333b.]
[33] [*Catena Aurea*—S. Thomas, *Opera*, Parma, 11:334a.]
[34] [Cf. *PG:* 57:587–604; and 61:54–68.]

teach, we concluded broadly earlier, means treating the mind quietly, tactfully, smoothly, logically, with precision, step by step, at a pace allowing intervals of time. To teach also means that the will of the learner is drawn by things with charm to them, gentle, tasteful things. So the form Christ set for preaching the gospel wins the mind with reason, wins the will with motive.

In sum: (a) Preach penitence and forgiveness of sins in the name of Christ. (b) Testify that He was appointed judge of the living and dead by God. (c) All the prophets prophesied that people would have forgiveness of their sins, all who believed in Him. (d) Those caught in various confusions and criminalities would be encouraged, emboldened to hope for forgiveness of past sins by the miracle of divine mercy. (e) Pardon was promised even to the Jews who crucified the Son of God, so they could be prompted to hope that their former sins would be wiped clean. To preach this way such declarations, promises, proposals, clearly implied that the mind be won over by reasons and the will won by attractive, compelling motives. The gloss cited earlier confirms this: "By gracious encouragement removing malice from people's hearts."

Conclusion: The form Christ, the Son of God, set His apostles for preaching His gospel everywhere, before His death, after His resurrection, was one and the same, to win the mind with reasons, to win the will with attractive, compelling motives.

And it is clear enough not to demand further proof, the conclusion that this way, this form of preaching the gospel holds good for all people, all races, no distinctions made. For Christ commanded: "Go everywhere, teach everyone." No one, no place privileged. So we are not to discriminate between place and person, not to choose.

It is further clear that Christ's way was to last into the future, after Christ's ascension, until judgment day, because the gospel is the law of Christ's kingdom. Compare Matthew 24:14: "This Gospel of the Kingdom is to be preached." But the kingdom of Christ is to last, so the gospel of Christ, the new law, is to last to the end of the world. As Matthew 24:34 puts it: "I tell you, this generation will not pass away before everything comes about." Chrysostom explains this as the generation of the Church, i.e., the kingdom of Christ.

St. Thomas gives the reason:

Since the new law supplants the old law as something more perfect supplants something less perfect, our present life can have nothing more perfect than the new law. For nothing can be closer to our ultimate good than that which puts us in immediate touch with it.

The new law does just this. Hence Hebrews 10:19 says: "So brethren, with trust that in the blood of Christ, the new way He initiated, we can enter the Holy of Holies," we approach God. Life lived in the new law is more perfect than any other now lived, because the most perfect life is the one closest to its fulfillment.[35]

Therefore we will keep to the same form and fashion of preaching the gospel, we must, while time lasts, i.e., until the day of judgment, with every people in every place. The conclusion stands. Just as Christ did not pick and choose between peoples or places, He did not between age and age. Given that the kingdom of Christ, the generation of believers, that is to say the Church of Christ, or the life of the new law, is going to last until judgment day, it follows that the law itself, the gospel of Christ, is to last as well until the crack of doom. Since, at Christ's bidding, we must preach, we must likewise keep to the same way in preaching, to the same form.

Let this be enough for the ninth argument we chose for proving part one of our conclusion, i.e., we preach at Christ's bidding in the way He set.

BY THE EXAMPLE OF THE APOSTLES

From Christ's bidding, from the fulfillment of it by the apostles in the way they preached the faith, we draw the next argument. It is quite sufficient a proof to lay out what the evangelist Mark says in the last chapter by way of brief summary: "The apostles set out and preached everywhere, the Lord helping them, backing their preaching by miracles that followed" (Mark 16:16).

Note here that they kept to Christ's way and form as they preached. They were true keepers of the works of Christ, and firm followers of His words. As in 1 Corinthians 4 and 11:1: "Be imitators of me, as I am of Christ." John 13:15 shows we need not prove that this was also a bidding of Christ: "I have given you my example—as I have done, you should also do." We are sure that they kept perfectly to all Christ bade them, and to the form Christ set for them to preach the gospel. They changed not the slightest detail. Otherwise we could not say they were true keepers of Christ's word and works.

And this makes natural sense. In the natural order of things, lower

---

[35] Cf. S. Thomas, *Summa Theologiae,* Ia IIae, q. 106, art. 4 [*Opera,* 7:276].

creatures imitate higher ones insofar as they can. Something by nature active, superior, makes something by nature passive a look-alike. The Son of God is the exemplar at the origin of all created things, as John 1 puts it: "Through Him all things were made." So He is the primordial model every creature resembles, "the true and perfect image of the invisible God, the eldest of all created things, on whom all creation is based." In a unique way He is the source of those spiritual graces which illumine creatures endowed with soul. The phrase is from Psalm 109:3, which says of the Son: "In the glow of holiness, before dawn, in the womb I conceived you."

This image of God was far from us at first. Listen to Ecclesiastes 2:12: "What can a creature do to approach the Lord who made him?" So the Lord willed to be human, to give a human norm to humankind. This is the reason Augustine says in his *On the Christian Struggle:* "What soundness there is in someone who spots the words, the deeds of that man, who loves and follows Him, the Son of God, who gave himself as a norm for your lives."[36] The angels are modeled on divinity directly, the rest of creation indirectly, as Denys says in *On the Angelic Hierarchy,* bk. 10.[37] So the apostles are given the model of humanity to imitate directly, as befits leaders, the subsequent leaders of the Church. That is why they were told: "I gave you my example. . . ." Next, the apostles, the leaders of the Church, fashioned on the model of Christ, become models for the life of their charges. In the words of 1 Peter 5:4: ". . . made the norm for the flock from your soul . . ." and of 2 Thessalonians 3:9: ". . . to give you in our conduct an example to imitate."

Given that Christ, the model of all graces of the soul, taught, set the form of preaching His law, worldwide—not just by word, but also by deed, winning people over gently, persuasively, attracting them— then clearly the apostles kept to that form unswervingly. They were the first leaders of the Church, they were placed over all the faithful, they were keepers of His words, His bidding. They were true followers of His deeds, they were set up as models to everyone else in preaching and portraying the law of Christ.

Every evangelist shows that Christ taught, that Christ set the peaceful way not just by His words but also by His deeds. He was humble and meek. He would teach others meekness and humility. From the outset of His preaching therefore, He dealt humbly and meekly with people so he could draw people to Himself with peaceful behavior, could get

[36] [*PL,* 40:298.]
[37] [*PG,* 3:271–74.]

them to trust being able to approach God. In the words of Romans 5:2: "We have an approach to God through Him." In the words of Matthew 9:10: "And as He sat at table in the house, behold, many tax collectors and sinners came and sat down with Jesus and His disciples." Jerome comments on the passage: "Publicans and sinners seem to have found in His quiet, gracious dealings with them room to turn from sin to something better, room for repentance. That is why they did not despair of salvation."[38] Luke 4:15 says: "He taught in the Synagogues. Everyone esteemed Him." He purposed to show that He was sent in a Spirit both gracious and kind. As He entered the synagogue—it was His habit—He was given the Book of Isaiah the prophet. He began to read at the passage: "The Spirit of the Lord God is upon me, because the Lord has anointed me to bring good tidings—that is, to announce the good news of peace—to the afflicted, to bind up the brokenhearted, to proclaim liberty to the captives, sight to the blind, and the day of vengeance" (61:1). He closed the book, gave it to a minister, and sat down. Everyone in the synagogue fixed their eyes on Him. He began to speak to them with these words: "Today these Scriptures are fulfilled in your hearing" (Luke 4:17–22). Everyone witnessed what he said, they were in awe of the grace-filled words he spoke, the easy, flowing, powerful wisdom words by which He won their affection.

That is the posture He used in preaching to persuade people, to win them over to Himself. That is the meaning in Psalm 44:8 of the words: "God has anointed you with the oil of gladness above your peers. Grace is poured forth on your lips." There is a gloss on the words, "The Spirit of the Lord . . ." from Luke 4:18. It says: "He was anointed in the power of heaven so he might suffuse the poverty of the human condition with the wealth of the resurrection,"[39] might lift forever the captivity of the mind, give sight to the blind soul, cure the crushed and contrite heart, and might usher in a year of the Lord by healing people's sorrows and forgiving their sins. The jubilee year, the year of true liberation, is a time of grace in which the Church on earth sets out from the Lord to preach and teach its truths and after the jubilee time to preach the time of judgment when the Son of Man will come in glory with His angels to judge each one according to his deeds. This is the way He was sent, He said, with this Spirit of the Lord upon Him.

In Luke 4:42 are also the words: "And the people sought Him and

---

[38] [*PL*, 26:56.]
[39] [Thus Ambrose in *Catena Aurea*—S. Thomas, *Opera*, Parma, 12:52b.]

came to Him and would have kept Him from leaving them." They were enchanted by the charm of His words, by His grace, His dignity, His ease . . . but He said to them, "I must preach the good news of the Kingdom of God to the other cities also. I was sent for this purpose." And He was preaching in the synagogues of Galilee. You know the passage—John 7:32—in which the leaders and the Pharisees sent subordinates to take Him. Once they heard Him speak they came back empty handed. They gave as their excuse for not bringing him back: "No mere mortal ever spoke as this man speaks"—such is the wisdom, the flair, the charm of His speech, the vivacity, the sense, the rightness of it, that He is unmatched. And no wonder at this utter felicity in word since He is the unique word of God. There is a statement of Peter in John 6:69: "Lord, to whom shall we go? You have the word of eternal life." Which means, You speak so attractively, so graciously, Your teaching about God is so appropriate, we find no one to match You. You are all we want. And in Luke 24:19, Cleophas speaks "about Jesus of Nazareth, who was a Prophet, mighty in word," because Jesus "began to do and teach" as someone gentle in His words and most wise, as His actions were before His speech. So praise of Him was great, as Matthew says in 5:19: "Whoever practices what he preaches shall be called great in the Kingdom of Heaven." For His life, Jesus won praise, won greatness; for His doctrine, admiration before God and the whole people.

And Peter again in Acts 10:38: ". . . He went about doing good and healing all that were oppressed by the devil for God was with Him. And we are witnesses of it all."

And in 1 Peter 2:22: "He committed no sin. No guile was found on His lips. When He was reviled, He did not revile in return; when He suffered, He did not threaten."

Look how He taught the peaceful way of preaching the gospel and made it mandatory, with His words, yes, but more fundamentally with His works. So by mandate, by the effect of His works, He bound His apostles and their apostolic successors to preserve the peaceful way.

What Christ did was law to us, more than what He said. He was the eternal law of the Father, the art, the wisdom, the word cloaked in mortal flesh. God the Father spoke to the world through Him. Whatever He told us derived from the mind and will of the Father, and so from the Most High Trinity. He is primordial truth incarnate. He cannot be deceived, cannot deceive, cannot falsify, cannot mistake His own evangelical teaching or be fooled in it. So it follows that it was with wisdom, with skill, without deceit, He arranged our renewal, our liberation from the law, arranged also the manner of manifesting His teachings. Not only that, but He also chose means for winning over people, no deception, no fraud. He set up means, shaped them, tempered them, shifted them so they were more apt, more concordant, more effectively fitted, so they were better in method and manner for winning over people to accept His teaching, His law, willingly, graciously, with little delay. Better means could not be thought up—temperate, concordant, fitting means.

So, since He was divine law, eternal but visible, cloaked as a man, whatever He said or did, the actions He performed must be considered no less a law than what He put into words, what His speech made manifest. This refers to good mores, to Christian life, to human dealings neighbor to neighbor, to those actions He wanted people to imitate Him in, excluding miracles and counsels. He did not oblige us to them, just in special cases, as we are to believe.

Words, deeds seem to have equally the force of law, especially when it comes down to us doing exactly what Christ did, the preaching of the gospel, the calling of pagans to the law of Christ, the return of the lost sheep to the sheepfold. Christ taught, Christ mandated the way, the manner in which we were to do this and do like things. There is support for this argument in St. Gregory, Homily 17, on the gospel passage: "Jesus designated a further seventy-two . . ." (Luke 10:1). He says this: "Dear brethren, Christ instructs us with words sometimes, with deeds other times. His deeds are His commands. When He does something without saying a word, He marks out what we ought to do." And in Homily 19: "His deeds show something on one level, power, and say something on another, mystery."[40] Christ's deeds are expressive. As expressive as His words. So Christ's deeds are His words. They are divine law, the source of law, they oblige everyone great and small, apostle, pope, bishop, emperor, king or prince, whatever, no matter their status, the lofty position they hold, no matter anyone's condition, or grade, or job, or life. It is the law of the Lord of them all, "and ruler of the kings of the earth" (Apocalypse 1:5). And there is the phrase in Hebrews: ". . . for them to see and imitate."

Especially since He often urged people in word to imitate what He did, an urging set out clearly in Matthew 11:29: "Learn from me, I am meek and humble of heart." And John 13:5: "I have given you an example. As I have done, so you also should do." And in 1 Peter 2:21: "Christ also suffered for you, leaving you an example that you should

---

[40] [*PL:* 76:1139, the 1st quotation; the 2nd is not an exact quotation but gives the gist of 76:1153–59.]

follow in his steps." And Paul to the Ephesians 5:1: ". . . be imitators of God, as beloved children. And walk in love, as Christ loved us."

He seems to have wished that what He did would hold us to the law, rather than what He said, what He ordered. First. Because the mind behind the voice is more powerful than the voice, however that mind makes itself known. The jurists say, "The letter should not be fixed on but the meaning." "What dominates is not letter over meaning, but meaning over letter." The reasoning is that words are invented so a speaker can communicate to someone else a knowledge of what he thinks.[41]

Second. Almost every human being eagerly seeks a knowledge of the deed done. There is nothing more powerful in prompting the human soul to do likewise than the deeds of bygone days. So, says Pope Leo, that is the reason why dramas are mounted. Through fictional characters we reinforce in people's minds the values we want them to have. And that happens because people move to some understanding through the use of their senses; it is natural. They communicate to others this way as well. Through sense-things we are led to mind-things and to the things of God. "The things invisible of God are understood through the things made visible" (Romans 1:20). Providence provides for people. Hints of the divine are put in reach of people's senses. That way people's minds are pulled toward the things of God.

This explains, says St. Thomas, the fabrication of images in Church life—to fix more firmly in our memory the mystery of the incarnation and the deeds of Christ and of the saints, and to affect piety which is more surely done through the eye rather than through the ear.[42] Luke the evangelist was careful to relate Christ's deeds prior to Christ's words, and his care was sound. He writes: "Jesus began to act and teach" (Acts 1:1). And in his last chapter: "Concerning Jesus of Nazareth who was a man mighty in work and word before God and humankind," he wrote "work" before "word."[43]

Gregory—in a homily on the gospel words "I am the Good Shepherd"—says: "He did what He advised; He obeyed what He ordered."[44] The implication being that we are linked to the law of Christ

---

[41] *Digest,* lib. 33, tit. 10, lex 7 [Krueger, 1:518b]; *Codex,* lib. 8, tit. 16 (17) lex 9 [Krueger, 2:342b]; *Gratian,* causa 22, q. 5, cap. 11 [Friedberg, 1:885–86]; *Decretals,* lib. 5, tit. 40, cap. 8 [Friedberg, 2:913–14]; *Gratian,* causa 22, q. 2, cap. 4 [Friedberg, 1:867–68].

[42] Commentary on *II Sententiarum,* dist. 9, art. 2, corp., and ad 1m, 2m, and esp. 4m. [*Opera,* Parma, 6:461–62].

[43] S. Thomas notes this in *Contra Gentiles,* lib. 3, cap. 119 [*Opera,* 14:370].

[44] [*Catena Aurea*—S. Thomas, *Opera,* Parma, 12:373a.]

more strongly by what Christ did than by what He said. It seems that Christ Himself wanted to give that idea, and expressly. To testify to the fact that He was God, that by all rights people should believe in Him, He referred to deeds, not words to bear witness, in John 5:36: "The deeds I do bear witness to me, that God the Father sent me." And in John 10:25: "The deeds I do in the name of my Father, these bear witness to me." And in 10:38: "If you do not want to believe what I say, believe what I do."

Likewise He got the disciples to show people through the deeds they did that He was the Son of the Father in heaven. As Matthew 5:16 says: "So let your light—your life—shine before people that they see your good works and glorify your Father. . . ." And: "Love your enemies . . . so you may be sons of your Father in heaven" where Matthew puts deeds above words.

So Christ taught, Christ set the way, the form for preaching the gospel: deeds first, words later. If Christ had done deeds only, the same way, same form would have the force of law. It would bind everyone to employ it in evangelization. It is the right means, the apt means, the one fitted to the purpose of preaching—to gather and unify all people in one faith—in fact a necessary means in our regard for reaching that very goal.

There were many ways, many other ways for Christ to have drawn people to Himself. Not for us. Only the way He taught us, the one He practiced, He put into operation and commanded us to practice in our activity. No one is allowed to take a different path, to invent a way different from Christ's, to use an opposed way in transmitting the truth of the gospel, the gospel itself. It is necessary to obey the law of Christ completely, to be faithful to the law of His words, and faithful to the law of His divine works.

The apostles had to follow the Master's lead. They had to imitate Him who made them leaders, the greats of the whole Church, living examples. They had to put into perfect practice the peaceful way, the form of spreading the law of Christ, the good news. We should take somewhat of a look at how effectively they did this, at them together, at them one by one.

Chrysostom, in a sermon on Pentecost, speaks as follows about the apostles as a group imitating the deeds of Christ:

> They were fishermen who went to the world. They found it sick. They brought it to health. They found it in chaos. They gave it order, not by rattling shields, by bending bows, by letting arrows fly, by passing bribes, not by rhetoric. They were stripped of this world;

they were cloaked with Christ. They were poor but rich. Penniless men, they owned the kingdom of heaven. They had not the comforts of home. They had the Lord for comfort, Who said: "I am with you all days even to the end of the world." They walked the broad world as sheep through a wolf-pack. He sent them, the sheep, to the wolves. They were not savaged by those beasts. The wolves were made over, meek as lambs.

Earlier in the same sermon he says:

They were fisher-folk for sure. They slept while their nets worked. They caught fish first and killed them. They caught people later and vivified them, made the lame walk, the blind see, the lepers clean, the demons vanish. Witness the throng who believed the things of God. They kept vines. In their physical absence, the vines flowered and grew grapes. They were vine keepers, fishermen, "towers" and "pillars" and physicians and chiefs and teachers and harbors and rudders and shepherds and athletes and pugilists and champions. Pillars, because the Church is of stone from their strength. They are the foundation. The Church is built on their belief, as the Lord said: "You are Peter and on this rock, . . ." Harbors, because they break wicked storms. Rudders, because they guide the world in a right path. Shepherds, they drive off wolves, they save the sheep. Farmers, they clear thorns. Vine keepers, they root out the wild grapes, they plant the grapes of piety. Physicians, they cure our sin sick soul. . . .[45]

When Chrysostom speaks of the apostles in his *Against People of Unbelief*, he says: "They did not resort to arms. Nor to bribes. Nor to muscle. Nor to military might. Nor to anything violent. They won the world over by straight talk, by great courage, by the evidence of miracles, the miracles they did, the Christ they preached crucified. . . ."[46]

Again, Chrysostom, commenting on Genesis, Homily 28, says of the apostles and their preaching:

It is amazing, amazing! The apostles soothed the savage beast. The language of piety made them peaceful, taught them to reflect. They gave up their savage customs. They turned to piety. As through the three sons of Noah the Lord of the universe repopulated the world, so He won the world back to Himself in faith through eleven raw and unread fishermen who feared to open their mouths. These raw and

---

[45] [*PG,* 52:803–8, at 805 and 804.]
[46] [*PG,* 48:820.]

unread fishermen surpassed the philosophers. They were winged; above the earth, they spread the word of truth. On the earth they plucked out the weeds of old and rooted ways, and planted everywhere the laws of Christ as seed.

And nothing stopped them, not their being few, powerless, uneducated, not their teaching of hard, new doctrines, not the deep seated customs of humankind. Grace preceded them, removed all obstacles; all they did was done without hitch, the obstacles gave them greater zeal. Example: They taught the truth joyfully even as they were flogged. Not because of the flogging. But because they were deemed worthy to suffer humiliation for the name of Christ. . . .[47]

Again, in his book *Against People of Unbelief,* he says:

Those who believed were locked in prisons. They were mocked, deprived of property, killed, burned at the stake, suffocated in water; they suffered every kind of torture, had humiliation heaped on them, they were persecuted as public enemies. Nevertheless more believers joined them. The torments to other believers did not stop the flow of the new ones. They came more eagerly, in fact, leaping into this glorious haul of fish. They caught the fisherman. The latter were not caught, not subjected to violence. They came spontaneously, grateful to those who netted them.[48]

Also in the first Homily on Matthew, Chrysostom says about the apostles:

The wise of the world never even dreamed what the apostles announced with confident, persuasive clarity, winning to the faith not just people of our era, but those of bygone eras who are now dead. And not a couple, or twenty, not a hundred, a thousand, ten thousand—but cities, races, land-peoples, sea-peoples, Greek and barbarian lands, livable parts of the earth, and the very desert itself. They won peoples to truths we know exceed our natural power.

And further on:

What these fishermen preached—harassed everywhere, often beaten, often pitched into peril, having to talk without education or

---

[47] [*PG,* 53:258.]
[48] [*PG,* 48:831–32.]

rhetorical training—others received with complete respect, the learned and the unlearned, the slave and the free, king and soldier, Greek and barbarian.

And further on, after other good comments:

> The primary teachers of this gospel are tax collectors, fishermen, tentmakers. Their lives were not brief things, they live still, live in eternity. Even dead they do their disciples good. The gospel is not at war with humankind, but it is against viciousness, demonry, against spirit powers. So the leader of the fight is no mere man or angel. God is the leader, beyond doubt. The arms of the soldiery in such warfare stem from the nature of the war. They are not clad in iron and leather. They are clad in truth, in faith, in justice, in all virtues else.[49]

The conclusion is clear, how the apostles kept to the form of preaching the gospel set by Christ, one He imposed on them by a clear-cut command, to imitate Him entirely. They drew people to the truth of salvation by patience, by humility, by faith, by justice. And by a gentle exposure of the truth. And by a gentle persuasion. And by a blameless life. Armed with straight talk, with devout discourse. Using no force, causing no harm, but giving gifts gratis. And drew the whole world, its varieties of human beings, kings, emperors, thinkers, Greeks, Latins, barbarians, the great and the small. Brought them under the culture of Christ so they gave thanks to God with willing voices, and to the teachers of the truth.

There is confirmation of this in Augustine, third letter to Valusian, near the end:

> The apostles were filled with the Holy Spirit. Suddenly they speak a common tongue. They combat error courageously. They preach the sobering truth. They urge repentance, they promise pardon from God for past sinful lives. What follows the preaching of prayer and true belief are visible effects and miracles. Bitter unbelief arises against them: they bear it; their hope is in the promises; their teaching in the precepts. Few in number, they scatter through the world. They win people with remarkable ease. Among enemies, they thrive. They thrive in persecution; oppression only spreads them far and wide. From being the dullest, the worst off, the smallest, they become the brightest, the best off, the biggest. They convert to Christ

---

[49] [*PG,* 57:18, 20.]

brilliant minds, brilliant speakers, brilliant talents among the sharp-
est rhetoricians and teachers, convert them to preaching the way of
prayer and salvation. In the shifts of good and bad times, they keep
an even patience and control. With the world coming to an end, and
telling tired creation the last age is here, the apostles look to the joy of
the heavenly city, confident the more in it "because this too was
foretold."

And further: "All come down, temples, effigies of demons, profane
rites—slowly, one by one, as the prophecies predicted."[50]

Augustine says the same as Chrysostom, but with fewer words. So,
changing nothing, the apostles use the method, the manner set by
Christ of preaching the gospel to people.

CHRIST'S KINGDOM OF COMPASSION AND PEACE

One more powerful argument can be added to fortify the position
outlined in the previous sections concerning the one peaceful, gentle
way of presenting the truth of salvation in Christ, of drawing people to
that salvation. It was the way to form a Christian people so Christ could
reign, something God foretold long ago. The argument is this:

When Christ came into the world to save humankind, He was to
have otherworldly power over the Christian people, not worldly—as I
will outline in broad strokes early in the next chapter, God willing.
Though He was Lord and Maker of both king and subject, though at
His coming He could have chosen the way of rigor and force if He
wanted, nevertheless He led a lowly life, a kind, peaceful, poor, a marginal life. That was His choice on coming. He submitted to king, pre-
fect, prince, to the pomp of power, fulfilling Zechariah 9:9 and
Matthew 21:5: "A just and saving king will come to you, meek and
poor, seated upon a donkey with foal." And John 6:15: "He left when
the crowd wanted to take Him and make Him king."

The saints, St. Thomas especially, give several interpretations for
this behavior. First, Christ wanted known the difference between His
power and the power wielded by earthly princes. Christ used His
power, His right to rule, to save souls, to provide the unseen goods of
the soul, though these imply the goods of the body, on condition that
they help the soul. Christ's ultimate purpose was to aim His kingdom
below at the kingdom above, the everlasting kingdom. The kingdoms
of the worldly, the carnal, the myopic are time-bound and evanescent.

---

[50] [*PL* 33:523.]

So He lived humbly in this world. He chose the way of poverty and meekness. Thus He could draw His faithful—who *are* His kingdom according to Augustine—more readily to follow His example and act out of strength. St. Bernard says in his letter "On Poverty": "When we were lost in a wilderness without water, He came to show us the way out to a city of life. (Psalm 106:4) It was the example of His life that showed us the safe and sure way there—He owned nothing in this world. He obeyed His Father even unto death. (Philippians 2:8)"

Second, Christ wanted to teach the princes of this world humility and compassion so they would be signs of love in their kingdoms, sources of blessing, because humility draws blessing. As Proverbs 29:23 says: "A glory will transform the lowly of heart." Also Ecclesiasticus 3:23, "Fulfill your duties with compassion: you will be loved more than the great of this world." And James 4:6: "God resists the proud, but yields to the humble."

Christ said emphatically that we had to learn these two virtues from Him—humility, compassion—because these virtues filled Him, overflowed from Him; they are the pinnacle of charity which is the greatest of all virtues. That is why He is the unique instructor who taught us these virtues by both word and deed. He urges us to practice these virtues for an important reason, because we are especially disposed by them for union with God. They clear the way to the kingdom above. St. Bernard shows plainly, in the earlier quotation, that Christ was sent for humility's sake. Bernard argues from the fact that humility is of such value and dignity it can be taught by no one else but God. So he says that Christ by His examples of humility showed us the right, the sure way to eternal joy.

The same thing is true of compassion. And since kings and princes tend more toward pride and haughtiness, they simply must practice humility and compassion. If princes of the world are prized for being humble, caring, for plain living, and for being gracious and lovable to their subjects and a source of progress for their people, why not prize Christ even more for His perfect humility, His compassion? Many leaders lived in poverty and humility for the salvation of their people and for the common good—which is superior to the individual good, according to Aristotle in 1 Ethics. They were compassionate, they gave up their lives for their people.[51] It makes greater sense that Christ should have lived in humility and poverty, that He should have taught

---

[51] Thus Valerius Maximus, concerning [the Athenian king] Codrus and other notables, lib. 5, cap. 6 [cf. Karl Holm, ed., *Valeri Maximi Factorum et Dictorum Memorabilium Libri Novem,* Leipzig, 1865, pp. 253–59, esp. 257].

these virtues with a mature concern, not just to peasants but to princes of this world, by personal example. He was born for the good of humankind, to be killed for its salvation, then to draw all eagerly to His grace and love and life of soul. It simply had to be that He excel in these virtues so He could be visible to all as lovable and gracious, so He could gather more and more people by this gracious and lovable way into His kingdom and make it grow and mature more easily, more fruitfully for all.

The third reason: the way of humility, peace, rejection of worldliness, fits with nature; it draws people to moral life quicker and better—the way Christ intended—than force of arms. We proved this earlier at length.

Violence cannot coerce the human will into doing good. "If you donate from terror, you do not donate."[52] "Anyone forced to shift home or belief, shifts neither home nor belief, but is shifted."[53] We can claim no reward from what we have done unwillingly.[54] "What you choose to do, you keep doing; what you are forced to do, you drop quickly."[55] And the law "Nihil consensui" says: "Nothing contradicts consent more than force or fear—and consent is the basis for judgments in good faith. Approval of force or fear is immoral."[56] And there are certain transactions which require express consent. Faith is one, and marriage, baptism, voting, jurisdiction, etc.[57]

Christ knew the human condition. So He fashioned a way of attracting people to Himself, to a moral life, by attachment to Him, compliance with His laws. The way was respectful, attractive, altruistic, germane to human kind. He ordered that this be the way people should come under His gentle rule of their own free will; the way His faithful should live under His law, the way the rest of the sinful world should be invited to live under it also, very gently, very openly; the way they would persist in belief and belonging, very strongly, very firmly. The best proof comes from when Jesus was at table. Publicans and sinners sat with Him as well as disciples. That could not have happened if He bore Himself as a king or led an upper-crust life, pompous and

---

[52] *Decretals,* lib. 5, tit. 41, cap. 8 [Friedberg, 2:928. Las Casas had erroneously cited a canon from the *Sext*].

[53] Gratian, causa 7, q. 1, cap. 34 [Friedberg, 1:579].

[54] Gratian, causa 13, q. 2, cap. 25 [Friedberg, 1:729].

[55] Gratian, dist. 5, cap. 27 [Friedberg, 1:1419].

[56] *Digest,* lib. 50, tit. 17, lex 116 [Krueger, 1:923b].

[57] *Digest,* lib. 3, tit. 3, lex 8, #1 [Krueger, 1:68a]; *Digest,* lib. 8, tit. 2, lex 5 [Krueger, 1:144]; and *Decretals,* lib. 3, tit. 42, cap. 3 [Friedberg, 2:644–46]; Gratian, dist. 23, cap. 5 [Friedberg, 1:81]; Gratian, dist. 45, cap. 3 and cap. 5 [Friedberg, 1:160–61, 161–62].

vain. That way people would have shunned His presence, His company, too frightened by His power to approach Him. And if they had first been ravaged by war and the effects of war, if wounded, if lashed to the point of hatred, they would have avoided Him with a passion.

The fourth reason for Christ's way was so that He could remove all suspicion from people's hearts that He was ambitious and greedy. So they would not think He carved out a kingdom in order to rule in this world, that He set His mind on it as other kings of the earth, that He had His eye on worldly riches and honor—something that would debase authority, the dignity of His preaching, something that would vitiate His goal, the riches of converting and saving precious souls.

St. Paul knew that suspicion of greed was the biggest obstacle to achieving Christ's goal. He feared it mightily, he treated it as poison, as the finish to preaching the faith: "I never flattered you, as you know, nor used you for greed's sake . . ." (1 Thessalonians 2).

The fifth reason: Because of the fruitfulness of peace. People need peace, peace and quiet, to worship God, St. Thomas argues in *Against the Gentiles,* bk. 3. It is clear from what we have said earlier that the souls of people cannot pay any attention to worshiping God in the conditions of panic, anxiety, unrest, and alarm—conditions that go with war. They fill with terror, with pain and sorrow, things of that kind, and many another which drives the soul to distraction, makes it incapable of doctrine and worship which demand peace and quiet.

So the King of Peace, the Wisdom of the Eternal Father who never fools us or betrays us, whom we can never fool or betray, Christ, chose a fitting way: one that was necessary, one He knew was germane to the rational creature He came to bring back to God—the purpose of the incarnation, the purpose of the redemption (Matthew 12 and Luke 3). With pure compassion He ordered His followers to be peaceful, to be modest and kind, as the introduction to the *Decretals* puts it. There the wrecker of peace suffers capital punishment. Many exceptions are granted for the sake of peace, but not otherwise.[58]

The sixth reason: It ill-suited the compassionate, gentle character of Jesus Christ and the scope of His kingdom, this theory of wars and subjugation, this option for such a horrid, detestable means to reach the rule of the gospel. Christ's kingdom is eternal, spiritual. War was a foul, a gruesome practice, no different in concept and kind from what Mohammed did, that foul and gruesome monster.

---

[58] *Digest,* lib. 49, tit. 16, last sentence [Krueger, 1:890a]; *Decretals,* lib. 3, tit. 5, cap. 21 [Friedberg, 2:472–73]; *Decretals,* lib. 4, tit. 2, cap. 2 [Friedberg, 2:673].

It was more suited to Christ to collect a Christian people peacefully, in the way I described Him doing above, to make it one, to make it grow, to make it safe. God wanted it this way, the prophets foretold it this way:

Behold my servant (He spoke in human metaphor) whom I uphold, my chosen, in whom my soul delights; I have put my Spirit upon Him, He will bring forth justice to the nations. He will not cry or lift up His voice, or make it heard in the street; a bruised reed He will not break, a dimly burning wick he will not snuff out . . . He will not fail or be discouraged [because He has a joy, a happiness, the interlinear gloss says] . . . and the islands wait for his law (Isaiah 42:1–4).

That is, peoples are called 'islands' because, Jerome says, "they are open to enemy attack on all sides. We feel the presence of a law given not by Moses but by the gospel."[59] The evangelists took up this prophecy, e.g., Matthew 12:19: "He will not cry or lift up His voice . . . till He brings justice to victory, and in His name will the Gentiles hope"—i.e., the pagans. Jerome says of the same Isaian passage:

The crushed or the broken, He will not further break. He will be a balm to all, He will be a grace to the sinful, as in the words to the woman, "Believe, daughter, your sins will be forgiven." He will not snuff out the lamp wick: "The mercy of God will keep alive those who have burned low."[60]

Jerome comments further on Matthew: "He breaks a bruised reed who does not steady a sinner or lift a brother's burden. He snuffs out a flax lamp who thinks worthless the spark of faith in the weak. The Lord came to save the dying sparks."[61]

Christ is not violent, He is peaceable to all, He came to save the sinner. So war is an obscenity, a contradiction of His peaceable kingdom—war, its tangle of turbulence, of heartlessness, and sadness, and lost souls.

And Chrysostom, on the same passage, Matthew 12, in Homily 41, says

The Lord lavished His mercy, His kindness, His awesome power on His people, He opened the door wide to pagan peoples, He laid out

---

[59] [*PL*, 24:422.]
[60] [Again, *PL*, 24:422.]
[61] [*PL*, 26:79.]

the future role of Israel. He foretold His own miracle of mercy, His kindness beyond telling, His utter altruism in the world: "He will not quarrel, He will not roar." He chose to stay with His persecutors and cure them. He did not reject His rejectors, nor repel those who drove Him away. Finally, the prophet Isaiah, to show the wisdom of Christ and the folly of His rejectors, said, "He will not break the half-broken reed." He could certainly have broken people, already like half-broken reeds. "He will not snuff out a smoking lamp." Isaiah sets before us the smouldering rage of sinners, then says that the power of Christ is so great it could easily snuff them out. That Christ did not is easily a sign of His infinite humility and kindness. . . .[62]

And Chrysostom in *On Damnation* uses these same passages as his authority. He says:

The Lord sees beforehand all our choices and what our future will be. He creates us nonetheless to show His kindness and generosity. He did not cease from creating because of foreseen malefactors. In fact He enriched them as He enriched all. How else can you act, if you attend church, if you offer the gifts of the Son of God? Can you forget that He did not break further the half-broken, He did not snuff out the smoking lamp?[63]

The same with Isaiah 2. The Holy Spirit taught the prophet the manner and means of forming the kingdom of Christ, the Christian people, of spreading it, of preserving it. Not by war. Not by force of arms. By the taste of peace. By an atmosphere of charity, by the works of kindness, of mercy, of modesty. This must be the way of calling and convincing people to believe in Christ. This way is suited to the compassion and generosity of Christ. Isaiah says: "They will beat their swords into ploughshares, their spears into pruning hooks. Nation shall not rise against nation [i.e., Christian against pagan, say, to propagate the faith] nor will a nation take to the sword for battle against another." Isaiah continues: "The nations will come to Him [to Christ the King, who is described symbolically as a mountain or a carved rock no human hand has carved]. And many peoples will gather to say, 'Come, let us climb up the mountain of God' [the Christ], to Jacob, the house of God [the Church]. God will teach us life. . . ." Jerome comments here: "The passion for war shall be changed into a passion for peace; harmony will replace warfare in the whole world. Swords into plough-

---

[62] [*PG,* 57:441.]
[63] [*PG,* 48:950.]

shares. Spears into pruning hooks. Gone fanatic warfare, its weapons will work the fields, will reap bountiful harvests."[64]

Clearly, if Isaiah prophesied that at the time Christ was to come peace would fill the world, he did this to make the quality of Christ attractive, His kingly compassion, even for narrow, unbelieving people —the world was then full of them, they had been at war a long time, here, there, and everywhere, yet there was a moment of peace—then clearly, it ill-suited to the generosity, the kindness of Christ to subjugate to Himself, by war and its weaponry, any people, any kingdom. His way was to draw people, to win them to Himself so they would flow to His side, to His teaching, freely, joyously. Isaiah illustrates this point well in the cited passage: "All people will flow together toward Him. Many nations will arrive and say, Come, let us climb up the mountain of God. God will teach us life." That voice would not have been if people had been unwillingly dragged in by war and the ravages of war, massacre, cruel massacre, if people were choking on their own disasters.

To flow, to run quickly like a watercourse, means to say how willingly, how naturally, greedily, bounding with joy they came to the mountain who is Christ. Isaiah prophesies a manner different from the way God chose for the Jewish people to take the Promised Land. People were to flow toward the Messiah, who was to unify, settle, secure His people without recourse to violence. The Jewish people took the land, settled and secured it by a series of wars. The future apostle of Christ is described in totally different terms. Not by force of arms does he win nations, does he settle and secure them. He does it by the doctrine of Christ which is fully gentle, fully peaceful, fully loving—to cite scriptural commentators on even the literal sense.

There is a superb reason for this: the weapons of war are physical things. Their nature is not to conquer souls but bodies, booty, buildings, material things they can reach. But it is through spiritual weapons that the Christian people are to be formed, gathered, settled, preserved —the way Christ wanted and still wants to gather, settle, expand, preserve those over whom He wanted a spiritual rule, so they might become His by faith, hope, charity, virtues of the free soul only. By spiritual arms, i.e., by a gospel message full of light, of gentleness, of kindness, by the sacraments, by the grace of the Holy Spirit, actual and habitual. As He Himself said: "Behold I am with you all days even to the end of the world" (Matthew 28:20).

---

[64] [*PL,* 24:45.]

These are the mighty weapons of Christ's army, powerful enough to reach God, to reach the soul, reach to the pure point of the soul, weapons for the soldier of Christ "to destroy strongholds, . . . to destroy arguments and every proud obstacle to the knowledge of God, and take every thought captive to obey Christ" (2 Corinthians 10:4–5).

No one should conclude from this that warfare is forbidden to Christian leaders when it is necessary for the defense of the nation. It is one thing to speak of the way to preach the law of Christ and thereby gather, settle, and secure a Christianity in which He rules spiritually. It is another to speak of saving the nation, of using sound judgment which sometimes dictates waging a defensive war, or offensive war, against tyranny. Grace does not contradict nature but perfects it.

You see what power the weapons of Christ have for conquering the world, you see what destruction, what captivity is worked on enemies! Different from the spirit of tyrants and slaughterers who cannot win the souls or affections of those they conquer, though they conquer body and property and locale and kingdom with their physical weapons. Physical weapons can bring ruin on people, irreparable harm, but cannot reach beyond body, property, or place, as I said earlier.

That rule is tyrannical, violent, and never long lasting which is acquired by force of arms, or gotten without some consent of the conquered.[65] Tyranny is the worst of all political systems of rule.[66] The rule which people grant to someone as a gift, grant it freely, with no force or fear or coercion involved, so someone rules willing subjects—that rule is a noble rule, natural, just, virtuous, and judged to be the best. Therefore, if everyone, everywhere, or if a plurality of nations should freely install the same someone as their lord and king, that monarch would be the best possible. All the philosophers think so, and the Catholic theologians as well. It is a clear teaching in St. Thomas.

A rule at its best is a rule constituted for the common good of the subject, not for the profit and glory of the prince, though profit and glory may come as a consequence.[67] So the more the subjects enjoy a liberty which does not ruin peace and tranquility, nor do damage to the common good, the better the rule is, the more noble, the more lasting. Thus a king or emperor in charge of the best realm has subjects so free that they cannot justly be deprived of their property or rights or freedoms, except through their own fault, and the fault must be proven.

---

[65] Thus Aristotle argues in *Politics,* entire bk. 3 [McKeon, 1176–1205].

[66] Thus Aristotle in *Ethics,* bk. 8 [McKeon, 1096].

[67] Thus Aristotle also states in *Ethics,* bk. 8, and argues in *Politics,* lib. 5 [McKeon, 1069–70, and 1232–1264].

And they acquire things for themselves, not for king or emperor. They can keep what they acquire as they will; they can hold on to it or give it to anyone they want.

This was the sort of rule Christ offered all people, it suited Him, it sat on His shoulders (Isaiah 9:6). His were the labors, His the death to undergo for our sins, for the common good of everyone, everywhere—though also for the deeper reason, to glorify the divine name—and that is the difference between His rule and the rule of worldly princes. Theirs is ordered solely toward the common good, His to God alone Who is over all, to Whom is owed all honor and glory and power (cf. Daniel 7:27 and 1 Timothy 1:17).

With this sort of rule, He left His subjects a true, a total liberty, with peace and tranquility. He forced no one. He took no one's property, or rights, or freedom. He deprived no one of wealth or rank by His primacy. He caused no one injury or trouble. He drew to Himself no one who was unwilling. He forced no one to submit to Him after first striking terror into Him with a weapon. People submitted to Christ the King avidly, viscerally, once they heard His words of eternal life, once they saw His miraculous deeds. And many later gave their lives to bless and honor Him—they loved Him so—and to keep safe and inviolable the faith He gave. The words of our Savior were truly attractive, truly effective, so much so that, as Isaiah prophesied, all who heard Him followed eagerly, delightedly after Him wherever He went, as the Gospels testify.

His life, His teaching were indeed hard, His commands difficult. Witness His words: "Whoever does not take up his cross and follow Me is not worthy of Me." And: "I have not come to send peace on the earth, but the sword, and to set a son against his father, and a daughter against her mother" (Matthew 10:38). And: "Whoever does not give up all he owns is not worthy of Me" (Luke 14:33). And like statements. These statements were rough going for those who knew how to fill their belly with food and drink and knew nothing else. Yet they did not pull back from His words, His teachings, nor from following Him. His words were gentle, compassionate, gracious, attractive. They were convincing. They were filled with divine inspiration, with the fire of the Holy Spirit.

One time some disciples abandoned Christ because of the difficulty of His words. These were the words: "Whoever eats my flesh and drinks my blood possesses eternal life." And these: "Unless you eat the flesh of the Son of Man, you will not have life in you." He said then to the twelve apostles: "Do you want to abandon me also?" Peter answered for the rest: "Lord, to whom will we go, You have the words of eternal life, and we believe, we know You are the Christ, the Son of God" (John 6:55, 54, 68–70).

This, therefore, is how the Redeemer Himself began to form the Christian kingdom. He laid the basis for its spread and its unity, gently, invitingly, appealing to free will. He left to each one the choice to kill the kingdom or to keep it. No force, no threat, no coercion on His part, no menace of war, so justice stayed intact. (I spoke earlier of this and at length.) Suffice it here to quote what James the Greater is supposed to have said to Hermosensus, a magician in conflict with the faith, after he was freed from the devil's clutches by a command of the apostle: "Be freed and go where you want. God wishes no one converted against his will."

THE IDEAL MISSIONARY

We can now select out five basic traits from all the material we have just presented, traits that reveal as a whole how the gospel must be preached according to the mind and mandate of Christ.

One. Those who hear the gospel preached, non-Christians especially, must sense that the preachers want no power over them as a result of the preaching. Chrysostom's view. He said that when Paul preached, Paul did not use the language of seduction nor the language of deceit. The seducer wants power, the politician wants control. "No one can say we lied to gain control of people." It comes down to Paul's statement: "We are not after glory from human beings; not from you, not from anyone else" (1 Thessalonians 2:6). Paul's success had provoked suspicion. Chrysostom thinks he said what he said to get rid of that suspicion.

Two. Those who hear the gospel preached, non-Christians especially, must sense that the preachers are not really itching after their wealth. So Paul says: "Preaching cannot be a cover for greed" (1 Thessalonians 2:5). Or, in Anselm's wording: We were not after what you had when we preached, it was not our wish; we kept to the Lord's instruction, the one which went to the root of all evil. He forbade the apostles to keep gold or silver or any coin. St. Jerome, reflecting on Matthew's Gospel, says that if the apostles made money, people would think they preached for lucre's sake, not for the sake of saving souls.[68] Whatever they then said would be laughed at as propaganda. Chrysos-

---

[68] [*Catena Aurea*—S. Thomas, *Opera,* Parma, 11:131a.]

tom says, about this second rule: (1) The precept of poverty frees the disciples from suspicion. (2) It frees them from worldly worry—their entire concern can be for the word of God.[69] Paul states the matter: "It was trust in God that let us preach the Gospel to you without stint" (1 Thessalonians 2:2). (3) He showed them that He, Christ, was their power. Christ's question later brought it home: "What else did you need that time you preached?" (Luke 22:35).

Three. Preachers should address audiences, especially non-Christian, with modesty and respect. They should create a climate of kindness and calm and graciousness so that their hearers would want to listen and would have a greater respect for the message. This is why Paul said: "I became like a child." Or a peaceful person, as I noted from Chrysostom: "I said nothing that smacked of arrogance" (Homily on 2 Thessalonians). And Chrysostom adds the words "in your midst," meaning "not wanting to lord it over any of you." He says the same in the next homily:

> A teacher must never harm students with truths intended to help them. To take care of a flock of sheep, Blessed Jacob wearied himself night and day. The one who has charge of a flock of souls should do more, much more, whether the job is hard or easy, when the one goal is involved, the salvation of the souls he teaches, and the glory that he thereby gives to God.[69a]

Athanasius comments also on [the Pauline phrase] "I became like a child": "Paul means kind, innocuous, even weak, i.e., incapable of evil, and dead to pride. Those who are like children never think evil, never think pride."

Chrysostom comments on the comparison, "as a nurse cares for her charges [1 Thessalonians 2:7] . . . so must a teacher. . . . Does a nurse tell lies so the children praise her? Does a nurse squeeze money out of nurslings? Does she batter and bruise them? Are not nurses better with children than mothers?" He speaks of the way love works. Then he goes on [paraphrasing verse 8]: "So if we base our service on love and care for you, we take no pay for it. Just the opposite, we would give our lives for you and nothing would stop us."[70]

Athanasius comments on the same comparison, "as a nurse . . .":

---

[69] [*Catena Aurea*—S. Thomas, *Opera,* Parma, 11:131a.]
[69a] [*PG,* 62:399–406, 405.]
[70] [*PG.* 62:403.]

"Now Paul shows the scope of his altruism. A true teacher treats peaceably, patiently, even the stubbornest student he finds, the way a nurse treats a child, even a child that kicks and scratches her." And Primatius says about the further phrase: "He simplified himself, he became childlike in all he did so he could draw someone higher by his example. The nurse prattles also, she eats in little bites, she takes little steps so the child feels easy with her."

And Anselm comments:

> She sits on the ground, takes the child in her lap and suckles it, she strokes it and makes sounds to teach it speech. We have sat on the ground for you. We took you to the bosom of belief like a loving mother long on patience. We breast fed you the faith. We stroked you with visions of the life to come. We told you about the human Jesus in infantile words, so we could lead you to adult speech about His divinity.[71]

So a preacher who draws people to the truth of Christ must treat them graciously, respectfully, especially those who are set against it, or not eager to hear it, or ready to laugh at it. This is what Paul taught Timothy:

> And the Lord's servant must not be quarrelsome but kindly to everyone, an apt teacher, forbearing, correcting opponents of his truth with gentleness. God may perhaps grant that they will repent and come to know the truth, and they may escape from the snare of the devil, after being captured by Him to do His will" (2 Timothy 2:24).

Chrysostom says, commenting on Psalm 119:

> Do not tell me someone is savage and unbearable. The time to show oneself peaceable is exactly when one has to deal with savage and unbearable people, hardly human, hardly civilized. Then a teacher shows his worth, then his efforts and his results become clearly visible.[72]

And Chrysostom says (Homily 58, *On Genesis*, ch. 32):

> It takes a great soul in us to go beyond loving and serving wholeheartedly those who love us, and win the friendship of those who hate us

---

[71] [Anselm's only treatment of 1 Thessalonians 2:7 is in his "Oratio ad sanctum Paulum." Cf. Franciscus Salesius Schmitt, *S. Anselmi Opera Omnia*, t. 2, 33–41 (Stuttgart, 1968, 2 tomes).]

[72] [*PG*, 55:343.]

by our unfailing charity. Gentleness is powerful. Throw water on a
pyre and it controls the blaze. Say a gentle word and cool a soul that
is hotter than a forge.[73]

Paul had that greatness of soul, gentleness. He used it without stint
toward those to whom he preached, his persecutors included, "that he
might gain everyone for Christ." Paul is like the father who loves
beyond love a son who is taken with a fit. The more the son lashes at
him, the more compassion he feels, the sorrier. Paul too, the more he
sensed the passionate intensity, the anger of those who harassed him,
the more he offered a healing love. Just notice the control, the kindness
with which he tells us about those who whipped him five times, who
loaded him with irons, or who bound him hand and foot, who thirsted
for his blood, who threatened to pull him to pieces every day. "I do
this," he said, "to draw them to act like God, though it is not within
their logic."

Four. There is a further trait to be drawn from the previous material about what is crucially needed in the way one presents the faith, if
the preacher is to save himself as well. It is the love called charity. Paul
sought to save the whole world with it. Gentleness and patience and
kindness are kindred spirits to charity. "Love is patient, it is kind, it
suffers all things, it bears all things . . ." (1 Corinthians 13:4, 7). If you
want proof of how his heart was on fire with charity, listen to him say:
"So being affectionately desirous of you, we were willing to have im-
parted to you, not the Gospel of God only, but also our own souls,
because you were dear to us" (1 Thessalonians 2:8). "Greater love than
this no one has than that he lay down his life for his friends" (John
15:13). And notice what he said to the Corinthians. It shows how kind,
how respectful his preaching was even to his persecutors, even to those
who refused the faith a hearing. "I am afraid that God will make it
humiliating for me when I come to visit you. I will be a reproach to
those many who used to sin but have done no penance since for their
former impurity and fornication and lewdness" (2 Corinthians 12:21).
And: "My little ones, I am in constant labor until Christ is born in you"
(Galatians 4:19). There was a lustful man whose lust grieved deeply.
Paul grieved for the man more than the man for himself. He prayed for
him: "Love this man even more" (2 Corinthians 2:8). And when Paul
was absent from the community of the Church he lived a sad and
lonely life: "For I wrote you out of much affliction and anguish of heart

---

[73] [*PG*, 54:512.]

and with many tears, not to cause you pain but to let you know the abundant love that I have for you" (2 Corinthians 2:4). "To the Jews I became as a Jew, in order to win Jews; to those under the law I became as one under the law; to the weak, I became weak. I am made all things to all people so that I might save all" (1 Corinthians 9:20–22).

Chrysostom, from whose book *In Praise of St. Paul,* Homily 3, the preceding [scriptural] citations were taken, says further:

> Do you know you are watching someone overcome selfishness completely? He wanted to bring everyone to God. He brought all he could. The whole world was like a child of his. He worried, he traveled, he hurried people into the kingdom of God with his teaching, his visions, his meditations, one minute praying for them, the next cajoling them, then scaring them, routing the demon ruiners of their souls. With letters he wrote, with visits he made, with a word here, with a deed there, done by himself or by a disciple, he tried to firm up the weak, to strengthen the strong, to raise the hopeless, to heal the penitent, to quicken the sluggish with the smell of praise. He had a harsh voice for enemies and a harsh look. As a good soldier or good doctor adept at his trade, he watched out for his men, watched out for his patients, unreservedly, one man doing everyone's job everywhere.

> He was outstanding doing the corporal works of mercy, and as outstanding doing the spiritual. He left ample evidence of his practical concern. For one woman's sake he writes to a whole community. Listen to what he says: "I am sending Phoebe, my sister in faith. She is from Cenchreae. Please receive her in the Lord as you would someone holy, and please help her whenever she needs you" (Romans 16:1–2). This kind of love is a hallmark of holiness.

> He prayed repeatedly for those his preaching could not persuade, stubborn people, hard people. He wrote: "I want deeply, I pray God for their salvation" (Romans 10:1). Paul, the insatiable servant of God, a parent to Christ's people—I say Paul, keeper of the world—has saved us all through constant, tireless prayer, his words to us always being: "For this reason, I bend my knee to the Father of Our Lord Jesus Christ, from whom all kinship, all paternity in heaven and on earth are named. That He might give you Christ to live in your inward self through faith, according to the riches of His glory and confirmed in strength by His Spirit" (Ephesians 3:14–17).

> Do you see how forceful constant prayer is? It transforms us into temples of Christ. We can further know the power of prayer when we

see Paul place no trust for saving humankind in his racing around
everywhere like a bird, in being jailed, or whipped, or chained, or
being in danger of life and limb; no more than in his casting out
demons or reviving the dead or healing the diseased. He worked on
the world with prayer; and after working miracles, after reviving the
dead, he sought help in prayer, the way a winning athlete goes right
back into training. Sometimes just prayer is enough to revive the
dead, and to revive everything else.

Paul nourished his soul by night with prayer. He could then bear
easily whatever came, however harsh—he could bare his back to
whipping as if he were made of stone. Though he was peerless in
every virtue, his charity burned brighter than any other. The way
steel put in a forge turns a total red, so Paul, fired up with love,
turned into total love. He became like a first parent, he became like
every parent in the love of all their children: his love, his loyalty
transcended that of carnal and spiritual parentage both. He spent on
them his money, his mind, his body, his soul. That is why he called
selfless love the whole law, the keystone of holiness, the mother-lode
of goodness, the first thing and the last. "The goal is selfless love
from a pure heart" (1 Timothy 1:5). And further: "Every law, i.e.,
not to commit adultery, not to murder, is based on the one law, Love
your neighbor as you love yourself" (Romans 13:9). Since love is the
first thing, love the last, and every good thing in between, we must
try to be like Paul especially in this, because he became what he was
through selfless love. Do not cite to me as more important the dead
he often raised, nor the lepers he often cured with his miraculous
power. God asks you to do none of these. But capture Paul's selfless
love and you will capture heaven. Through it Paul reached the peak
of perfection and nothing made him more worthy of God than did
the virtue of perfect love. . . .[74]

Five. It is found expressed already in Paul's words cited above.
"You witnessed, as did God, the way I related to you who came to
believe, how respectfully, how carefully, how honestly, how blamelessly" (1 Thessalonians 2:10). Words added to the text say: "both
before and after your conversion."

"How respectfully," i.e., under God, as the gloss in the text notes,
and St. Athanasius says also, doing all that has to be done with due
reverence for God. And Anselm interprets it: "How respectfully . . . I
related to you through the openness of all my dealings." "How care-

---

[74] [*PG*, 50:483–87, at 485–86 passim.]

fully," is interpreted by the gloss on the text and Athanasius to mean, "doing right by my brethren, not wronging them, i.e., putting the squeeze on no one for their money." "How blamelessly," meaning a harm to no one.

Or, as Anselm reads it, "How carefully" keeping the balance of justice toward neighbors by doing right; and "How blamelessly, how straightforwardly and honestly I treated you, not to give you cause for complaint against me." Or, "How blameless I was toward you. I never criticized you when I had to live with your shortcomings. There was a reason to act this way toward you, to help you: something you all recognize, you know this, and something in addition, that it was with love I brought each of you around. . . ."

Take 2 Thessalonians 3:7: "You yourselves know how you ought to imitate me." Take the words, "in order to give you in my conduct an example to imitate." Ambrose says in his commentary:

> Watch how Paul is influential in what he does as much as in what he says. A good teacher practices what he preaches. Clearly what is taught is learned, but let the teacher neglect to practice it and the pupil profits little thereafter. You move an audience by what you do more than by what you say. Give those great credit, who profit from words their teachers fail to practice. Paul set the example, for the weak members of the flock, on how not to lose one's influence.[75]

And Anselm again: "I need not explain to you a tradition you know. We must set the example, so those who want to follow the right way should walk the path we do." Polycarp, disciple of John the Evangelist, says about Paul's words to the Philippians: " 'All of you, defer to one another in your dealings; be blameless among non-believers, so you gain their praise for your good deeds, and God is not mocked because of you.' Woe to those who make God's name a mockery. Teach everyone the good behavior you yourselves practice."[76]

Clearly, the fifth element prescribed for the preaching of Christ's gospel is living example: a life visibly virtuous, a life that harms no one, a life blameless from any quarter. A teacher must live his own words, must teach by practice more than by presentation. A teacher who talks, only talks, has a frigid effect; in fact is not a teacher but a faker and two-faced. So apostles teach first by deeds, second by words. No need

---

[75] [*PL*, 17:459.]

[76] [In these multiple brief commentaries on three words of St. Paul, Las Casas gives no lead to any standard compilation he is using. It may have been either a manuscript source not currently available, or Pedro de Córdoba's jottings on the ideal missionary from such a source.]

for words when their deeds did the preaching. The evidence shows they led such holy lives that those who carped at them carped at their doctrine not their decency. As Chrysostom puts it: "They put up with being called seducers and quacks for the Gospel's sake, but no one could ever scoff at their lives." No one ever called an apostle guilty of lust or greed, the accusation "seducers" described only their doctrine.

[Chrysostom continues:]

> You must respect someone whose moral life is a beacon, whose truth stops the critique even of enemies. It is not right to attack such people with curses and slander, the ones who live faultless lives— you can hear Christ saying as much: "So let your light shine before people that, seeing what you do, they may give glory to God the Father who is in heaven" (Matthew 5:16). No one but a blind man would call the sun black; what everyone else sees would shame his contention. The same concerning a man of great dignity, of great moral life, no one but a blind man would dare blame him. It's rather to attack the teachings that non-believers loose their barbs. They dare not loose them at the purity of his life. The life, they hold in awe and admiration, as does everyone.

Therefore Chrysostom says:

> Live so the name of the Lord is not mocked: let us not accept people's adulation, but let us not lack their esteem, let us do what is good and right. Let us be honored for both principles—"You will enlighten people of the world like lamps," says Paul to the Philippians (2:15). God chose us to be such, like stars; to become like yeast as teachers of others; to be angelic with people on earth; to be men with a man-child; to be almost a soul for the soulless; so people profit greatly from our company; so we can be seminal; so we can produce a bountiful harvest. No need of a word if the life we lead is a beacon of holiness. No need of a teacher if we act out of integrity. There would be no non-Christian if we cared to be Christian as we ought, if we kept to the counsels of God, if we did not return blow for blow, if we blessed when we were cursed, if for evil given we gave back good. Only a wild beast would not come at once to believe the truth of salvation if he saw believers act as Christians ought.

> The proof is, there was but one Paul, yet he brought many to know God. If we were Pauls, what a world we could attract! There are more Christians than pagans. One teacher suffices for a hundred pupils in other schoolings. In this schooling, the teachers being so many, the pupils ought to be so many more, but not a one comes, not a one is attracted. Pupils watch the lives of teachers; if they see us itch for the same things as they, lust for the same, long for primacy and prestige, what esteem could they have for Christian doctrine? They see the

sordid lives the Christians lead, base souls wallowing in mud, loving money as much as anyone, much more in fact, equally fearful of death, equally fearful of impoverishment, equally impatient of illness, equally avid for fame and power as anyone else, equally cutthroat of each other for lucre's sake. How can pagans acquire belief? By miracles maybe? We are past miracles. By seeing holiness of life? Holy life is plainly gone. Prompted by charity? There is not a trace of it visible. We will surely answer not just for our own sins but for others' failures also—we caused them!

I beg that we come to our senses, we open our eyes, that we act on earth as if in heaven. And say with Paul: "Our way of life is the way of heaven; let us sustain it in the struggle, the struggle on earth." Maybe someone objects: "We had our holy people once. A pagan could now come and say, Why believe? You do not do what you say [your apostles] did, I can see it. If we are to believe just stories, we can bring in stories of philosophers to tell you, great people, of wonderful life, of moral probity. Show me another Paul, another John. You Christians today are ready to kill or be killed for a pittance, you sue and sue for a foot of ground, you are reduced to total chaos over the death of a child."[77]

Chrysostom again, on 1 Corinthians 1 (Homily 3):

This is the way we win them, this the way we struggle, by holiness of life we gain their souls, a far better way than with words. This is the struggle at its best, the argument at its surest, the deeds we do. It is no gain at all for us to talk much and often yet show no improvement in our lives. People watch what we do, not what we say, then respond: "Take your own advice before you insist with others." If you say heaven holds limitless goods and you seem to fixate on earthly goods as though there were no hereafter, your fixation will convince me, not your words. When I see you lifting others' goods, see you distraught over your losses, see you many times over a criminal, why should I believe your talk of resurrection?

Pagans do not actually say this, but they think it, in their souls. It is this behavior that keeps the pagan from becoming Christian. Let us recall them by our living example. Many an unschooled man has moved a schooled mind this way, as if to show philosophy the reality itself; goodness of life has a voice clearer than a trumpet or schooling, more powerful than a tongue. So if I say be angry at no one, and then unload a thousand angers on the pagan I preach to, how can I pull him with good words when I pelt him with wicked deeds?

---

[77] Thus Chrysostom on 1 Timothy, chap. 3, in Homily 10. [*PG*, 62:551–2.]

So let us draw pagans by the good life we lead, let us build the church through their conversion, let us grow rich this way. There is nothing to equal soul-worth, not the whole material world. You could shell out huge sums to the poor, you do more if you convert but one soul: "If you draw worth from the worthless, you will be a messenger from me" (Jeremiah 15:19). It is a high and holy thing to help the poor; higher, holier to fetch back a soul lost in error. Whoever does so is a Peter, a Paul. We can accept their counsel, not to endanger ourselves as they did, putting up with famine, disease and the rest—our time is a time of peace—but to intensify our apostolic desire. This way, even housebound, we can fish for souls. For a friend, a relative, a neighbor. Whoever does, acts as the disciple of Peter and Paul.

Why do I remind you of them? The answer will be Christ's: "If you draw worth from the worthless, you will be a messenger from me." If today you win no one, you will tomorrow; if you win just one, yet your reward will be full. You will not win all, yet some from all. Not even the apostles won the world. But they broached the question universally, and they gained their reward for each one. For God rewards what we purpose to do, not the profit we gain from good works. Though you as teachers give a pittance, God will reward you as the widow was. Though you cannot save the globe, do not think less of small efforts, do not let global desires distract you from local ones. If you cannot carry a hundred, take care of ten; if not ten, then look to five; if five are too much of a demand, look to one; if you cannot care for one, keep hope, keep trying.

You know, do you not, that merchants use silver as well as gold in their transactions? If we grasp the small we will grasp the large; if we ignore the small, the large will be hard to grasp. Those who grasp small and large come out enriched. It is the way we also must proceed, so that enriched by small and large we may enjoy the kingdom of heaven given by the grace and kindness of our Lord Jesus Christ.

Thus Chrysostom.[78]

PAPAL ENDORSEMENT OF PEACEFUL CONVERSION

Finally, to close the first part of our argument, we have but to support it by reference to many church decrees. There are truly many.

"Whoever sincerely intends to bring non-Christians to the Christian faith must bring them to it by kindness, not by cruelty." This is found in Gratian. And further on: "We must so act that they want to

---

[78] [*PG*, 61:29–30.]

follow us, moved by meaning and mercy, not to flee us. . . ." And in the subsequent chapter: "When priests do blameable things, kindness does more to correct them than harshness, bolstering more than bullying, charity more than force. . . ."[79]

And from the Fourth Council of Toledo, the chapter "De Judaeis":

> From this point on no one is to be forced into the faith, so the Synod decrees. God forgives whom He wishes, He leaves in sin whom He wishes. The willing, not the unwilling, are saved; that way justice is kept intact. We perished as people obeying the serpent of our own free will. We are saved through belief, called by the grace of God to the conversion of our own minds. So people are to be persuaded to conversion by the power of their free choice, not by force, not by compulsion.[80]

Pope Leo is quoted in the following chapter:

> Kindness does more to correct than harshness, bolstering more than bullying, charity more than force. And those who choose themselves and not Christ are quickly spotted by this law, they want to dictate to subjects, not care for them. Honor flatters them, inflates their pride; the sources of harmony turn noxious.[81]

There is a remarkable text from Pope Nicholas:

> What someone does not choose, not opt for, he loves not. What he loves not, he scoffs at. No good not chosen. So the Lord said take no staff for the road in order not to do violence to anyone. You would do wiser to light in them a celestial love by preaching in gentle terms a contempt for worldliness and a love for God than by unleashing violence on people.[82]

The true agrees with the true. The truths of mission all agree that the way of teaching, of drawing people best to God and the knowledge

---

[79] Gratian, dist. 45, cap. 3 and cap. 4 [Friedberg, 1:160, 161. See also *PL*, 77:1267–68, for the quotation from Gregory].

[80] Again Gratian, dist. 45, cap. 5 [Friedberg, 1:161].

[81] Once again, Gratian, dist. 45, cap. 6 [Friedberg, 1:162]. Also relevant are Gratian, dist. 43, cap. 1 [Friedberg, 1:153–55] and causa 8, q. 1, cap. 12 [Friedberg, 1:594].

[82] Gratian, causa 20, q. 3, cap. 4 [Friedberg, 1:849–50, esp. 850, the passage beginning "Quod enim quis"].

of the truth has to win the mind with reasons and win the will with motives that are compelling and attractive.

The last decree left to cite is a new one. Pope Paul III issued it, in the year 1537, as a specific and general policy, occasioned by the following situation.

Corrupt men wanted riches, in this world, whose litter they are, and pleasures, in this world, not in a future life with God's elect enjoying the delights of paradise, seeing God, enjoying God to overflowing. They wanted to be freer, to be unchecked in getting what they wanted as their paradise, gold and silver, their object of faith. They wanted to extract these riches from the sweat, the hard labor, the durance vile and death, death replete with torment and torture and wide-scale injury, the brutal burdening of masses of human beings, practically everyone around. So they concocted a novel way of masking their injustice, their tyranny, and giving credence to their decision.

It was this: They put the lie on the Indian peoples that they were so lacking in the common traits of humankind that they could not govern themselves, that they needed overseers. And this is how far their mad, their damnable impudence went: They said flatly that the natives were brute beasts or next to being so. They flatly defamed them, so it was right to conquer such beasts in war, to hunt them down, to break them for service, then have them for use at will.

The truth is that many a native could rule us, in a domestic, or a mercantile, or a political life, could educate us to the moral life, could surpass us in natural reasoning, as Aristotle said about Greeks and barbarians in 1 *Politics.*

When this posture was denounced to the pope by a member of the Order of Preachers, the pope was shocked, naturally enough, at the sacrilege, the rashness of these disgraceful men. He knew at once how human nature was maligned by this posture, the nature the Son of God did so much for, suffered so much for. He knew the stoppage put to the propagation of the faith by satanic representatives. By a decree sealed in lead, he renewed former decrees: and he declared the posture just presented erroneous, something detestable, something the hearts of the faithful should utterly reject. These are his words:

> Paul, Bishop, Servant of God's servants, to all Christ's faithful who will read these words, health to you and my apostolic blessing. God, though beyond us, so loved humankind that He made us able to share in reachable, visible goodness with the rest of creation—but further than that to share in the highest goodness, unreachable, invisible, and see Him face to face. Sacred Scripture also testifies that we

were created to attain eternal life and eternal bliss. And no one is able to reach life and bliss in eternity except through faith in Jesus Christ. So we have perforce to admit that we humans are of such nature and condition that we can receive the faith of Christ. Anyone who is a human being is capable of receiving that faith. No one but a fool would think he could attain a goal, and not use the means absolutely necessary to attain it. So Truth Incarnate, Who is never deceived or deceiving, said, as we know, when He sent preachers out to preach the faith: "Go, and teach everyone." All, He said, without exception, since all are capable of learning the faith. Satan saw and was jealous of humankind. He fights goodness always to destroy it. He concocted a novel way to prevent the word of God being preached to people for their salvation. He got certain of his lackeys, who wanted to satisfy their lust for riches, to affirm rashly that East and West Indians—and others like them who came into our ken recently, and therefore lacked a knowledge of our Catholic faith— were brute beasts, were to be subjected to our control wherever they were. These lackeys reduce them to slavery, they load them with afflictions they would never load on any beast of burden.

We are the unworthy Vicegerent on earth of the Lord. We try with all our might to lead into the flock of Christ committed to our care, those who are outside the sheepfold. We are aware through what we have been told that those Indians, as true human beings, have not only the capacity for Christian faith, but the willingness to flock to it. We wish to provide apt solutions for the situation. The Indians we speak of, and all other peoples who later come to the knowledge of Christians, outside the faith though they be, are not to be deprived of their liberty or the right to their property. They are to have, to hold, to enjoy both liberty and dominion, freely, lawfully. They must not be enslaved. Should anything different be done, it is void, invalid, of no force, no worth. And those Indians and other peoples are to be invited into the faith of Christ by the preaching of God's word and the example of a good life.

The same credence is to be granted copies of this present decree as is granted to the original—copies notarized by a notary public or by the seal of any person empowered by ecclesiastical office. This we declare through the present decree, notwithstanding earlier ones or whatever else to the contrary. Given at Rome, St. Peter's, in the year of the Lord's birth 1537, the 2nd of June, the year 3 of our pontificate.[83]

---

[83] [For a critical edition of *Sublimis Deus*, see *Las Casas en México*, Apendice 14, which details the copyist's error in the original bull and the errors in most printed copies.]

What is pertinent to our purpose in the document is the following: (1) The Indians and others are to be invited to the faith of Christ, (2) by the preaching of God's word and by the example of a good life. In these two principles everything we argued earlier is included: People are to be drawn to Christ through a way that wins the mind with reasons and wins the will with motives. An amply proven argument.

SUMMARY

The purpose of this past chapter was to lay out fully, text by text, what God wanted as the natural way of teaching the world true belief, true Christianity. It was to serve for all, in one and the same fashion; it was not optional. We were to invite people to a wedding feast, that of Christ, the Son of God. We were to invite them to recognize that this world Savior, this Savior of humankind, was God, was truly God, one with the Father and the Holy Spirit. Anyone who knows this, who then accepts and keeps the laws of God, opts for eternal life. "It is eternal life," John said, "to know you, true God, only God, and Jesus Christ whom You sent to us" (John 17:3). "Go teach people everywhere to keep the commandments I gave you." The texts require of us both faith and works. They give the lie to the strange heresy abroad which holds as dogma that faith alone can save us.

I am speaking about the way Divine Providence proposed to draw people toward Christ. It was to be attuned to the souls of those approached. It was to breathe peace and love and kindness. It was the fittest means for God's purpose, the conversion, the salvation of humankind, a means steeped in love, grace, charm, humanity, joy, a means worthy of anyone's choice.

PART TWO: FALSE EVANGELIZATION

The Opposite Way: Violating the Mind and Will

The opposite way would clearly be this: If a group whose duty it was to preach the gospel to pagans, or to send them preachers, decided it would be quicker and better done if they subjected pagans willy-nilly to Christian political power. Once the pagans were beaten, they could be preached to without trouble. And they would not be coerced into belief. The preaching would appeal to their minds and draw them gently once the conquest had removed their political defenses.

No pagan in his right mind, especially a pagan prince, would surrender to political control by a Christian people or a Christian prince. There would have to be war.

War brings with it cannon fire, surprise attacks, shore raids that are lawless and blind, violence, riots, scandals, corpses, carnage, butchery, robbery, looting, parent split from child, child from parent, slavery, the ruin of states and kingdoms, of lords and local rulers, the devastation of cities and towns and people without number. War fills here and there and everywhere with tears, with sobs, with keening over every pitiful spectacle possible.

People the world over know too well the evil effects war causes or brings to birth. Let me name a few of the many listed by jurists: War, like a tornado, like a tidal wave of evils, runs amok destroying everything, whole cities, whole regions.[84] War paves the way for atrocities, it causes bitter hatreds, it makes people boldly vicious.[85] It beggars a people, it torments them, etc.[86] In war cattle are raided, crops ruined,

---

[84] *Sext,* tit. 14, cap. 2 [Friedberg, 2:1008–11]; *Decretals,* lib. 2, tit. 13, cap. 19 [Friedberg, 2:290–1]. Also *Digest,* lib. 49, tit. 15, lex 21, #1 and lib. 47, tit. 10, lex 1 [Krueger, 1:887a and 830a].

[85] *Clementines,* lib. 3, tit. 7, cap. 2 [Friedberg, 2:1162].

[86] Authentica "De armis," beg., coll. 6 [Novella 85/i.e., Authent. 86, coll./6, tit. 13—Krueger, 3:414b et seq.].

peasants slaughtered, ancestral villas torched, and prosperous cities leveled by the one blast of all those deplorable hostilities. War is a curse not a blessing. Families live in fear, they feud, they carp; everything is depressed; the crafts go dead; the poor are forced into starvation or into a lawless life; the rich resent their loss of wealth, they fear further loss, they are doubly trapped. Raped women marry, though seldom and sadly; and widow women live in barren homes; law is gagged, decency ridiculed, justice pitched out, religion mocked, nothing is sacred, everything is up for grabs. Each nook and cranny of war is stuffed with crooks, with thieves, with rapists, with arsonists, with killers. War is a license to kill and steal; what else can it be? The wider the war, the wickeder, the more thousands of innocent victims are dragged into the lethal conflict and they gave no cause for the harm. People lose their souls in war, they lose their lives and their livelihood.[87]

The next step is to see how opposed to the peaceful way of preaching the faith, how utterly opposed the violent way is. It is the dead opposite, the reverse of preaching the faith and drawing people gently into the flock of Christ, of reaching the goal God wants from the preaching, honor for the divine name, change of heart and eternal life for the human soul. The proof runs this way:

First. We worked out in the preceding chapter how a rational creature is born with a free will and therefore must be treated as free, must be drawn, led, moved toward what is good gently, gently, without pressure, delicately. Now take pagans who have just been subjected to the horrors of war: they are crushed; they are bleak; they are helpless; they despair of their lost children, their lost homes, their lost liberty; they curse their evil luck. How could they possibly want to hear what we would want to teach them about faith, religion, justice, truth? How could they possibly accept such teaching? Again, if a kind man makes many friends, and a violent man forces quarrels and quarrels create enemies (Proverbs 15:18; 10:12), what about words and deeds that are cutting and harsh and cruel and acid to the core—how many enemies will they create? And men gone mad in war, how much violence, how much hatred will they engender?

Conclusion: A creature with a mind and will has to be drawn through its own nature to what is good—i.e., to belief, to religion—drawn gently, without pressure, respectfully. If such a being is driven against its nature by the dogs of war, if it is forced by brutal means, by

---

[87] [Here we have omitted Las Casas' supporting par. citing the jurist Baldus de Ubaldis' commentary on the _Sext,_ describing natural calamities caused by war.]

cruel, heartless, vicious, violent means, it is inevitable that such means, in essence unnatural and inhuman, will produce unnatural, inhuman effects, i.e., people who are deaf to the faith, or who despise what they hear of it. They may be forced to listen, but not forced to agree to what they hear. And that is belief, to accept willingly an understanding of the faith. No one believes without choosing to. Just as sense creates sense, nonsense creates nonsense. If sense is the cause of sense, nonsense is the cause of nonsense. Contrary causes produce contrary effects.[88]

Someone listens willingly to things that are new, utterly new, because they are attractive, noncoercive, respectful. Someone believes these things for the same reason. And just the opposite, if things are the opposite. So the use of war to subject pagans to Christian control, in order to make preaching the gospel possible, is the dead opposite of the natural, normal, pre-established way.

Second. I also worked out in the preceding chapter how someone under instruction in religious faith must think through the doctrines presented. They have to question, they have to discuss the way one teaching connects with another and whether what they hear has a basis in the truth or not. Then they can conclude it is good to believe in that religion. But if someone has seen the hideous effects war brings indiscriminately on himself and his people, what will be on his mind, the horrors he knew and knows or the points of Christian doctrine—a doctrine he never heard of, never believed in, never dreamed of, a doctrine not found in the nature of things? How do you catechize someone who lives with such horrors in his mind?

Like intellect, like will, whose job it is to steer the intellect. Will is freedom. It does not make choices unless it is intrigued or excited or drawn by things which have an appeal—tasteful, attractive things, things present in the mind with the look of goodness about them. What appeal, what taste, what attraction will things have for victims of war who see themselves, their wives, their children, their friends, their neighbors savagely slaughtered? Who see enemy swords disembowel them, quarter and kill them? Who see heads lopped from shoulders with one stroke and pitched as far as they can go? Who see the human body chopped in pieces every which way? Who see some die run through, some die cremated alive? (I have! I have often seen cremation

---

[88] Thus Aristotle in: *De caelo et mundo,* lib. 2; *Posteriorum analyticorum,* lib. 1, and *Metaphysicae,* lib. 9; and *De generatione et corruptione,* lib. 2, and *Physicorum,* lib. 2. [For all but the first of these principles, cf. McKeon, 110–58; 820–34; 468–531; 214–394. Las Casas is simply applying Aristotelian principles of logic to processes of faith, as our version makes clear; these are not citations.]

alive!) Who see blood dripping off everything? Who see those still breathing dragged off to a filthy slavery, a slavery without end?

And what about the deposition of authorities, kings, princes, judges, driven from power, from position, from place, from region and realm given them by the law of nature? Is this the kind of thing, attractive, appealing, charming thing in and of itself which can (I repeat) intrigue, excite, draw the human will so it steers the mind because of its own freedom to consider freely, to accept freely the doctrines of faith it hears preached? And what will they do afterward, those who are treated to the horrors of war, so they can think freely about the heaven-sent gift preached to them by pawns of their tormentors? Yes! Consign it to oblivion! And which way will those sufferings lead them? Yes! To hate the faith, to think of it as raving madness and damnable lies!

Name a people that does not appreciate friendship, kindness, civility and civilized ways! Name one that does not detest people who are arrogant or criminal or cruel or brutal or bestial!

Conclusion: The practice of subjecting pagans to Christian political power by the awful engines of war and thus to make them willing to hear the gospel and to become Christians, is the utter opposite of the natural, normal, pre-established way.

Third. I explained how the human mind is the root source of freedom in what humans do. Freedom is intrinsically linked to knowledge, to a mind not clouded by prejudices born of the passions. Once prejudice rules, the power to think things through, the power to draw conclusions, the power to choose what is good, all three powers are blinded and baffled. The thinking mind must have calm and quiet and enough time if it is to do what it does freely. It must be free as well of fits of passion. Then the will is safe from all coercion, from all harassment.

War breeds traumatic, evil effects. These in turn breed rage, hatred, vengefulness, depression, sorrow, fear, horror, despair, and a thousand more passions in the mind. Is such a mind supposed to think through what it hears told it about religious faith? Is it supposed to judge that faith sound and worthwhile choosing? Take the man who rages against another man, who festers with a mortal hatred against that other because of all the suffering he has seen that other cause: injuries, irreparable losses, brutal hardships, humiliations, beatings, rapes, tortures, murders, jailings. If his mind is filled with grief, with loss, with fear, with horror, with desperation, will he listen peaceably, will he reason calmly, will he conclude, will he choose with ease? Will he admit as true what he hears of religious faith? Will the truths touch him? Will he want them, want them as precious to him? Will he take the plunge and believe them? Will not the contradictory occur?

Conclusion. The practice of subjecting pagans to Christian political power by means of war to make them hear the gospel preached, is the dead opposite of the natural, normal, pre-established way.

And earlier I argued that whoever wants to convince people to accept what he proposes must set their souls at ease right away. Then he has their attention, their willingness to listen and to learn. He sets them at ease by a calm voice, a kind face, a modest bearing, a peaceable language. Only then does he teach them, attract them, convince them.

The same approach must be used, it must, to preach the faith, to lead people to the right religion. The truths of the faith, the truths of the Christian religion are beyond our natural grasp. They are so difficult that they are not really understood. They are believed, and only by an act of the will. I said already how hard they were to live, how otherworldly for our hopes.

WARS FOR CONVERSION CONTRADICT THE HUMAN WAY

What pagan soul would want to hear about our faith and Church if he or she is horribly harmed by the cruel weight of war, the brutal, unbearable waste of war? The voice of war is not calm; its face is not kind; it has no modest bearing, no peaceable language; it does not attract, does not convince with charm. War is a frightful chorus of yells. Its face is a gruesome glare, as fierce as hell; its angers like those of men gone mad, crazed like beasts, bitter, bitter men. War is all curse and catcall; it is the grating, fearsome screech of weapon on weapon left and right and dead men falling. War is hardness and harshness and hurt. It lashes everything, it panics everyone, mainly through fear, then pain, then sorrow, then bitterness, the whole gamut panics people. War is weeping and wailing everywhere. What balm or blessing will it take to make victims of war willing and able to learn religious belief?

The human mind is shattered by terror, by bedlam, by fear, by violent language. Torture shatters it even more, depresses it, crucifies it. So it blocks its ears and eyes. Sense experience is distorted, outer, inner, its synthesis in imagination distorted. Result: Reasoning is in the dark, the mind cannot see in the imagination something it can understand and love and want. It can only see something painful and odious. It sees things as they are, and these things are wicked and hateful. It is useless for anyone to try and placate souls who have suffered the effects of war, to calm them, then win their good will, then gain their attention, then teach them.

It makes perfect sense for them to be forever implacable, unyielding, to be hostile, unteachable, dead set against hearing anything called Christian, to be future enemies of that name.

Is there anyone stupid enough as to think that he can savage his audience before he instructs them? They will hear him with disgust, they will never open their minds, they will believe nothing!

Conclusion: The practice of preparing pagans to hear the gospel preached and to accept the Christian church by subjecting them to the deadly force of war is the utter opposite of the normal, the natural, the gentle way.

Fifth. I made the argument earlier that the way one draws people to faith and to the Christian religion is like unto the way one draws pupils to knowledge. A pupil has to concentrate intensely, he has to focus his attention constantly on what the teacher says and does. A pupil must have quiet, leisure—a soul free of emotional upset born of fear, depression, sorrow, fury, outrage, despair, humiliation. Any of these can ruin concentration, partially or wholly. The different powers of the soul have a common root in the essence of the soul itself. The focus of the whole soul is affected by violence from outside it. People likewise who are lashed by the violence of wars, by the damages, the crises caused by wars, harried, beaten people who live as a result in sorrow, fear, pain, rage, resentment, people who abhor the savagery of Christians, clearly focus their whole outward and inward selves, their whole attention on thinking about, on deploring the evils they undergo, the sufferings and loss through no fault of their own. The life that is left them they live for revenge on their enemies. So whenever they hear teachings on faith and church they take little or no notice, make little or no effort to learn. They are not about to fix on what their teachers say or do. Just the opposite: what they hear they ridicule as nonsense, as make-believe, the stuff of fools. The unforgettable evils they have suffered command their whole attention and all the strength they have left.

Conclusion: The practice of subjecting pagan peoples by war, and so to make them hear the gospel preached, then accept the faith, is totally unlike the true way, a contradiction of it.

Sixth. There is an art one must use in drawing people, however barbaric they are, to a moral life, to any goodness at all. It is the way of nature. The best philosophers used this art. Each sets out his theme often. He explains it, breaks it down, recasts it, reasons to it, wins assent, asks questions, exhorts, invites, charms, even spoonfeeds his pupils. Most of the time it is done with a soft voice, an eager look, graciously, with quiet argument and suitable language, with lively and lovely benevolence. This is in order to create comfort and familiarity in the souls of his hearers, so he or she is then comfortable and familiar with the doctrine they hear, that it is on their level, that it is easy to hear, easy to approve, easy to perform. But that art would be useless to any missionary if pagan peoples had first been ravaged and ruined and beaten and bruised by the wave of hideous effects that follow in the wake of war. They would not want to hear, nor trust anything of what they did hear. The one thing they would do is deplore their awful state, their awful lot. They would use violence on them to make them listen, pile an evil on an evil, and they would not offer you one iota of interest or effort or concentration. That is so clear from previous proofs. Violence only intensifies conditions of sorrow and sadness and deprivation. Violence creates nothing able to last. This is Aristotle's view in 5 *Metaphysics.* He speaks of violence there and what brings violence of itself. They are both deplorable. His proof is from the line of a poet who says that every fated thing, every violent thing is deplorable. "Fate is a kind of violence, as a certain poet states: I was forced to act"—i.e., fated.

St. Thomas says on that very point that violence, as something alien to the normal tendency of a nature, either puts a brake on the will when it is already moving toward some purpose, or never lets it start. So violence is a force on the attack. It is a deplorable thing, nothing else. So it is clear that if violence is used to make people listen, it is evil added to evil, and fruitless for anyone to try. Thus this method is the utter opposite of the normal, the natural, the gentle way.

Seventh. The practice of subjecting pagan peoples by war first, so they will listen later to the faith preached and accept the Christian religion, contradicts the method the holy patriarchs used from the dawn of time and in every age since, up to the coming of Christ. The patriarchal method appealed to the mind; it was kith and kin to human nature everywhere, a method made by Divine Wisdom for shaping and teaching religious truth to all people, for drawing them persuasively toward truth and virtue. We made this clear before. So the method of subjecting pagan peoples by war first, etc., is a new method. It is mindless, unnatural, inimical to human nature, without precedent, and therefore dubious, against the way Divine Wisdom intended. So, as a result, a contradiction of the normal, natural, peaceable way.

I showed above that it was a contradiction to conquer pagan peoples first so as later to evangelize them and bring them into the true faith. I showed it was a contradiction of the normal, intelligent, peaceable way—the way suited to human history and human nature—

through proof from philosophical reasoning, from the practice of the best teachers and the ancient patriarchs, century after century, up to the time of Christ.

WARS CONTRADICT THE WAY OF CHRIST

I must further the argument and prove how the war/conversion approach is a flat and absolute contradiction of what Christ wanted and willed.

The first proof is easy enough. Christ willed it, through the way He did His own preaching, that the preachers of His law, before they said or did anything else, should offer peace to the pagan people of whatever place they entered, fort or farm or city, even before peace was offered them. And Christ forbade His preachers to carry even a staff, so that they could be seen as peaceful men right from the start. But the method we contradict says we should conquer pagan peoples, should call down on their heads a welter of suffering and death. This way pagans are not only shamed and cursed by the words we bring; but also they are beaten, bruised, wounded and killed, by our deadly deeds. Conclusion: The way of war contradicts the way Christ willed, the one He taught when He preached His gospel.

Second. Through His own way of preaching the gospel, Christ commanded His apostles and those who later carried on their missionary role, to heal the sick, to raise the dead, to cleanse the lepers, to expel the demons. War says and does the opposite in fact. It makes pagans who have done Christians no harm—to my knowledge—undergo a living death first, then die. It makes sound and healthy people sick unto death through the horrors they are forced to accept. It makes those who were leprosy-free suffer worse leprosies, those caused by the plagues the warrior brings. There is no doubt of it.

The way of war provides a shortcut for demons to pour into people's souls, whose bodily health prevented it before then. The victims will surely hate, with an implacable hatred, those who wage war against them, hate them as enemies. The next thing is that the victims who are killed are damned eternally since they die in unbelief. And the killers, no doubt of it either, they are possessed by demons in the waging of war. They will burn in the same eternal flames along with their victims, if they do not repent. And so this new, this bizarre way of conversion contradicts the way Christ wanted and willed it to be when He Himself preached the gospel.

Third. Again, by the way He preached the gospel, Christ willed that His missionaries should be meek as lambs, simple as doves. His words were: "I send you like sheep among wolves" (Luke 10:3). And: "Be simple, like doves" (Matthew 10:16). He further willed that they should learn from Him to be meek and humble of heart, both in word and deed. But the way of first conquering pagans in war does not smack of the meekness of lambs nor the simplicity of doves. It is all a roar of lions, bears, tigers, all a howling of wolves, a howling of horrible monsters, it is crafty as a fox at maliciousness. It almost outdoes the devil himself in pride and ferocity of thought and word and deed. Warrior preachers are—or are sent as—ravening wolves among flocks of sheep, not flocks of sheep among ravening wolves. And that is an utter contradiction of the true way.

Fourth. Christ also forbade His gospel preachers to have gold, silver, money; forbade them, and forcefully, to exact money even peaceably from those they were to evangelize or those who might be tightfisted, or even to take money from those eager to give it. On the contrary they, the missionaries, should give freely of the goods they received from God—goods given for the sake of other people. But war, the new, bizarre way of preaching the faith, it teaches people not just how to rob the tightfisted—violently, cruelly—of gold, silver, money, the essential support of people's lives, and of all kinds of stuff of little value. It teaches people also how to rob kings and legitimate rulers of the dignity of office, of title, of respect; rob them of right and rule, then pitch them down to a wretched, debased level of life, one of total misery, more bitter than death by far. Because, to quote Boethius' work *De Consolatione,* "It is bitterest to have been happy once but now sad."[89] And so the way of war is a contradiction to the normal, peaceable, natural way Divine Wisdom began with, the way Jesus Christ reaffirmed.

Fifth. Christ also wanted His missionaries to be careful of their good name, their reputation, and careful to be held in high esteem by everyone. So they would be thought of as holy and sincere men by the pagan, as sober and sound, without the print of narrowness and passion on them, so the pagan would love them and respect their teaching more. Therefore He ordered them to look for the right host wherever they stayed, then opt to stay with him and not to leave lightly, so the host is not embarrassed, not made suspicious, not scandalized. Missionaries coming in to convert pagans on the heels of warriors who have conquered them—even if the missionaries are not personally re-

---

[89] [*PL,* 63:677.]

sponsible or involved in the war—become odious because of their own behavior. Pagans judge them to be unjust also, to be tyrants, robbers, brutes, boasters, brawlers. The horrors that happened force the souls of those who saw and heard to see warrior and missionary as one and the same, seething with wicked vices. They feel an eternal hatred for the two: And more than against them—against the whole of Christianity also. They think all Christians behave violently. You should have no doubt that what follows is contempt, disgust for Christian doctrine and everything associated with it. "Despise what someone does and you despise what someone says," to quote Gregory. The way of war contradicts the way of Christ.

Sixth. Pagans see how wonderful God is through the way of preaching initiated by Divine Wisdom and expressly willed by Christ. Pagans are drawn by it powerfully and peacefully to faith, to Christianity. This is clear from Matthew 5:16: "So let your light [that is, your life] shine before people, that people will see your good works and glorify your Father in heaven." The gospel also refers to the way one preaches. Contradictory causes produce contradictory effects; we explained this earlier. The words and deeds of Christian war, against the pagan who never harmed the Christian—i.e., without just cause—are evil in themselves, worse than evil, they are damned by every law. They will therefore surely cause the pagan to blaspheme God, to despise faith and Church, to recoil from hearing or heeding either. The way of war contradicts peaceful preaching, the kind initiated by Divine Providence, and wished and willed by Christ.

Seventh. Christ did first, then said what He wanted the fundamental way of preaching the gospel to be. He took His own advice, He obeyed His own command. On His journeys He taught people humbly, gently, generously. He healed those in the grip of demons. The way of war, by contrast, teaches arrogance, it kills and kills insanely, cruelly, brutally, harshly. It does people the ultimate evil, people who could have been won for Christ—it puts them to an unjust, untimely, unnatural death and into the hands of the devil in hell, there to suffer eternal torment. The way of war contradicts the way of Jesus in the preaching of the gospel, the one He taught by deed and word.

I ask you why should a peaceful king, a kind, rare, strong, good, all-powerful king—a king who shows power solely by pardon and compassion—choose such a wretched, rotten, pestilence-ridden, vice-ridden instrument, I mean war, the refuge of robbers, the road the rottenest of the godless take? Why choose it as the instrument with which to form His lovable kingdom in the minds of thinking creatures, ones He had made originally free, with wills of their own, creatures born ready to be drawn to goodness by goodness, kind, gentle goodness? Christ is "the Prince of Peace, Father of the life to come," is He not? In fact as well as name? (Isaiah 9:6). It was foretold of Him before He was born, was it not? "When He comes, justice and peace will dawn" (Psalm 71:17).

At His birth the angels sang peace, not war songs, not songs of victory in war! (Luke 2:14). When alive, He offered peace and He ordered it offered (Luke 10:5–6). When dying, He bequeathed peace (John 14:27). When risen, He repeated His offer! (John 20:26). Scrutinize His whole teaching once again. You will find nothing that is not redolent of peace, that does not ring with friendship, that is not rinsed with charity. For this one reason He gave His command to love—filled with love Himself—for it to produce peace, for it to nourish the peace produced, for it to preserve the same! (John 14:27; 15:13).

The kingly dignity of Christ, His kingly generosity would not stoop to using war as a way to gain a people, nor war to expand, enrich, ensure a kingdom. Only through peace. So it is not the way of Christ or Christian or apostle, the way of war, with its fearful clash of weaponry, to gain a kingdom. It is the way of robbers, of pirates, of tyrants, of heretics, of faithless people, of ravenous, murderous wolves who come only to rip, to madden, kill, wipe out the flock of Christ, the flock that exists, and the sheep on the threshold of the flock who would enter it with little trouble if not blocked, if not slaughtered by such hoodlums!

By contrast, the Lord Himself, the Good Shepherd, came "that people might have life and have it abundantly," to use His own witness (John 10:10). His responsibility, when it was laid upon His shoulders, was to bear our burdens, our labors—the prophecy went, "He took on our sorrows, He Himself bore our sins" (Isaiah 53:4 and 1 Peter 2:24). His responsibility for our salvation had to be kingly, had to be kind, gentle, easy, tactful, the best of any! It is a contradictory way, the one we deny, it is brutal, unnatural, fearsome, riotous, bitter, terror-filled. It is sorrow and tears, it is tyranny, the epitome of evil, it is the worst of any, and thus from beginning to end a kingdom so constituted is bereft of blessing. As Proverbs 20:21 says: "An inheritance gotten by shortcut in the beginning will not end as a blessing." For "a kingdom ill-gotten by plot or ill-gotten by ambition, even if later its morals and manners do not offend, is nonetheless, right from the start, a bad precedent."[90]

The goodness of Christ, His kingly dignity, would not stoop to gaining a people, to making it grow, to making it safe, by the metallic

---

[90] Thus Gratian, causa 1, q. 1, cap. 25 [Friedberg, 1:369].

might of weaponry, by human slaughter, by massacre, violence, havoc, by other and kindred calamities, but by the opposite—by kind teaching, by the sacraments of the Church, by forgiveness, by compassion, by generosity, by peace, by mercy, by charity, by graciousness.

Eighth. The apostles were chosen to be luminaries, exemplars. They came from a world of fishermen, vinedressers, fort builders, column makers, captains, doctors, gatekeepers, governors, shepherds, runners, and boxers. They followed exactly the footsteps made by Christ, their model of goodness and grace. They kept to the manner and mode willed for them by His word and deed when they evangelized the world and built churches everywhere. They used no weapon, no mercenary. They did not subdue the world by physical force or by massed battalions. They did it by preaching the crucified Christ in simple words, loving words that had miraculous power. They made the savage breast of barbarians calm and open to Christ. The way of war is novel, it is bizarre, it contradicts the works, the example, the "fishing for souls," the doctrine, the governance, the preaching style practiced by every one of the apostles.

WARS CONTRADICT THE WAY OF THE MISSIONER

Paul the apostle worked harder than anyone else at converting people, at keeping to the form of preaching expressly willed by Christ. He was by special grace the teacher of the Gentiles. And he spoke and wrote more than anyone else about this characteristic preaching. He said clearly that Christ's way had five key elements to it. The way of war contradicts each key element. It was and is therefore a flat contradiction of the way Paul the apostle, teacher of the Gentiles as he is popularly called, thought and preached during the time he evangelized the Gentiles.

(1) It is clear how war contradicts the first key element. Namely, that pagans understand the preachers of the gospel have no intention of gaining power over them through the gospel. What else could they think when they see themselves invaded so callously by Christians without cause, so fiercely conquered, killed, looted, cruelly enslaved, and everything about them flattened? Is there any obscurity about it? About how war contradicts the peaceable way fashioned and fostered by Divine Wisdom, renewed by Christ whose word and deed are revelation and commandment? About the way practiced to the letter by every apostle, signed, sealed and delivered a thousand times over in the preaching practice of St. Paul?

(2) And the second element. Namely, that we give pagans no cause for thinking that our preaching is really done for lucre's sake, to squeeze them for money or the goods of this world. You can guess what pagans would think—it is so obvious!—when war is waged against them for no cause but the greed of the attackers who are out to get gold and silver and whatever else has any monetary worth, the greed of looters who spare nothing after loot.

(3) And it is clear as the light of day that the works of war contradict the third key element of Christian preaching. Namely, that the missioners be mature, humble, kind, gracious in their dealings with pagans, be simplicity itself, as though the pagans were schoolchildren, so that they will listen willingly to Christian doctrine, and take no offense or feel any burden imposed on them by the missioner, or sense self-will in them.

(4) We now have to show what love of charity men could ever possibly have had, who came using the way of war for imposing the mysteries of faith on pagans. For it surely clashes with the fourth key element of preaching, charity. But we must know what charity is first, as defined by Sacred Scripture and by the teaching of the saints.

Charity is the love, the affection, by which God is cherished directly, and humankind indirectly on account of God. As in Matthew 22:37–40: "You shall love the Lord your God with all your heart, and with all your soul, and with all your mind. This is the great and first commandment. And the second is like it. You shall love your neighbor as yourself. On these two commandments depend all the law and the prophets." And 1 John 4:21: "And this commandment we have from Him, that he who loves God should love his brother also."

Augustine treats these passages in his book *On the Christian Life,* chapters 8 and 9.

> The whole teaching of the law and the prophets comes down to these two commands. So whoever loves both God and neighbor lives up to the teaching. The old law wanted nothing else than love of God and love of neighbor. Whoever sins not against God or neighbor is a consummate keeper of the law. But we cannot simply pretend we know what love of God and love of neighbor mean and skip on. We love God when we keep all God's commandments. We love God when we keep God's laws and counsels. We love God when we are holy as God is, and God is holiness itself. The Scripture passage says, "Be holy, for I am holy, the Lord your God" (Leviticus 19:2). We love God when we fulfill the dictum of the prophet who said, "Hate evil if you love God" (Psalm 96:10). We love God when we think only of high and holy things. God's primary love is for holiness and

justice and fidelity. We love God when we do nothing but what we think God loves. Our Lord and Savior tells what it is to love God when He says, "Whoever hears My words and keeps them is the one who loves me" (John 14:21).

So whoever keeps God's commands loves God; whoever does not, does not love God. You either love or you hate. It is clear, obvious; people hate God in not keeping God's law. The prophet spoke about such people, I think: "Do I not hate them who hate thee, O Lord? And do I not loathe them that rise up against thee? I hate them with a perfect hatred; I count them my enemies" (Psalm 138:21-22). A sinless prophet hates sinners, hates adulterers, hates criminals and those who scorn God's law. The same prophet says elsewhere: "I saw liars and I seethed" (Psalm 118:158). And: "I hate the wicked; I love your law" (v. 113).

Look how sinless, how holy and whole we ought to be! We cannot do evil. We cannot deal with evildoers. The holy apostle makes this more than clear when he says we should not even break bread with sinners, i.e., "If someone you call brother is a fornicator or a miser or an idolater or a blasphemer or a drunkard or a robber, do not even eat with him" (1 Corinthians 5:11). God wanted a people holy and free of all taint of sin and evil. God wanted them such—sinless, faithful, innocent, pure, open—so no one would find anything to blame, but rather something to admire and praise. "Blessed is the nation whose God is the lord, the people He has chosen as His heritage" (Psalm 32:12). Lovers of God, humble servants, ought to be serious, prudent, faithful, blameless, clean, sinless, so anyone who sees them will be astonished, will admire them and say: "The life these people lead is truly from God."

The people of God should so comport themselves, that everyone should want to see and hear them, and no one should mistake them for other than children of God, a people who fulfill truly the prophecy: "His speech is most sweet and he is altogether most desirable" (Canticles 5:16). If a Christian, a servant of God, lives a life exactly like that lived by devotees of demons and idols, the latter will start to curse God and say: "O Christian, O servant of God, what a wicked life you lead, what wicked deeds you do, what filthy things, what faithless, foul, filthy, fetid things you do!" The prophecy will be true of such Christians: "Because of you people will blaspheme the name of God" (Isaiah 42:5). Damnation on those through whom God's name is blasphemed! God wants, God asks of us only that what we do should cause people to honor the divine name, as Scripture puts it: "A sacrifice of praise will honor me" (Psalm 49:14). It is the sacrifice of praise that God wants and God loves, better than any beast offering. Through the goodness of what we do, God's name will be honored everywhere. The truth of God will be proven in the behavior of God's servants. We love God truly when we do only that which brings honor to God's name.[91]

Augustine also says in his book *On Loving God,* concerning charity toward God:

Lord, no mind filled with the sweet taste of your love is trapped by fear, or spattered by lust, or ripped apart by anger, or blasted with pride, or giddy with glory, a glory empty as smoke. No such mind boasts, or whips into rages. It is not gutted by ambition, or throttled by avarice, or flattened by despair, or hollowed by envy. No vice corrupts such a mind while it keeps the taste of your love.[92]

So what kind of charity do they have who use the method of conquering pagans first, in order then to preach the faith to them? And how much, how much charity toward God? You can tell by matching the quality of their lives, the morality they exhibit in war, with the qualities the love of God requires. The contrast is stark.

The warriors keep not one shred of God's commands in even the least of the things they do, not one shred of divine law or precept. Just look at what they do when they invade and conquer the countries of pagans who have given them no cause. God, through law, through precept, through command, forbids us to dishonor the divine name, or to scandalize others into dishonoring it, or to give creatures greater honor than God—the subject of the first commandment—or to curse in the name of God, or to work for profit on holy days. We are to do spiritual works, ones that glorify God. We are not to kill. We are not to commit adultery. We are not to steal. We are not to give perjured testimony against someone. We are not to covet our neighbor's goods. Nor lust for his wife; nor his servant; nor his maid; nor his cow; nor his mule; not for anything he owns, as Exodus 20:7–17 forbids.

And Exodus 22:21–24 forbids us to harm or hurt a guest, or widows or orphans. For if we do injure them, they will invoke God and God will hear their cry for help. God's wrath will rise and wreck us with the sword. Our wives will be made widows, our offspring orphans.

And Exodus 23:2–9:

---

[91] [*PL,* 40:1038–39.]
[92] [*PL,* 40:861.]

We are not to follow a crowd in the doing of evil. We are not to agree to the verdict of a mob if it departs from the truth. If we find the stray ox or donkey of even our enemy, we are to return them to him. If we see the donkey of even our enemy burdened to breaking, we are to lighten that burden, not pass by. We are not to kill the innocent, the sinless. God turns on such wickedness. We are not to harm the stranger."

And Leviticus 19:11–19:

Be holy, because I am holy, Your Lord and God. Do not steal, do not lie, do not swear in my name, defiling the name of your God. Do not lie about your neighbor nor do him physical violence. Do not keep the wages of your workers one extra night. Do not mock the deaf nor trip up the blind. Respect God, your God, as God. Commit no crime, no wicked judgment. Judge your neighbor justly. Let no lie of yours cost him his life. I am the Lord. Do not hate your brother secretly. Do not seek revenge. Love your friend as another self. Keep my commandments.

Isaiah 1:16–17, also: "Cease to do evil, learn to do good, seek justice, correct oppression, defend the fatherless, plead for the widow."
And Jeremiah 7:5–11:

If you mediate between a man and a man, if you put no lie on the stranger and the orphan or widow, if you shed no innocent blood, if you chase after no false god to your own harm, then I will let you live. . . . [But no], look what you do! You trust in lying words, they profit you nothing. You steal, you kill, you commit adultery, you perjure yourselves, you offer to Baal, you chase alien gods, in igno-rance of their evil. Then you come and stand in my face, in my house, and say to me, "We are free of you. Our crimes have set us free of you." And you look on my house where my name is invoked in prayer as your house, your den of thieves, do you not? I am who I am. I am not blind, says the Lord!

And Ezekiel 18:4–9:

All souls are mine. The soul that sins will die. If a man is righteous and does what is lawful and right . . . does not defile his neighbor's wife or approach a woman in her time of impurity, does not oppress anyone, but restores to the debtor his pledge, commits no robbery, gives his bread to the hungry and covers the naked with a garment, does not lend at interest or take any increase, withholds his hand from iniquity, executes true justice between man and man, walks in my statutes and is careful to observe my ordinances—he is righteous, he shall surely live. If however he does all these horrible things, he shall surely die; his blood shall be upon himself.

These are the rules anyone must keep who loves God, who holds to God in charity.

You have to watch how they act, those who urge conquest of pagan peoples prior to converting them to the law of Christ, how they keep God's counsels and commands. Either they are blasphemers in their own right—that kind of person blasphemes automatically, have no doubt! Or they provoke it automatically, a contempt for the faith of Christ, a blaspheming of the King of Angels and Lord of Creation. I gave ample evidence of this earlier.

You can readily guess, from how they neglect God's commands, that the riches they honor most are not that of God but that of gold, silver, and other things out of which one makes a pile of money. The Lord God is a curse-word they use a thousand times a day; feast days are work-for-profit days. So you can see from this the way they behave all the time—again, have no doubt!—and see from the foul crimes they later commit.

For this kind of man brings cruel war to bear on those who never harmed him, never insulted him, people he never knew before, of that we are sure, people who never plotted evil against him. He kills, he slaughters human beings—never mind their sex or age—with a sword, with a spear, off with their heads! One stroke head from neck, and plunges the souls of his wretched victims into instant hellfire. Disgusting!

Conquerors steal others' wives, force them into adultery. They don't have to steal! They own everything! And incest, and lewdness, and concubinage, up to the minute they die! I tell you they steal servant and maid and ox and ass and anything else on the landscape! I say not a word about stripping legitimate kings and princes of the honor and respect due to them, not a word about those who survived the sword to lead a life more bitter than death. And not a word about the wounded, their arms cut off, their hands or feet or other parts, then plunged into perpetual slavery, slavery they can never hope to escape except through death.

As if this is not enough, missionaries fanatic for the spread of faith in Christianity, so that they themselves can apply the full weight of divine sanction, malign the natives a million ways, even to the point of perjury, calling them dogs, idolaters, accomplices in rotten crimes, stupid morons, unfit, incapable of Christian faith and moral life. The things they then do to these people under the pretext of a lie—a false, a wicked, a heretical lie, a deadly detestable lie—might then seem just, or at least pardonable. "But I am who I am, I am not blind, says the Lord!"

Do you call this doing no harm to the stranger, doing him no hurt? And the strangers are natives, they are fellow citizens! Do you call this doing no harm to widows and orphans as the divine command enjoins? And those who suffer what I just described, the victims, will they not invoke God, will God not hear their invocation, will God not be infuriated against us and cut us down with a sword, will our wives not be widows and our offspring orphans? Do you call this not following mob violence, not yielding to mob rule, not departing from the truth? Does this square with the precept that if we find the ox or ass of our worst enemy lost, we should bring it to him? Or down under too heavy a load, so that we should help the beast up and not walk on by? Do you call this not killing the just and the innocent? Which is what these pagans surely are for us—they have done nothing to us! This is wickedness supreme! God is dead against it! Do you call this not preying on strangers? In fact they are citizens, in their own country, in their own cities and towns, living peacefully! Do you call them holy, these marauders, holy as God is holy, as God wishes Christians to be? Could we not say they malign their neighbor, they violate their neighbor, the men who bring the evils of war down upon pagans? If we must not hold back the wages of our hired hands even until dawn the next day, with what justification does our military hold under an unjust occupation a mass of people? How do they hold kings and peoples great and small in subjugation, realms and regions, treasure taken violently; and not just until dawn the next day, but until death, forever in fact, and do it without scruple, as if they inherited their holdings rightfully?

God forbids that we should mock the deaf and trip up the blind who are within sight and sound of us. Imagine the prohibition forbidding us to smear by false testimony someone not within sight or sound of us, deaf, in this case, because absent and unable to deny the charge! Imagine the prohibition forbidding Christians to trip up the blind, blind in this case to the law, to the power of God, since all pagans are (at least those we speak about) in common ignorance of divine things! Especially those who have not come into the Church because of the torture, the torment, the horrors they suffer from people who glory in being called Christians!

Do you keep the command—"You are not to shed your neighbor's blood"—by mass slaughter in which everything reeks of human blood? Or do you keep it by not slaughtering innocent life, by not betraying your kindred, by suppressing your bad behavior, by getting justice done, by helping victims, aiding orphans, protecting widows, keep it by not harassing others—no violence, no robbery—by feeding the hungry? Or do you rather keep the bread, and so create famine and death for thousands and thousands of people, men and women of every type and rank and age? And what about the command not to put faith in a lie since it leads us nowhere? Do you obey it by stealing, robbery, murder, adultery, lewdness, by fouling everything with incest all around, by lying under oath, by the cult of Baal, i.e., the special idol of marauders, who has a hold over them as over subjects, who possesses them? A Baal is a lust for power, a huge hunger to get rich; limitless lust, hopeless hunger, and "that is an idolatry" (Colossians 3:5). "A Baal is something I so idolize that it dominates me, it possesses me," Jerome says. Baals are kith and kin to lustful, hungry, greedy men, to preachers of war, to rotten and damnable tyrants.

I think you see clearly enough what little or no obedience marauders give to divine law and precept. You see if they love God, if they hate evil, if they think about high and holy things, if they love sanctity and justice and fidelity, if they do what they think God loves, if they hear and heed the word of Christ the Savior, if they do whatever God commands. Or you see if they do the exact opposite, hate God, hate God without cause because they scant God's law even in trifles. You see how holy they are, how free of any taint of sinfulness and crime. You see how just they are, how clean, how untouched, how guileless. You see how little the pagan peoples can reproach in them, how much they should admire them, exclaiming, "A happy people! This people whom the Lord God has chosen as an inheritance."

The first ones whom pagans should meet, of those who call themselves Christians and who preach the faith, should be the distinctive ones, i.e., kind, humble, peaceable, prayerful, above reproach, careful, blameless. And anyone who meets them should be impressed enough to say: "Only people of God lead such a life!" It was the way the people of Iconia spoke about Paul and Barnabas. They had believed in the gospel, they had known the holiness of the apostles. They had seen miracles. So they burst into praise, "Gods in the likeness of humans have come down to us from heaven." They called Barnabas Jove. And Paul Mercury because he was a word-bearer. "When they wished to offer sacrifice to the apostles as to gods, the apostles put a stop to their mistake by saying, 'What are you people doing? We are as mortal as you are, mortals telling you to turn from idols toward the living God who made both heaven and earth . . .' " (Acts 14:10–11; 14).

That will not happen to these warriors. They will be called devils, not gods, and rightly so, named from their own terrible deeds, their filthy behavior, from their lives, faithless, foul, criminal, cruel, brutal, beastly lives—devils, not gods! Pagans are forced to burst out into blasphemy, to curse the Creator since they think the awful injustice they undergo comes from that Creator's law or precept or prior and wicked command. They will go on then to detest faith and salvation in Christ as a fake, a lie. And that is the sacrifice of praise through which Christ will be honored and glorified by those subjected to war so as to come under Christian control before the faith can be preached to them!

All those who wage wars of conversion, all those who unleash them, have no love of God; they have a hatred of God, they live without charity.

It will not be difficult to know those who embrace their brethren in charity. The description just given is ample concerning what the love of God means, and who they are who really love God, who they are who really hate God and consequently live life without charity. Love of God cannot exist without love of neighbor, love of neighbor without love of God. "Love of God, love of neighbor, simultaneous loves!" says Chrysostom.

The one who loves God does not hate the brethren, does not prefer material to spiritual wealth, but always behaves generously, recalling the phrase of Jesus: "Whoever helps one of the helpless, helps me" (Matthew 25:40). That one thinks that his ministry makes him a servant alongside God.

And Augustine says in his *Commentary on John,* Tract 65: "Each law is found in the other for those who understand the two correctly. One who loves God cannot ignore that God commands love of neighbor. And someone with a high and holy love of neighbor, what else is that but a love of God?"[93] And in Tract 87: "If you love God, you love your neighbor as yourself. If you do not love God, you do not love yourself."[94] And in *On the Trinity,* book 8., chapter 8, part way into it: "Therefore we find that the two precepts cannot exist the one without the other. The reason: God is love. Whoever loves love, loves God. Whoever loves the brethren has to love love."[95] And further on: "The more we love God, the more we love ourselves. It is with one and the

---

[93] [*PL,* 35:1809.]
[94] [*PL,* 35:1852.]
[95] [*PL,* 42:958.]

same love that we love God and neighbor. God for God's own sake, our neighbor for the sake of God."[96] It is clear then that the warriors we talked about do not love God, they hate God, they live without love. So it follows from what we proved, they do not love themselves, they do not love their neighbor.

The one point I want to develop is that warriors do not love either themselves or their neighbors with the love of charity. To prove it, just think how God was so concerned to have people love one another with a mutual charity that through Scripture He showed how the whole law was contained in loving one's neighbor, that alone. Even though there are two precepts, even though the one can be understood in the other, nonetheless the two are made into one, compressed: "Love your neighbor as yourself," as in Galatians 5:14: "The whole law is contained in one statement: Love your neighbor as yourself." And in Romans 13:8–10, Paul says:

> Whoever loves his neighbor fulfills the law. The commands, do not commit adultery, do not kill, do not steal, do not bear false witness, do not yield to lust, or any other commands, are summed up in the statement: Love your neighbor as yourself. You do not do evil to someone you love. Law is love to the full.

On Paul's words to the Galatians cited above, Jerome says:

> The goodness in charity is so great it contains all other law in itself. The apostle speaks in another place of the good that charity is: "It is not fanatic, not wrong-headed" (1 Corinthians 13:4). Further on he says: "Our Savior said in the gospel that love of neighbor was the hallmark of His disciple" (John 13:35). It is the same thing but in different words in the sayings: "Do not do to others what you do not want them to do to you" (Tobias 4:16), and "The way you want others to behave towards you, you should behave towards them" (Matthew 7:12). I do not want my wife abused. I do not want my goods stripped from me. I do not want to be lied about. In brief, it angers me when I am the victim of any injustice. If I do or want to do positive things to my neighbor through the charity working in me, I fulfill the law.

It is not hard to show how every law—not to kill, not to abuse, not to

---

[96] [*PL,* 42:959.]

steal, not to perjure oneself . . . (Exodus 20:13–14)—is kept by keeping the law of charity.[97]

Augustine treats the same theme extensively in his *On Christian Discipline and Christian Life,* written to his sister.

I will explain as best I can, what love of neighbor as oneself means. The command is: "What you do not want done to you, do not do to others" (Tobias 4:16). Our Lord, Our Savior also said, "Everything you want others to do towards you, do likewise towards them" (Matthew 7:12). No one wants someone else to do him harm. Whoever treats his neighbor the way he himself wants to be treated, loves his neighbor as himself. He gives freely what goods he has even as he hopes to receive as a gift what goods others have, because a Christian is asked to do more than avoid evil. He is asked to do good. Those who do neither evil nor good are not let into heaven but are let into hell. It is as we read the Lord saying in the Gospel about those who do neither evil nor good: "Get from me, you damned, into the hellfire my father prepared for the devil and his like. I was starving. You fed me nothing. I was thirsty. You gave me no water . . ." (Matthew 25:41–2). They are damned, not for doing evil, but for not doing good.

Anyone with any sense can guess what hope of heaven they have, who are steeped in evil, when heaven is even withheld from those who do neither evil nor good. God does not just want us to avoid evil but also to do good. We call them wicked who do wicked deeds. Likewise we call them good who do good ones, the opposite of the first.

And further on Augustine says:

Let no one foster an illusion in his own mind; let no one fool himself with an unfounded feeling. No goodness, no heaven. No works of justice, no works of mercy, no kingdom with Christ. No escape from the fire of hell, if no humanity, no fidelity, no hospitality, no kindness, no compassion.

And further on when he urges a larger moral innocence in everything people do.

---

[97] [*PL,* 26:409.]

With the command on you to be good even to enemies, when can
you possibly not be innocent, when can you possibly harm someone? Can you hate a friend and you forbidden to hate a foe? Can you
torture a brother and you forbidden to touch a stranger? Can you
call yourself a Christian and you heedless of the covenant, Old
or New?

Listen to what the apostle tells you so you will not be a Christian who
has no reason to be, a Christian in name only: "If you stole, steal no
more. Make your goods with your own two hands so you have what
to give when someone begs you. Let no destructive word leave your
lips, only creative words that build faith, so you may give grace to
your hearers. Do not darken the Spirit of God. You were marked by
the Spirit on the day you were baptized. Be kind to each other as God
was kind to you in Christ, be merciful, be generous to each other"
(Ephesians 4:28–32). Furthermore: "Be imitators of God, be like
beloved sons, live a life of love, love the way Christ loved us . . ."
(Ephesians 5:1).

Augustine goes on:

He has reason to think himself a Christian who keeps the commandments—someone holy, humble, modest, fair, someone active in
works of justice and mercy. Now do you think someone is Christian
who never does a Christian thing, whose life never involves justice,
only wickedness, infidelity and crime? Do you think someone is
Christian who harms the helpless, who milks the poor, who itches to
steal, who makes other paupers to make himself rich, who harbors
stolen money, who takes his bread from others' toils, who profits
from the deaths of victims, who lives with a mouthful of lies, whose
lips unleash nothing but filthy and foul and fetid profanities—someone who takes what others own when told to give others what
he owns.

This someone walks boldly into church and boldly spreads his
impious palms toward heaven in prayer, palms stained with stealing
and with the blood of innocent victims; and with the same filthy,
curse-filled mouth still hot from lying and lewdness, pours out
prayers to God unaware of any evil in himself. You poor fool! What
are you doing? Why do you bury yourself under a pile of sins? Why
do you add injury to insult toward God? Why do you lift your
impious hands to God, the very evidence of your guilt, as if to provoke God's wrath more quickly. God sees no prayer in them, the
God who ordered only holy and clean hands to offer prayer. What
good do you ask from God with a mouth still warm from evil words?

However many prayers you mouth, God detests them. As scripture says: "When you pray with hands outstretched, I will look the other way from you; pray as much as you want, I will be deaf to you. You pray with bloodstained hands" (Isaiah 1:15).

Whoever prays in the following way can truly open his hands to heaven, can pray God in good conscience: "The hands I reach to you, O Lord, you know they are clean, they are innocent, they are guiltless of theft, torture, violence, and my lips, you know they are pure, free of the taint of lies, the lips I use to ask your mercy." The deep darkness of evil and greed have blinded some people I know. So that when they succeed in overpowering the poor or overpowering the weak, or wrecking innocence with perjury, when they steal or ravage, they give God thanks, they think their succeeding is due to God's help. And God is that wicked, they think, as to be their partner in crime! What miserable fools, so blinded by their crimes they do not see God cannot be partner to what God forbids! Their crimes are not enough, they have to add another, attributing evil to God!

Some think to justify what they do. They give a little in charity of the lot they stole from the poor; or give a pittance to the one, out of what they took from the many. One mouth eats the food of many. Many are stripped so one can dress. God does not want charity to be like that. God does not want kindness to come from killing. Better to give no alms at all than the kind that strips the many to clothe the few, that dresses the one in the many's stolen robes. And if the one blesses you, what good is it? The many curse you! What grace do you get for giving as alms what you stole from someone else?

And further on: "Some think a person can be saved without having done charitable deeds." Augustine argues broadly that faith without works of charity is futile for salvation, then gets pointed:

Fool no one on this, delude no one: whoever is not holy is not saved. Whoever does not keep the law of Christ in everything here, can have nothing to do with Christ hereafter. Whoever does not spurn the earthly, cannot espouse the heavenly. Whoever cannot let go the human, cannot lay hold of the divine.

No one can call himself a Christian but the one who keeps the truth of Christ and follows His example. Can you call him Christian who never gave a bite to the hungry? Who never gave a drop to the thirsty? Who never set a meal out for a pauper? Who never gave a roof to guest or pilgrim when they knocked? Who never gave a stitch

to the needy? Who never gave a hand to the helpless? Whose goodness no one feels? Whose mercy no one knows? Who acts in no way
like good people, but laughs at them, ridicules them? In no way call
that kind a Christian, in no way call that kind a child of God!

A Christian is someone who walks in the way of Christ, who is like
Christ in all things. Witness the Scripture: "If you claim to be in
Christ, you walk in the way of Christ" (1 John 2:6). A Christian is
someone compassionate with everyone, someone hurt by another's
hurt; someone who stops oppression in his presence of the poor, who
lifts the helpless, who often aids the indigent, grieves with the griev-
ing, sorrows with the sorrowing, weeps with the weeping others
weep. Someone whose house is everyone's house, whose door shuts
no one out, whose board takes everyone in, whose gift is bread for
the world. A Christian is someone whose goodness everyone knows;
someone who harms no one, who serves God day and night, day and
night thinks on the teachings of God; poor on earth to be rich in
heaven, a trifle in men's eyes to be a treasure to God and God's
angels. Someone whose heart is not a fake; whose soul is clean and
straight, whose conscience is pure and steadfast, who has a mind
only for God, who has hope only in Christ, who wants a heaven not
an earth, not things human but things divine. Those who love
earthly things, who revel in the glories of time, should listen to the
warning: "Do you not know it? The friend of this world is the enemy
of God?" (James 4:4)[98]

Augustine, in the preceding citations, distinguishes quite clearly
between those who love and those who hate their neighbor, between
those who act as Christians, and those who are Christians in name only,
who make a false, mocking, sacrilegious use of the name. I need say no
more about what love marauders have for themselves and their neighbors, since the facts speak so much for themselves.

Nevertheless, I want to interrogate those who want to draw to
Christ by means of war the many neighbors committed to their charge
—to ask them if they love themselves, and therefore love their neighbors as themselves. If they answer yes, God says immediately that they
lie, in the words of Psalm 10:52: "Love evil, hate your soul!" Is it not
evil to be the cause for people to blaspheme God and detest salvation
and the Christian name? Is it not evil to panic peaceful people, who live
quietly in their own places, their own homes; to demoralize them, to

---

[98] [*PL*, 40:1039–41.]

attack them, tear them from their ground, their goods, ownership, honor, wives, children, life, liberty; to loot them, to lacerate them a thousand different ways? Is it not evil to rob them, rape them, massacre them? Not evil to seethe with lust for power, to crush defenseless victims, to get filthy rich on stolen goods, to totter the world with wicked, obscene works—and because of putrid behavior, to make people think that salvation in Christ is a disgusting, a criminal thing?

Self-hatred is rife in this behavior. Whatever they say, they hate, not love themselves—love evil, hate your soul! Hate your soul, hate your body next! The body is the tool of their filth, says Augustine in his book *On Christian Discipline.*

This is the love of self they have, who are in charge of the neighbor they are supposed to love with the same love of self! It is shameless of them to argue it is the same love!

So let us refute them. Would they themselves want to have been softened up by torture and terrible harm before being made Christian? As we just described? To be cut, bruised, panicked, trapped, robbed, enslaved, killed in body and soul? To see wives raped, children, parents killed in front of them, infants plucked from the nipple and brained on rocks? To hear the world filled with chaotic screams and wails and a million other sounds of horror never heard before?

In no way would they opt for these evils on themselves. Nor evils far less, even if faith were to follow for them in the wake of evil. Especially since so many of the dead during war would be damned—a certainty for all those who have not yet received faith and die unconverted. So they should not wish these evils on their neighbors, even less should they inflict them. Love of neighbor does not do what is evil! Just the opposite, they must keep evil from harming their neighbor as much as they can! Thereby they prove they love their neighbor as much as they can! Otherwise they prove they love their neighbor not, not as they love themselves. They are bound to love "in word and speech" but also "in deed and truth" (1 John 3:18).

Love includes wanting what is good for another. It is as Aristotle says in 2 *Metaphysics:* To wish what is good for someone is to love someone. To be free of what is bad is like having what is good, Aristotle also says, in 5 *Ethics.* So it would be love on our part to want those we love to be free of what is bad. To want for someone is futile and false, if it tries to effect nothing. So an effective and true love tries to do good to those we love and also to keep them from harm—again Aristotle, in 9 *Ethics.*

For human beings there are three 'goods' and three 'evils' to conflict the 'goods'. The first good deals with life-supports, and it is basic.

One human must help another who has lost his life-supports. See 1 John 3:17: "Someone who has the goods of this world, and sees another in dire need and refuses him help, how can the love of God remain in that someone?" By the same token, someone must help prevent damage to another's basic possessions. Deuteronomy 22:1 insists on it: "If you see a lost cow or sheep you must not ignore it, but bring it back to your brother, its owner." I cited other passages earlier.

The second good is a life-defense good in which someone must help another against adversity. This is clear from Proverbs 24:11: "Free those doomed to death; make every effort to free those headed for destruction."

The third good is a life-transforming good, the good of the soul. The evil of sin and hell conflicts with this good. To achieve this good, to avoid evil, there is a greater obligation to help another. It is based on the law of charity, on the essence of why someone should love another. In 9 *Ethics* Aristotle says: "One helps a friend avoid the loss of his money. The closer the friendship, the more one helps a friend avoid the loss of his soul." So the law of love obliges us to help another to believe, to grow in goodness and deportment, and to help another avoid sin— the evil that destroys goodness—to avoid hell, for charity's sake.[99]

Conclusion: The satanic champions of war, the wreckers of Christ's holy Church, in no way want pagans to have these three human 'goods'. They ravage these pagans with war—they choose not to provide these goods effectively, they choose not to prevent the evils that conflict with these goods. Just the opposite. They doom pagans to death themselves, they unleash on pagans destruction and damnation, irreversible things. They do it pitilessly, implacably. They cause the ultimate evil to countless souls. They do not love, they hate their neighbor, that is so evident! Champions of war are alien to charity, always, they cannot be described in the terms Augustine used above for the good missionary. No way! Nor can their method for preaching the faith be anything but a contradiction of the fourth key element in the method of Christ and His apostles, a complete contradiction of charity.

WARS CONTRADICT THE WAY OF THE CHRISTIAN

It is clearer than sunlight how wars to convert flout the fifth and last key element in the way Christians are to preach the law of Christ. How much proof there is in the many materials cited above, solid

---

[99] Cf. S. Thomas, *De virtutibus*, q. 3. art. 1, c.

proof! This fifth key element in preaching is a sine qua non. Without its presence, pagans who are to be drawn to the faith by the invitation of love will hardly believe what the Christian missionary says is true.

It is a just life, a blameless, model, holy life, this fifth key element. And the one who thinks he is called to preach the gospel, who thinks he is sent to illumine the pagan world, must be aglow with such a life. By a just life I mean one that causes no complaint or embarrassment, one that deals honestly with the world, that keeps the missionary free of accusation. "Holy" means like an angel on earth, a likeness of God come here below. It is someone who treats the profane and passing world as if it were dung, wants no gold, no silver, no power, no primacy over people, no mortal glory or glitter. It is someone manifestly at home with others, peaceful, dignified, unassuming, patient, pure, honest, spiritual, someone intent on heavenly things, not on earthly goods.

People are attracted to such fruitful lives. It soon follows that their faith turns toward the doctrines preached, and toward the missionary's life as worthy of following. When they see the missionary expecting little in this world and much in the next, when they see him graced with a virtuous life, they will believe what he does far more than what he says. They will be drawn to the truth, they will come freely, though they be savage as beasts.

But what can one expect from militant missionaries of the gospel who have concocted the new policy that pagans ought to be flattened by war before being catechized? They are not warriors for Christ, but for anti-Christ, who also attacks pagan peoples by force of arms—war, one of his many wicked tricks—to damn them. "It is the satanic method!" (2 Thessalonians 2:9). Forced conversion undermines the Church of God, Paul says.

Militants mimic Mohammed, clearly the falsest prophet of them all. He took the world apart. I say they mimic him in the policy he used to convert people to his belief; and in his practice of violence, his savage, outlaw behavior. We cite a book containing the debate between a certain Saracen and a certain Christian from Arabia, a debate about Saracen law and Christian faith. The debaters were learned each in his own belief, both were close friends of the Saracen king, Emir el-Momini, both dear friends of one another, as Vincent tells us in *The Historical Mirror*.[100]

Al Erqumetu argued that the way of God was the way of the sword

---

[100] Vincent de Beauvais, *Speculum Historiale*, lib. 23, cap. 40. [I.e., *Biblioteca Mundi seu Speculi Maioris*, the fullest medieval encyclopedia, 1st ed. 1473–76. In the Douai 1624 ed., this cit. to the historical. vol. is 4:913a.]

against people, devastation against infidels and their allies until they accept faith in God—until they admit there is no God but the God of Mohammed, that Mohammed is the servant, the messenger of God. Either accept this or pay the price of subjection!

The Christian then said to the Saracen:

> Show me what evidence, what miracle, your prophet has performed that would warrant our belief in him. He has done nothing but kill people so far, rob and loot them, enslave them parent and child. This is nothing but evil. Worse than evil, because it is done against God's people, a people with no other defense than its belief in God. (And we can add to fit it to our own argument: against a people living at peace, ready to accept the worship of God, a people with no other safeguard than the divine and natural law God made.)

> Is it not bad enough without calling it the way of God? God forbid that it should be God's way, or that any of God's special people should declare a war, much less one of God's prophets. Yet you invite us to kill people with the sword, to ruin their resources, to level everything, until they come twisted into belief, the unwilling subjects of your laws, forced to a public confession. You have never read in Scripture that anyone was converted by violence, forced by law, sword, kidnap or captivity—the way your kinsman did and made you do!

> There were heretics in the past. No one of them used a sword or violence to win a follower. They used lies. Whoever wanted followers, for his truth or his lie, had to win them at least through some semblance of preaching. We know they all did this. Your kinsman did not. He did not win followers that way, not with the play of warmth and words, but with swordplay he won them, with oppression, with genocide. What he said to the world was unheard of before: Whoever does not admit that I am the Prophet of the God of Ages goes down under my stroke. And those who follow me will do the like, strike the infidel's house and haul his household off to captivity.[101]

Vincent also writes in ch. 49 what the Christian said to the Saracen about his criminal deeds:

---

[101] [After the debate is announced in Vincent's *Speculum historiale,* cap. 40, the life of Mohammed and the early history of Islam is told in subsequent chapters. This long quotation is from cap. 62—in 1624 ed., 4:920b. *N.B.* Las Casas is attacking the *jihad* method of conversion in order to damn the use of that method by Spaniards against innocent Indians.]

I cannot help but wonder how anyone could consider that man a Prophet, not just anyone intelligent, but anyone who thought he had a trace of human feeling! That man's life, his doctrine are such utter contradictions, not just of divine religion but also of human integrity, that even brute beasts can almost see it! On the gentler side, what saint or missionary, whom we know God sent, ever said he was sent with a terrible swift sword? Whoever lived as wickedly as Mohammed? Whoever taught so many obscenities? Whoever reduced the human race to just belly and loins?

And back in ch. 42: "Think if such raids ought to be made by a Prophet of God, raids replete with trickery and violence and bloodshed and everything else robbers and hijackers can perpetrate!"[102] The above may all be found in Vincent's *The Historical Mirror* in the places we cited.

The author of a book called *Fortress of The Faith* provides a broader assessment of what was just said about Mohammed—and so does the author of another work *On the Peace of the World.* In it they cite what Mohammed said repeatedly in the Koran, when people would ask him to show the signs that Moses and Christ and other prophets showed. He answered that God forbade him to perform miracles lest what happened to Moses and Christ should happen to him. The world did not believe them. The world said they were wicked, not miraculous. "They would never accept me," he said, "so I came by force of arms!"

Those who were not converted he ordered killed unless they paid a tax. He allowed robbery provided a fifth part of the steal went to God, which he called the fee of God and His messenger. He ordered it given out to paupers, orphans, and widows. He made God an accomplice in vice, Whom he could not make an accomplice in virtue. He said in effect: "You good, God-fearing men, dare to do things that bring you near to God—in God's name be piratical and slaughterous, to the pitch of perfection and ecstasy!" And though he has some reserves on plunder and perjury and certain other crimes, the reserves come down to being a permission. For he said: Do not do certain evils, they displease God. But should you, God is merciful, compassionate, God readily forgives.

He made no rule of restitution for robbers, so they do not practice restitution. It suffices for a Saracen to say: there is no God but God and

---

[102] [*Speculum historiale,* 1624 ed., 4:916b, 914a.]

Mohammed is His Prophet. He said expressly about perjury: "God does not blame you for it, but for the lack of it." He really said: "Perjury is not wrong. Getting caught at it is!" Then he adds: "For punishment, feed ten paupers, or clothe them, or ransom one captive. If you cannot do this, fast for three days." His followers rob with no hesitation, they deceive, they perjure themselves, they do not keep to the faith they promised, though they should, by natural law, even toward their foes. This is what the two authors cited say.[103]

Now to see how those who war on infidels mimic Mohammed and his followers: also those who urge war to subdue infidels as a prior condition for preaching the faith. It is manifest in the policy Mohammedans call the way of God: subjection of infidels to their power by the slash and slaughter of the sword, by the rape and robbery of a people's livelihood, by captivity of parent and child, by the outright murder of many, never mind their sex or age! May the war the Christians wage—those who vaunt the name of Christ—be not more vicious than the wars of the Mohammedans! And though many Christians and their backers say it is not their intention to force-convert pagans through war, but simply to remove obstacles to preaching—though there are a few stupid enough to say pagans ought to be forced to believe—that is a willful deception. It does not excuse their blindness, their rotten deviation. Mohammed forced no one to join his belief, he also. But he attacked and terrorized pagans violently, with fearful weapons, with robbery, ruin, with other flails of war. And though pagans did not profess him as the Prophet and Messenger of God, so long as they remained subject and paid taxes, he forced them no further—as it is clear from his own words cited earlier, something we now see in those who believe in his law. And the subject peoples are forced to live in terror of the welter and weight of evils, irreparable evils brought by war, and in fear and trembling of greater evils, if such there could possibly be.

All of us know they will harbor an undying hatred and bitterness against their oppressor. There is no need to repeat how opposite war is to liberty, liberty so crucial for believing the essentials that constitute faith and salvation in Christ. The result is that, even if people say they want to convert to Christianity, and from all appearances seem to mean it, yet we ought to be duly suspicious that their wish to convert comes not from the core of their free wills but from the hope of escap-

---

[103] [The two authors are: Fray Alonso de Espina, whose *Fortalitium fidei* was printed in Lyons in 1511, 1525, and 1529; and Guillermo Postel, *De Orbis concordia*, Basel, 1544 and 1551. Las Casas cites from Postel's lib. 2, cap. 6, no. 6.]

ing further damage which they fear will recur, or from the hope of
escaping some of the misery they suffer in the state of slavery.

It is right to fear the total loss of one's goods. Jurists maintain this,
as in the chapter "Abbot," with the notes they place there.[104] It is more
right to fear the loss of all respect, dignity, status, princely position.[105]
Loss of authority is like loss of life. Fear of the total loss of goods is like
fear of death.[106] For the question of goods, all or most, is a question of a
person's hold on life.[107] And fear of the loss of personal liberty? Fear of
horrible enslavement for oneself, for one's family? Fear of the loss of
wife and child? Fear of torture and death? What will such fears do?
Augustine says somewhere in a sermon,

> It is no easy thing to give up a sure thing for an unsure thing, to give
> up a known thing for an unknown thing. Who gives up the sure
> without sorrow, who walks away without tears? Name one for whom
> it is not torment to leave the parents who saw him to birth, the
> beloved house and home that holds the memory of his parents and
> his infant years? . . .

And these same surrenderings, will they not be worse—harsher,
sadder, bitterer, more a cause for grief, tearful choking grief—for those
who will be defeated Mohammedan-style by Christian power before
Christianity will be preached? Should we not guess that people will not
accept with a whole soul what they hear about faith after the conquest?
That they will never convert truly to the true God? What is the difference between this policy and practice, and the policy and practice concocted by Mohammed for the propagation of his faith—that faithless,
foul man! Who can gainsay the above?

Christian warriors are the vanguard of anti-Christ. They also
match Mohammed in the policy he fashioned to force-convert people
to his faith.

I think it is evident also from example and argument made earlier

---

[104] *Decretals,* lib. 1, tit. 40, cap. 2 [Friedberg, 2:219].

[105] Thus Baldus, commenting on *Decretals,* lib. 2, tit. 24, cap. 31 [Friedberg,
2:372. See Baldus de Ubaldis, *Super Decretalibus,* Lyons, 1551, fol. 314ab]. Also Jason,
at the beginning of his coll. 3 on *Digest,* lib. 45, tit. 1, lex 134 [Krueger, 1:781b. See Jason
Mainus, *Secunda super Digesto novo,* Lyons, 1542, fol. 187rb, par. 7 of coll. 3].

[106] Cf. Bartolus on *Digest,* lib. 12, tit. 5, lex 6 [Krueger, 1:201a. See Bartolus a
Saxoferrato, *Commentaria in secundam Digest. veteris partem* Lyons, 1555, vol. 3, fol.
52rab-va.]

[107] *Digest,* lib. 27, tit. 1, lex 21 [Krueger, 1:397a], also the canon "Abbas" I first
cited here. [See above note 97.]

how Christian warriors well match him in violence, savagery, in criminality. Mohammed and his armies once attacked (and still do) people
who never harmed them, fortified though those people were, and leveled them by the edge of the sword, by force of arms—to force-convert
them, to swell the faithful, even just to satisfy the itch for power. So also
does the pseudo-vanguard of our faith behave. They make the excuse
that they are clearing the way to faith. They are removing the roadblocks. Far be it from a mere lust for power, or to squeeze riches out of
people's blood!

Mohammed and Mohammedans decimated infidel peoples. For
shame, so have we! We have devastated lands and regions and provinces and kingdoms teeming with innocent people utterly open to our
teaching!

It is the legacy of Mohammed and Mohammedans to massacre
people, to steal, to loot, to ravage, to raze, to enslave parent and child.
For our part, what miracle of holiness and justice, what legacy do we
leave? A like one. We cut people savagely to pieces. We spare no one
for their sex, their dignity, their age. We tear sucklings from the teats of
their mothers and brain them on rocks. We fill straw-roofed log huts
with men, women, children, babies, mothers of many or pregnant
mothers, we set fire to the huts, we burn them alive. And we have other
ways to torment them living.

The living torments, in number, in kind, in novelty, are so cruel,
so damnable, they cannot be described in words, one by one or all
together. They are unbelievable except to the eyewitness! Even so, people are stunned just hearing the story. Who can say how many the
warriors doomed to slavery? And what about the natural resources?
What about the gold, the silver, the stolen kingly robes, the pile of
wealth removed? What about the theft of power and position and esteem and rank, even royal rank? What about all the viciousness—the
adultery, the rape, the incest, the bigamy—the warriors thought nothing of committing right before pagan eyes?

These Christians are a match, are more than a match for Mohammed and Mohammedans in savagery, in violence, in brutality, in
criminal behavior! And shame again to say, when they are at death's
door they regret nothing of what they did Mohammedan-style, not a
whit of the scale and scope of raping and cursing and destruction and
irreversible harm. They do not admit these are sins. They make no
restitution, no satisfaction. They leave life calmly, loaded with sins,
dying dumb like animals.

They die calm as anchorites who lived long in the desert practicing
severe penance! They blithely confess that God is merciful, compas-

sionate. So they think God will not impute their sins to them, their evil deeds committed against God to the damnation of thousands upon thousands of their neighbors. They append to their last will and testament the command to clothe ten or twenty paupers from their estate, or to endow an altar in some monastery on which three or four masses a week can be said for their souls. Look at it! I ask you, what difference is there between a nominal Christian and a Mohammedan except greater punishment, greater torment in hell?

You blind, miserable fools, you worse than pagans and Moors, who will spare you the wrath to come on the day of sorrow and almighty ruin? "You would justify Sodom!" as the saying goes. That is: "Your deeds make Sodom's look good!" (Ezekiel 16).[108] This condemnation is meant for you: "Damnation for you also! You close the Kingdom of God to people. You will not enter it yourselves, you will be stopped at the door!" And Paul in 1 Thessalonians 2:16: ". . . by preventing us from preaching salvation to the pagans" you drown in your sins. The wrath of God will pursue you to the end because you hated your own salvation, and also because you blocked belief and thus salvation for so many thousands of people.

And they burn in hell! Not just those you killed with cruel swords and other murderous means, an enormous number of people! But also those who dodged your cruel swords, those who then refused belief or faked it, scandalized by wickedness. The word of God, the source of belief for everyone, must be offered to everyone (last chapter, Mark and Matthew). Yet you blocked its being preached the way God wished, the way God willed. Thus you are the common enemy of all people, the offscouring of the earth, just as Chrysostom said, and Paul in Thessalonians.

If, as Chrysostom said about Matthew 23, they are unpardonable who just withhold their charity, what pardon will they have who do positive damage? You will suffer torment as the damned, not just for damning yourselves, but also for damning others. You cut off with a quick death the time they needed for conversion and repentance. You sent them straight to the torments of hell. You damned also those who grew to hate our faith because of the awful example you gave, grew to ridicule the universal Church, grew to blaspheme God.

The Second Council of Braga agrees with the above. "If anyone shall leave this life unbaptized, frightened from it by fear of be-

---

[108] *Gratian:* causa 1, q. 1, cap. 37 [Friedberg, 1:372–73]; also, dist. 40, cap. 5 [Friedberg, 1:146]; and causa 24, q. 1, cap. 21 [Friedberg, 1:973–74].

ing robbed, those who caused the fear assure damnation for themselves."[109]

How utterly clear it is that Mohammedans and those who copy their methods suffer hellfire for causing the loss of pagans—the already damned, the damned to come—pagans who despise faith because of the terrible crimes of the faithful, pagans who refuse to believe because of the blot on the whole Christian people, and because of their detestation of God!

These missionaries ape the anti-Christ and Mohammed and Mohammedans—both in the principle he set for forcing people into his religion and in the savagery, the criminality, the wickedness of his practice—and are thus Christians in name only. So it is dead certain that the policy they concocted, of having war precede gospel preaching, contradicts the fifth key element of preaching the gospel in the method begun by Divine Wisdom, renewed by Christ, practiced by the apostles. That key element is a life of purity, full of justice, of love of charity, a blameless life, an exemplary, holy life, one that gives no cause for quarrel or offense or harm or trouble.

In total contrast, the warriors' lives are degraded, vice-ridden, godless, choked with violence, injustice, robbery, rape, cursing, killing, cruelty, hideous crimes. They cause damage of enormous kinds, they shock, they injure, they decimate countless peoples, not just peoples—regions, kingdoms, provinces also. I repeat, their lives are frightful, hateful, base, and tarnished beyond that of any other godless men. The conclusion is clear. The war-first policy totally contradicts Christ's way, the apostles' way, of preaching the gospel in all five key elements.

THE BRUTAL MISSIONARY

The religious, then, who work to catechize the Indians of the New World, while working also to reform them by bodily torture—whips, chains, chastisements done with their own stroke or at their command —are guilty of grave wrong. And of graver wrong if they try to punish those Indians for any sin whatever they committed before or after conversion, even if the religious are authorized to do so by the bishops.

Proof of this corollary: We speak of sins after conversion, bad as they may be, because we cannot consider the sins that were or are committed prior to the reception of baptism. The reason: The natives had then no civil or ecclesiastical judge outside their own.

---

[109] Gratian, causa 1, q. 1, cap. 103 [Friedberg, 1:199].

There are many proofs for the present corollary. Briefly, the first: As we have already demonstrated, whoever wants to teach others, to win them over to some value, especially a gospel value, must win the souls of his hearers right at the start. An audience in a state of good will opens to a preacher. The preacher produces good will by the warmth of his voice, the joy on his face, the gentleness of his bearing, etc.

But if the preacher of the word of God treats his neophytes to bodily torture—whips, chains, chastisements, done with his own stroke or at his command, for sins the neophytes committed after conversion—if he punishes them, pounds them, they will have to hate him for it. As a result, they will not want to hear a word, nor believe a word said to them further. They will not want to retain what they heard and believed in the past. "No choice of a thing, no say in it, no love of it. No love of a thing, easy scorn of it. No good not chosen. The Lord commanded: Take no staff for the road, you could do someone violence with it. It is wiser to enkindle contempt for the world and love of God and heaven with prayerful, persuasive preaching than by unleashing violence on people, etc."[110]

Even children can turn angry under punishment and be insolent and rebellious toward their parents. That is why Paul warns parents not to provoke their children. He says: "Parents, do not provoke your children to impotent rage, you will make cowards of them" (Colossians 3:21). He could have said, make mean and mocking spirits of them. The standard gloss on the passage is: "He required parents to be restrained with their children. Or the children treated strictly would react against them and offend God. Anger is heedless. Often the angry person harms himself."[111] The newer people are in the faith, the truer the cautions of St. Paul. So the religious, the missioners who try by violence, etc.

The second proof. We also concluded in Part One that intellect and will must be free in those who hear the faith proposed to them. The intellect is to be free of disturbance by the four dominant passions of the soul, free of any interference. The will is to be free of whatever goes counter to it. Neither of these powers should be impeded in their activities, because the truths of the faith are accepted only in freedom. The two powers need peace and tranquility. If the preacher of the gospel terrorizes his hearers, hearers who have newly entered the precincts of the Church, if he tortures them with harsh beatings, imprisonments,

---

[110] Gratian, causa 20, q. 3, cap. 4 [Friedberg, 1:849–50].

[111] [Nicholas of Lyra, *Bibliorum Sacrorum cum Glossa Ordinaria*, Lyons, 1545, 137rb.]

with such like afflictions, if he punishes them for any sin whatever, they will of necessity be filled with anger toward the missioner, their tormentor, their punisher, and be filled with grief, sorrow, fear, hatred, as well as anger.

The human mind is panicked by terror, by strife, by fear, by violent language. It is panicked most by wounds inflicted on the body. The mind is saddened, hurt, angry. The outer senses close off hearing and seeing. The inner—the imagination and its products—are shattered, so mind and its reasoning go blank. It is not possible for these powers, battered and hobbled as they are, to make judgments on experience. The will shrinks from such effects, they repel it so much. So what is left for it to do but refute, repel, hate the truth of faith it hears, it has to hear, and with it, its missioners. So the religious, the missioners, are guilty of grave wrong who do such things, etc.

The third proof. Again through the teaching of St. Paul in 2 Timothy 2:24, where he says: "The servant of God should not be quarrelsome. He should be peaceable towards everyone, ready to teach, patient, able to correct gently those who resist the truth." If he must not be quarrelsome, much, much less can he strike, can he punish backsliding converts in his audience with whips and painful punitions. Athanasius says: "It is right for a teacher to be kind and gentle even to those he finds recalcitrant, the way a nurse behaves toward the child she minds, even if it scratches and kicks her." As we said before, you will not find Paul, or any of the saints, inflicting punishment on anyone, by their own hand or on their own orders, however gravely the person may have sinned.

That St. Paul punished someone who turned to vice, giving him over to Satan to trouble him in body for a time, was an exception to the rule, and needed for an exceptional circumstance (1 Corinthians 5:24). If missioners had such power these days, they would do well to use it. The evil results would not ensue which follow from the missioners' own punitive action or punitive orders. In fact evil results would cease. Great fruit of souls would follow. Maybe the "giving over to Satan" meant excommunication, as St. Thomas says about this Pauline passage. If so, it was a spiritual punishment, one vastly different from material, corporal punishment. That is self-evident. It is not what we are speaking of here. If he has the power and authorization from pope or bishop, a missioner can judge it meet and just to excommunicate some of the newly converted who lapse back into sin, without doing any physical damage. And only if the newly converted understand the meaning of excommunication, and it is likely they will not think it worthless.

The fourth proof. The corollary is proven by the severe complaint St. Denys wrote to the monk Demophilus. The reason: Demophilus treated with unbending anger a certain convert who fell back into sin. Demophilus cut him off completely. It is a famous case and the letter is both beautiful and devout. It is a fulsome confirmation of our corollary. Please look at the whole of it. Denys says, among other things: "Better to teach the ignorant than torment them. We do not lash the blind, but lead them by the hand." A little further on, he says: "It is a thing of utter horror that you should damn, disclaim, drive out someone the all-good Christ sought among the mountains, found fleeing, and, fresh from the find, brought back on his sacred shoulders." Chrysostom uses the same theme of leading the blind: "Therefore, just to do our duty, we offer him an arm and we speak to him warmly." Therefore missionaries do a grave wrong if they want to punish physically, by their own hand or someone else's, the newly converted natives who sin again.

The fifth proof. The same conclusion is proven through much that the saints have written—we cited them often above, especially the writing of St. Gregory: "The preaching that produces faith by the cudgel is willful and bizarre." And: "Whoever with sincere attention . . . wants to bring those who are strangers to Christianity into the true faith, should try with gentle means, not with severity. . . ."[112]

The sixth proof. The wrong we spoke of can be shown amply through the teaching of Blessed Prosper [*sic:* Julianus Pomerius]:

> I say that if you recall what the dispute about holy priests was, you have a sufficient response. As I said, the teachers in the Church must have the power to judge so they can be involved, they must have patience so they can bear with those who are unwilling to reform. Thus they fulfill the Pauline instruction given to Timothy in these words: "Convince your peers, your elders, correct your juniors" (2 Timothy 4:2). Then Paul quickly added: "in true patience and teaching."

> Someone who is corrected gently shows respect for his corrector; someone subjected to harsh and hyper-correction takes no correction, no message of salvation.

> Paul says somewhere else: "Let the stronger among you bear the

---

[112] As quoted in Gratian, dist. 45: cap. 1 and cap. 3 [Friedberg, 1:160].

failings of the weaker" (Romans 15:1). They can bear easily with
them as weak, not with them as incorrigible. . . ."

And further on:

For if the weak are cut off from communion with the Church, those
whom castigation could not cure, they will sink under the excessive
weight of sadness. They will avoid meeting the holy people through
whom God could restore them. Or else, if driven to it, they will leap
at every chance to sin, shamelessly, and the evil they did in secret
they will do openly. Thus, in despair of regaining grace, they fall into
such a craziness that they switch the words of those who warn them
into wicked puns with a "who cares" attitude. And the reproaches
made against them, for boasting of their badness, feed their terrible
lives with wicked delights. To avoid these consequences, therefore,
the weak are to be borne with calm faith—they cannot be castigated
for their weakness.

The truth is, that if you induce a healthy shame in a sinner because
of the shame you feel for his sin, if you infuse in him the disgrace you
take on for his sin in the soul of your compassion, you will suppress
in him easily all desire to sin, you will remove the whole rebel urge
which is at the bottom of badness. Then a sense of shame, the watch-
dog of morality, hangdog shame will clothe his actions. What disgusted him earlier, when he was disgusting, will attract him now.
What attracted him earlier, when all that was good disgusted him,
will disgust him now. He will copy holy people willingly. In becoming like them, he will slowly transform his prior ways. After the hard
work of reaching the heights of virtue, it would be equally as hard for
him to return to the vices he was so happy to leave behind. As virtue
weighs on vice, so the pleasure of vice tastes bitter to the lover of
virtue. The person who has in mind only the salvation of the sinner,
who wants to help him, treats all sinners, confronts all sinners
peaceably.[113]

These are the principles of Prosper [*sic:* Julianus Pomerius].
I beg my brothers to meditate these principles often, often, and not
let themselves become torturers of the children they begot for Christ in
the Church, children they must beget again and again until the time
Christ is formed in them. Let my brothers become weak with the weak,

[113] [*PL,* 59:449–50.]

let them bear everything, with warnings, with beseechings, with tears openly, as Paul did, in order to save others.

Let them lead a holy and pure life. Let them be exemplary in their speech, in their relationships, in their charity, in their faith, in their chastity, so no one may demean their person. Let them be as Paul described to Timothy (1:4): as angels who deal with humankind, as men who raise their young, as spiritual kind who deal with material kind. So that the material kind feel uneasy in their presence, and are filled with shame and confusion if they do not follow them, do not believe in them—the way we just described it, the way Chrysostom did earlier. No need for the missioner then to inflict physical punishment, wielding the switches, whips, with his own hand or having another do it.

And yet they may put the fear of God into the fractious if they think it will help—i.e., describe the frightful judgment to come, the torment the fractious will suffer forever. If they think their efforts are useless, nonetheless they did not labor in vain, the damnation is due to others, not to themselves, their own reward is reserved in a safe place. That should be no small consolation.

PAPAL CONDEMNATION OF ARMED OPPRESSION

Finally, we recall the papal encyclical "God Who is beyond us," which insists on peaceful conversion. The High Priest and Vicar of Christ Himself gave teeth to that decree [*Sublimis Deus*] when he made the archbishop of Toledo the judge and executor of it. The archbishop was in Toledo at the time. The pope gave him complete power to force the tyrants not to injure, not to oppress the Indians as they had done against every law. And power to give relief directly to the Indians concerning their freedom and ownership of their own goods. His commission to the Archbishop says this:

> To our beloved son, health and apostolic benediction. We have a pastoral duty to perform with all zeal towards the flock confided to us by God. We are made sad by the loss of them, made happy by the gain of them. We do praise the goodness of their works, but we make suggestions derived from the wider scope of our apostolic responsibility. It comes to our attention that our beloved son Charles, ever august Emperor of the Romans, King of Castile and León, to check those who seethe with greed and take a brutal stance toward humankind, forbade all his subjects, by public edict, to make slaves of the

Indians, East or West, or to dare deprive them of their personal goods. So we are mindful also of those Indians, though they are outside the flock of Christ. They are not for that reason deprived or to be deprived of their liberty nor the ownership of their possessions. They are human beings, therefore capable of faith and salvation. They are not to die in slavery. They are to be invited, through preaching and by example, to live. So we also condemn the outlaw acts of such wicked men. We want to prevent it [from] happening that the Indians find it harder to embrace the Christian faith because they are demoralized by pain and loss. To you, then, in whose character we have a special confidence in the Lord—for your probity, your providence, your piety, your experience of these Indians and other peoples—to you, through this document, we make the following commission and command: (1) That you become a bulwark of defense for the aforesaid Indians in the aforesaid circumstances, yourself, or through another, or others. (2) That you strictly forbid anyone to make a slave in any way of the aforesaid Indians, or rob them of their goods under any pretext—anyone at all, whatever their dignity, their status, their condition, their grade, their nobility—forbid on penalty of excommunication, a judgment already made and incurred *ipso facto* if they act against this. They cannot be absolved from this penalty unless by Us or by a reigning Pontiff, except at the moment of death and after previous repentance. (3) And against the disobedient, you are to proceed to publish this threat of excommunication; and proceed further, to other measures apt for the circumstances, measures necessary and in any way suitable as you may determine, ordain, dispose, which will seem to you consonant with your prudence, your probity, your piety. By this commission, we give you full, free control in these matters against those who do the opposite. Given at Rome. . . .[114]

The last way of proving our proposition is now laid out, through the decrees of the Church, its succession of saintly popes.

---

[114] [See the definitive text of *Pastorale Officium* in *Las Casas en México*, Appendix 12.]

EPILOGUE: RESTORATION
OF THE INDIANS

*Restitution Required from All Because: Wars for Conversion are
Mindless and Unjust*

It is mindless, wrong, evil, tyrannical to wage war on pagans who
never heard of our faith or our Church, the fourth type of infidel we
analyzed earlier, the type who never harmed the Church—and to do it
so that once subjected to Christian power by war their souls would be
prepared to accept salvation in the Christian religion, or at least the
impediments to faith would be removed. There are many proofs one
can give for each of the four charges just listed.

Take first that it is mindless. A mindless war is one waged in
defiance of law. Such war is forbidden by divine, by natural, by human
law. Therefore such a war is mindless.[115]

The conclusion is clear, the minor premise proven. Mindless war
is forbidden by the natural law, because it contradicts the very way
Divine Wisdom deals with all creation, contradicts especially the way
established by Wisdom for drawing, for guiding rational beings toward
goodness—by the mind. Mindless war negates the normal way of
drawing people to goodness, a way common sense teaches all teachers
of others. Mindless war negates the way used by the wisest philosophers
who know what they know by the light of reason. They caused the most
barbarous peoples to lead civilized lives.

The law of nature is violated by a war in which a sovereign people
—not living under Christian rule, without provoking a thing—is struck
down by a horde of irreparable harms: murders, massacres, muggeries,
lootings, enslavements and such like. Cicero thinks that to take some-

---

[115] Hostiensis comments thus on the *Sext,* lib. 5, tit. 4, cap. 1 [Friedberg, 2:1080.
See Henricus de Segusio, Cardinal of Ostia, *In Sextum Decretalium Librum commentaria,* Venic., 1581, cap. 1, col. 28.]

158

thing away from another, or to profit at the expense of another, is more against nature than death, or poverty, or grief, or anything that can happen to body or property, because human relationship, human society, is wiped out.[116] How much more unnatural, unbearable, is it to inflict death itself, to make off with property, to plunge free peoples into slavery, to force them to suffer all that was listed earlier? How grievously, how pitifully unnatural to be the reason for countless kindred souls to perish forever! So mindless war is truly forbidden by natural law, there is no doubt!

The ancient law is against it, the Old Testament, which forbids not just that a neighbor be killed, above all an innocent neighbor, or that his goods be looted—not his slave, not his maidservant, not his oxen, not his donkey, not anything he has—forbids not just calumny, not just violence, not just mortal perjury, not just the gutting of a guest and like crimes, but forbids even being troublesome to anyone. What is forbidden is done in war and by war. Warriors violate the divine orders, the Ten Commandments. Our earlier proofs are cogent. So mindless war is forbidden by the ancient law, the Old Testament.

It is forbidden by New Testament revelation as well, and a flat contradiction of the way Christ wanted things done. His deeds as well as His words made mandatory the procedures He taught so strongly. What they were is clear: Christ established procedures, or rather He gave new force to the time-honored, humane way of drawing people to the truth of salvation. He told His apostles, and hence their successors, not to be bellicose missioners but gentle missioners, kind, humble of heart in word and deed, to be like a flock of sheep with a pack of wolves. He forbade them to carry a staff or anything that could seem to express violence; forbade them to have gold, silver, or anything a pagan could attribute to greed or profiteering. They should not own stolen goods, they should not accept such goods from thieves willing to give. That way, all suspicion that they preached for lucre's sake and their own advantage would be banished from the hearts of their pagan hearers.

He ordered them to be of good character, to be doers of good deeds, so they would be lovable to pagans, so pagans would believe their doctrines, so pagans would bless God as the superb Father of a superb family.

He ordered them not to give the slightest scandal whereby the weak and wavering nonbeliever could be kept from belief, or held back, or confused. He clearly lived a life that harmed no one. No one could take a whit of what He said or did as a cause for scandal, or as a reason

---

[116] *De Officiis* lib. 3 [cap. 5, nos. 21–23—Loeb, 288–91].

for recoiling from His words or His way of life. He willingly paid His taxes so citizens would not be scandalized, though He had no obligation to, for Himself or for Peter, as is clear from Matthew 17:26 where Jesus says: "So we do not scandalize them, go down to the water. . . ." Also Acts 10:38: "And He went about doing good, offending no one." He gave the command: "So let your light shine before the world . . ." (Matthew 5:16), to prevent scandalizing pagans.

Take Luke 12:35: "Be dressed and ready with burning torches in your hands." Gregory comments: "We hold burning torches in our hands when we illumine the way for our neighbor with good example."[117] Paul speaks in a similar vein when he says in Romans 12:17: "Doing good deeds not only in the sight of God but in the sight of people as well." And in 1 Corinthians 10:31–33: "Do all things for the glory of God, even to eating or drinking. Be not a trouble to Jew or Gentile or to the Church of God—I adapt myself to everyone in all I do. I am not after my own good, but the good of all the others, for salvation's sake. Imitate me, just as I imitate Christ." And in Philippians 2:15 and 4:5: "Be blameless among bad and blameful people." And: "Let your dignity be known to everyone." And in Titus 2:7: "In your teaching, in your life, give an example of goodness." Also in 2 Corinthians 6:3: "Give no one cause for offense so our ministry will not be blamed [i.e., our missionary effort], so we present ourselves as ministers of God in all we do, bearing up patiently in trials and tribulations and troubles and torments, in prisons, in works, in prayerful watches, in charity without guile. . . ." And in 1 Peter 2:12: "Be holy in your dealings with people."

Our Savior showed how much we should avoid confusing weak Christians and scandalizing pagans when He made known the severe penalty by which agitators and scandalous people were to be punished: "If your eye scandalize you, pluck it out. Better that, than to have your whole body burn in hell" (Matthew 5:29). And: "Whoever scandalizes one of these small children who believe in me now or later, he should have a millstone hung around his neck and be tossed into the deep. Woe to the world for scandals. Woe more to those who scandalize. See that you do not damage a one of these children" (Matthew 18:6–7). Chrysostom says the word "woe" is a horror-filled, terrifying word: the word of someone keening, promising scandalizers an eternal punishment they will not escape.[118]

---

[117] [*Catena Aurea*—S. Thomas, *Opera,* Parma, 12:149b]

[118] [In this one sentence, Las Casas summarizes Chrysostom's Homily 60 on the Matthean passage—*PG,* 58:573–84.]

So Paul took great pains to warn the faithful to avoid giving scandal:

Rather decide never to put a stumbling block or hindrance in the way of a brother. . . . If your brother is being injured by what you eat, you are no longer walking in love. Do not let what you eat cause the ruin of someone for whom Christ died. Do not let the good we do be blasphemed. Do not, for the sake of food, destroy the work of God . . . it is right not to eat meat or drink wine or do anything that makes your brother stumble or be scandalized or be weakened (Romans 14:13, 15, 20, 21).

And in Corinthians 8:9–13 he says:

See to it that this looseness of yours does not scandalize the weak. For if anyone sees you, a man of knowledge, at table in an idol's temple, might he not be encouraged, if his conscience is weak, to eat food offered to idols. And so by your knowledge this weak man is destroyed, the brother for whom Christ died. Thus sinning against your brethren and wounding their conscience when it is weak, you sin against Christ. Therefore if food is a cause of my brother's failing, I will never eat meat, lest I cause my brother to fail.

In Deuteronomy 27:18, there is a curse laid on the one who sends a blind man down the wrong road, the right road being the road to God the blind man was on. Or should have been on had he not been sinfully misdirected.

You see how scandal is scored, punished severely, or at least severely condemned. The worse the punishment, the worse the kind of crime.[119] You must give up doing whatever could cause scandal, if you can do so without sinning, according to Jerome.

Augustine, in his work *On the Words of the Lord,* Sermon 6, "On the Child of the Centurion," says:

Thus sinning against your brethren and wounding their conscience when it is weak, you sin against Christ. What more do you need to hear, brethren? You are Christians. Demean nothing if you want not to be deleted from the book of life. Watch your step, those of you who do demean things, you sin against Christ. We want to convert the rest of pagandom. You are roadblocks. Those wanting to convert run smack against you and recoil. They say to themselves: "Why give up gods for Christ if Christians want our gods?"[120]

---

[119] Gratian, causa 24, q. 1, cap. 21 [Friedberg, 1:973–74].
[120] [*PL,* 38:418.]

Add to this what Augustine says in Sermon 19 of *On the Words of the Apostles:*

> If someone is damned to hellfire by Christ saying to him or her, "I was naked and you did not clothe me," to what hellfire will they be damned to whom He says, "I was clothed and you stripped me!" Maybe to avoid Christ's condemning voice, "I was clothed and you stripped me," you think to strip a pagan in order to clothe a Christian. And Christ will reply to you—though His reply will be mediated through some minister of His—He will reply and say: "Even here beware of my punishments." When you as a Christian strip someone for being a pagan, you cancel a convert.[121]

And so those who wage wars of conversion, also those who order such wars waged, work against the tradition of Christ, against the love and the law He started, or rather renewed, concerning gospel preaching —not war first, but peace first, not wearing weapons to use against innocent pagans, as is clear from the preceding chapter. Warriors are not meek and mild, they are like wolves, maddened with hunger, slashing in among a flock of sheep. Again and again they slaughter people who have done them no harm. They loot gold and silver, anything anyone has. They sell free people into slavery, put them in dire straits. Because of this behavior of theirs the whole world rightly thinks the worst of them, rightly hates them, and by implication also the teachings of the faith on their account. Also the whole Christian Church. They cause the true God and Christ the Lord to be blasphemed thousands of times, tens of thousands, hundreds of thousands of times. With their hideous, heartless, damnable deeds, their disgusting lives, they scandalize the weak, the wavering pagans who know not the truth yet, but easily could. They create a mighty obstacle, scandal—unspeakable, raging—enough to horrify anyone, enough not just to keep pagans from coming to believe, but more, enough to close them off forever from the way of salvation. Yesterday, today, tomorrow, they destroy the work of God with their assaults and batteries, their craving for piles of gold, silver, wealth, their lust for power over foreign kingdoms, that is to say over the vast number of souls made in God's image. Many weak souls are thus damned because of the unholy, the damned soul of the brutal warrior, weak souls Christ the Son of God died to save. War for conversion contradicts the divine will revealed in the New Testament. It contradicts flatly the way, the wish, the will of Christ.

It contradicts positive law as well. It will be made clearer in a subsequent book, God willing. What is now clear is that war to convert

---

[121] [*PL*, 38:963.]

is mindless—a contradiction of natural law, a contradiction of positive law.

War is mindless for another reason—it is waged counter to the condemnatory stance of so many holy and learned people, though these were not inspired as were the evangelists.

War to convert is unjust. First of all: A war cannot be just unless there is a reason for waging it—some group against whom the war is waged provoked it by attacking some other group. But take pagan people living beyond the boundaries of Christendom. They are targeted for military action for the sole purpose of subjecting them to Christian control so as to wipe out all obstacles to evangelization in the Christian way of salvation. They have not provoked the Christian people, in any way, to merit a military action against them. So there is no reason to wage the war. So the war is unjust.

Secondly: The reason given for the war has been thoroughly undermined by the accumulation of arguments in these chapters. People not yet evangelized are to be invited to faith, to salvation, not by war but by peace, by good will, kindness, generosity, credibility, by charity from the heart. Absent the reason for war, absent the justification for it.

Thirdly: Justice means a kind of right order. Justice directs the deeds of people according to some norm relative to other people. A war to convert is monumentally normless relative to innocent pagan peoples. Belligerents attack them, conquer them without cause—what is inflicted on them is not provoked by them, the intensity and scope of the damage, wound and welt and waste. So such a war is monumentally unjust.

Fourthly: "Do injury to no one" is a norm of justice.[122] But in wars to convert, warriors cause people countless injuries without a reason— grievous, gruesome, permanent injuries. Such a war is therefore unjust, abhorrent to the very nature of justice.

Fifthly: Grant to each what each owns and keep it so. That is another norm of justice. But in wars to convert, militants wreck all the rights, all the goods the people they attack possess. They ravage and ruin as described earlier. So such war is unjust and fraught with evil.

Sixthly: We proved above that such war is unnatural. It is further clear because nature itself has created a certain kinship between human beings. According to that kinship we are forbidden to violate one another.[123] This right of kinship is so rooted in nature, so supported by the

---

[122] *Digest*, lib. 1, tit. 1, lex 10, and the same in *Institutes*, lib. 1, tit. 1, introductory sentence, #1 and 3 [Krueger, 1:29b, and 1a].
[123] *Digest*, lib. 1, tit. 1, lex 3 [Krueger, 1:29a].

Lord's command "Love your neighbor as yourself," that it can be confirmed but not abrogated by treaty.[124] War to convert breaks with the law of kinship, it ruptures every right. Such war is unjust. It is abhorrent to all law.

We conclude to the wickedness of such wars for a further reason: Wars destroy respect, for one thing, respect for God. By blocking or hampering the praise, the honor which would accrue to God from the spread of the faith and the conversion of the people, the militants kill and maim and scandalize, they destroy respect for God. They destroy equally respect for the Christian religion, a respect built on our good name, as a jurist calls it, our reputation for sanctifying life. It is the reputation of the whole Christian people they blemish irremediably by the scandalous deeds they perform, reversing the precept of the apostle: "Be blameless toward Jew and Gentile, toward the people of God, so your ministry is not mocked . . ." (1 Corinthians 10:32). "We must believe we cannot do those things which harm the respect we have, the good name, the bearing, nor, in a larger sense, those things contrary to good morals."[125] For this reason also war to convert is evil.

Ultimately it is tyranny: firstly for being violent, ruthlessly cruel, reckless—the stuff of robbers, looters, huns, who have no cause for the hideous, harmful swaths they cut, the welter of wounds and sufferings and disasters they inflict on people. They act as if they were the refuse of almost the whole human race, as they are.

It is tyranny, secondly, because the militants prefer their own particular worldly profit to the common good of all—to the honor due to God, to the salvation, the spiritual and temporal well-being of countless groups and individuals. That is the way tyrants behave. Sovereign power acquired in such a war is unjust, it is evil, it is tyrannical, it is totally cursed by God, it can in no way endure—we proved that earlier.

WARS FOR CONVERSION ARE MORTAL SIN

Those who wage wars of conversion, those who are in any way the cause of such wars being waged on unconverted peoples—those who declare war, counsel it, push it or supply it—all of them commit mortal sin of the worst kind. There are many proofs of this.

The first: They commit mortal sin who violate by deed the law of

---

[124] Nor by mutual consent, see: *Digest,* lib. 2, tit. 14, lex 38 and 34 [Krueger, 1:60b]; and *Codex,* lib. 8, tit. 46, lex 6 [Krueger, 2:357b].

[125] *Digest,* lib. 28, tit. 7, lex 15 [Krueger, 1:433ab].

God, that based on nature, that based on the two Testaments, and who violate international law as well. Now those who wage wars of conversion do violate by deed the law of God, that based on nature, that based on the two Testaments. They do violate international law as well. The proof is found in the preceding section. Therefore such warriors commit mortal sin.

The second: They commit a mortal sin who violate legal justice or a specific law on a key issue. Those who wage wars of conversion violate legal justice and local law. We just proved that. They therefore commit mortal sin.

To the major premise: First, the person who does something unjust violates thereby some precept of the law of God—i.e., the act is eventually classified under theft, adultery, homicide or some such. Each is a classification of mortal sin. Whoever therefore does something unjust sins mortally.

Second, injustice always involves injury inflicted on someone else. Injury inflicted on someone else is repugnant to the essence of justice. The essence of it is not to inflict injury on anyone, to give everyone what belongs to him or her, not take it away. Injustice is always a mortal sin.

Third, justice implies something owed. It is generally thought of in terms of what we owe another. A just act is one that gives what is owed to someone, to do him or her no harm. We have spoken of this. Injustice does not give what it ought to another, it does harm to him or her, it takes someone else's something. Justice and injustice cause contrary results. We touched on this in the preceding chapter. Therefore to act unjustly is to sin mortally. This is further proved because to deny someone his due falls under the prohibition of Paul to the Romans 13:8: "Retain nothing of anyone else's." And the further prohibition concerning harming, injuring another, taking what is his or hers: "Steal from no one" (Exodus 20:15). Therefore, etc.

The proof of the minor premise: The warmongers we spoke of cause willy-nilly the monumental injustices of war, violent crimes against general justice—i.e., against the legal structures of peoples and states, against the honor due to Christ, against the respect, the good name of the Church; violent crimes likewise against the specific laws dealing with countless individuals. Warmongers all commit mortal sin.[126]

---

[126] On this point see S. Thomas, *Summa Theologiae:* I^a II^{ae}, q. 60, art. 3, corp. [*Opera,* 6:389]. Also II^a II^{ae}, q. 58, art. 11, corp. [*Opera,* 9:18]; q. 66, arts. 3 and 5, corp. [*Opera,* 9:86, 91–92]; and q. 59, art. 4, corp. [*Opera,* 9:24].

When the salvation of the soul is at stake, every violation of the law of God is a mortal violation—here understanding the law of God in its broadest sense, the Ten Commandments for example—because one has to sin grievously in order to violate the law.[127] So what is right to do, is commanded.[128] It must be carried out. Mongers of wars to convert violate one way or another the counsel of Christ to preach the faith peaceably, to avoid scandalizing pagans, etc. In fact they violate every one of the Ten Commandments—witness what we argued earlier —because they kill, they massacre, they loot, they do infinite evil—we have made that clear already. So warmongers commit mortal sin.

Fourth, a sin is utterly mortal when the sinful act committed removes a person from submission to God and to the social compact, both of which stem from keeping God's law. There are certain things one must do in order to remain submissive to God and to the social compact with one's neighbor. If one sins against those necessary things, the sins are mortal in essence. They are called malicious by Aristotle. He means that every malicious act is an evil act. In this case, someone cannot be duly submissive to God who does not believe in God, who does not obey God, etc. The social structure of human life cannot be maintained unless the rights of each person are preserved. Homicide, theft, such like, all are kinds of injustice. All are mortal sins.[129]

Mongers of wars to convert show they are not submissive to God. Look at the unbelievable injustice, the criminal injustice they let loose in the wars they wage on pagan peoples. They violate the law of God and every commandment, that is clear from the previous descriptions of them. And they destroy the bond of human society when they kill people and have no reason to, when they strip, destroy, erase whole populations. Their sin is mortal sin.

Fifth, all who instigate wars of conversion in any of the above-mentioned ways abandon love of God and neighbor. We showed that in the preceding chapter. They thus commit a mortal sin. They are already damned.

Sixth, they commit serious mortal sin who do, or order done, a thing which leads people straight and sure to endanger their physical lives, even more their spiritual lives, leads especially to the sure damna-

---

[127] *Clementines*, lib. V, tit. 11, cap. 1 [Friedberg, 2:1193–1200].

[128] *Gratian*, causa 14, q. 1, cap. 3, #2 [Friedberg, 1:733]. On this point, cf. S. Thomas, *Summa Theologiae*, Ia IIae, q. 99, art. 1, corp., and art. 5, corp. [*Opera*, 7:199–200, 203]. Also IIa IIae, q. 44, art. 1, corp. [*Opera*, 8:331]; and q. 80, art. 1, corp. [*Opera*, 9:174–75].

[129] S. Thomas, commenting on *II Sentences*, dist. 42, q. 1, art. 4, corp. [*Opera*, Parma, 6:762–64].

tion of huge numbers of them. This goes also for those who counsel the thing, or aid it, or share in it in any way, unless a law allows them. The people who wage wars to convert, who order them waged, whose help makes them possible, unless the law allows it, lead their neighbors in large numbers straight and sure to endanger their physical lives, their spiritual lives, unto the certain damnation of many—many innocent infants, and many innocents like them. We have made it clear. They give such scandal to the surviving adults who have escaped their swords, that these adults will rarely convert to our faith. The mortal sin committed is gross and grievous. The major premise is quite proven in the evidence laid out earlier—and also from the effects war generates.

The minor premise is obvious: The warrior spares no one, man/woman, old/young, prince/pauper. They leave this life without the faith, without the sacrament. They go surely to hell, the ultimate evil. Innocent children, unbaptized, still in original sin, adults immersed still in idolatry and the sins that stem from it as a matter of course—they are damned eternally, no doubt of it in Christian doctrine.

The warriors effectively prevent the conversion of those who escaped death. The survivors hate our belief, hate the Christian religion. One: They have suffered for it calamities horrible in number and in kind. Two: They see the devilish behavior of the Christians. They are confirmed in their own, in their wrong-headed, superstitious belief. They think ours is bad, brutal, hypocritical. Three: They are, many of them, so mightily tormented and terrified by evils undergone that they flee to the woods to avoid worse. They hide in caves and hollows. They are thus deprived of all means of saving their souls. So people who bring on wars of conversion, by command, by counsel, by complicity, lead their many neighbors directly and surely to the loss of body and soul. That is most grievous sin.

Clearly. Because sins committed against our neighbor must be judged essentially in terms of the harm they do to that neighbor. The sin derives from the harm.[130] The more good taken, the more harm given. There are three types of human 'good,' we described them earlier—soul good, the highest; body good, the next in rank; thing good [possessions], the lowest ranked. These three 'goods' and any good else are taken from pagans whom the Christians attack to convert—taken by death, taken by theft of goods, of ground they govern, of political liberty, taken by the theft of living-time, the kind needed to accept the faith, accept baptism and repentance. It is therefore clear that those who wage wars of conversion, and the others who foster it by com-

---

[130] Thus S. Thomas, *Summa Theologiae*, II[a] II[ae], q. 74, art. 3, corp. [*Opera*, 9:140].

mand, by counsel, by complicity, commit sin whose gravity is mea-
sured by the greatness, the grandeur of the 'goods' they take away with
one stroke.

Soul good is the greatest good, as we said. We say nothing here of
body good or thing good—possessions. No greater harm can be done
than to take someone's life, no greater unless death finds that someone
not in the state of grace. To do that to someone is the absolute opposite
of charity by which the soul lives. It is therefore the worst of sins.
Therefore the one who causes damnation for his neighbor commits the
worst of sins. Aristotle says the better a thing, the nobler, the worse its
corruption. The human soul is worth more than the body or all that
one can see.[131] As Chrysostom says about the *Acts of the Apostles* in
Homily 3:

> I say no more than this: if even one dies unbaptized, is not the whole
> salvation of the one responsible for it compromised? The loss of a
> soul is such a loss that reason cannot fathom it. If the saving of a soul
> is worth so much that the Son of God became man and suffered
> great torment, think what the punishment is for damning one. If a
> killer in this world is deemed worthy of being killed, how worthy of
> being damned the one who causes damnation.[132]

The warmongers we spoke of are all guilty of damning souls, the
souls of those whom they killed in war, the souls of those who died
without faith or sacrament, young, old, boy, girl, victims all of scandal.
The Second Council of Braga is clear on this. And its argument is
quoted in the canon "Placuit": "If certain people die without the grace
of baptism while they are refugees, then damnation will be required of
those who caused the refugees to go beyond the pale of baptismal grace
out of fear of being ravaged."[133]

There is a neat description of the grievous guilt of the sins of those
who cause wars of conversion or are accomplices. They will fall under
the same verdict, damnation, who cause damnation because they did
deadly damage.[134] "There is no difference in the guilt if you kill or
cause a killing."[135] There is another fine text where Jerome comments
on Micah the prophet: "Those who ordain some of their followers

---

[131] Cf. *Decretals,* lib. V, tit. 38, cap. 13 [Friedberg, 2:888]; and Gratian, causa 12, q.
1, cap. 24 [Friedberg, 1:685], and causa 24, q. 3, cap. 1 [Friedberg, 1:988–90]; also *Codex.*
lib. 1, tit. 2, lex 21 [Krueger, 2:16ab].

[132] [*PG,* 60:40.]

[133] Gratian, causa 1, q. 1, cap. 103 [Friedberg, 1:399].

[134] Gratian, causa 23, q. 5, cap. 8 and cap. 19 [Friedberg, 1:932–33, 936]; and
Decretals, lib. V, tit. 36, cap. 9 [Friedberg, 2:880].

[135] *Digest,* lib. 48, tit. 8, lex 15 [Krueger, 1:853b].

priests, and expose their people to the scandal of these priests' lives, are themselves guilty of the loss of faith of those who are scandalized."[136] So the warmongers commit a serious mortal sin.

We have to show now that all the accomplices to a war are on the same level of crime and each one on the same—or greater—level of culpability before God. Paul, to the Romans (1:32), says they are worthy of death, "not just those who commit crimes, but those also who consent to crimes."[137]

The teachers of the law say someone can consent three ways. First, cooperation in crime. Examples, simony, incest, kidnapping a virgin, robbery, and false verdict.[138] Second, someone consents when he does not set straight those he must, ex officio.[139] Third, someone consents when he protects the sinner or abdicates authority.[140] The protector is more to be punished than the perpetrator. Consent is fourfold: carelessness, complicity, cooperation, cover-up—the misuse of authority.

In the case of carelessness, consent is less of a sin than commission, unless maybe the carelessness was gross negligence, say in a prelate or a prince. Thus the canons: "Someone seems to consent who does not hurry and halt what ought to be halted."[141] "Not to halt the criminal when you can is nothing else than helping him. He is suspect of complicity who does not interfere in an obvious crime."[142] "The faults of lessers must be blamed more on their lax and lazy leaders. Often the latter nurse the sickness under the pretense of providing it a harsh cure."[143] "He has the guilt of a criminal, who neglected to stop what he was able to stop. And he opens the door wide to criminals, who gives perverse consent. It is useless to escape punishment for one's own sins only to be punished for someone else's."[144]

---

[136] Gratian, causa 1, q. 1, cap. 44 [Friedberg, 1:375–76].

[137] Thus Gratian: causa 2, q. 1, cap. 10, and causa 3, q. 4, cap. 4 [Friedberg, 1:443–512]; also *Decretals,* lib. V, tit. 12, cap. 6 [Friedberg, 2:794–96]; and *Decretals,* lib. 1, tit. 29, cap. 1 [Friedberg, 2:158].

[138] Gratian: causa 1, q. 1, cap. 8 [Friedberg, 1:359–60]; causa 3, q. 4, cap. 4 [Friedberg, 1:512]; causa 36, q. 2, cap. 4 [Friedberg, 1:1290]; causa 17, q. 4, cap. 5 [Friedberg, 1:816].

[139] Gratian: dist. 83, cap. 3 [Friedberg, 1:293–94]; and dist. 86, cap. 1 and 3. [Friedberg, 1:298].

[140] Gratian, causa 11, q. 3, cap. 100 [Friedberg, 1:671]; and causa 24, q. 3, cap. 32 [Friedberg, 1:999].

[141] Gratian: causa 1, q. 1, cap. 101 [Friedberg, 1:398]; and dist. 83, cap. 5 [Friedberg, 1:294].

[142] Gratian, dist. 83, cap. 3, already cited [Friedberg, 1:293–94, cf. note 103 above]; also cf. cap. 6 on the shepherd who praises the wolves [Friedberg, 1:294].

[143] Gratian, dist. 86, cap. 1 [Friedberg, 1:298].

[144] Gratian, dist. 86, cap. 3 [Friedberg, 1:298].

Complicity is punished less than commission, the second kind of cooperation, but more than carelessness.[145]

In the third kind of cooperation, the perpetrator and the cooperator sin equally. Under this heading are to be understood all those who wink at what is done. Experts say they are equally punished.

In the fourth kind of cooperation, cover-up by authority, the one who uses authority as a cover-up sins more than the doer of the deed and is to be punished more.[146] We have the following verses:

Complicity blinks, invites, approves, protects.
Is liable, sometimes less, sometimes equally,
Sometimes more.
It consents by deed, defense, or a deaf ear.

The primary criminals are those who order the crime and those who advise how to do it. St. Thomas and all the doctors agree. Whoever commands or counsels the committing of a crime, by that very command becomes a primary cause, therefore a primary criminal, as the rule states: Whoever commits a crime through an agent, commits it himself.[147]

So it is clear that the instigators are primary causes of the great wickedness and devastation worked on pagan peoples in the wars of conversion waged against them. The instigators sin worse than the rest.

We say whoever counsels crime, causes crime, as much as the one who gives the command. So everyone who counsels a war to convert commits grave mortal sin, akin to those who commanded it, if the counsel proves efficacious in causing the war or something likewise wicked. These are the proofs:

First. The counselor is an essential cause of whatever is done by the one who acts on his counsel. That is clear from Aristotle 2 *Physics*. Other participants, who give aid and comfort, do not seem to be so

---

[145] Gratian, dist. 86, cap. 24 [Friedberg, 1:303].

[146] Gratian: causa 24, q. 3, cap. 32 [Friedberg, 1:999]; and causa 11, q. 3, cap. 100 [Friedberg, 1:671].

[147] Thus S. Thomas, *Summa Theologiae*, II^a II^{ae}, q. 62, art. 7, corp. [*Opera*, 9:58]; and his commentary on *IV Sententiarum*, dist. 15, q. 1, art. 5, qu^a 3 [*Opera*, Parma, 7-2:713–14]. *Digest:* lib. 26, tit. 7, lex 5, #3 [Krueger, 1:378b]; and lib. 43, tit. 16, lex 1, #12 [Krueger, 1:736a]; and lib. 50, tit. 17, lex 152, #1 and lex 180 [Krueger, 1:924b, 925b]. Also *Sext*, lib. 5, tit. 12, i.e., "De regulis iuris," reg. 72 [Friedberg, 2:1124]. [Following these citations which are germane to the par. above, Las Casas adds two full pages of supporting law citations from Roman and canon law, and the commentators Baldus and Bartolus.]

essential to causing the criminal damage. Innocent and other authors give the reason for the difference. It is because counsel covers every aspect of the criminal behavior, while aid does not, it is restricted to the job for which it is offered. So counselors of war to convert sin grievously, more than the rest, except for the instigators.

Second. Counsel is consent to a thing. Consent to a wicked, an unjust thing, is the cause of the thing when the thing is carried out because of the counsel. Example: The military counsel an unjust war; the government considers it; the government consents to it. The consent is the cause of the unjust war. Those who counsel an unjust war sin mortally, a graver sin than the rest, for the reasons stated.

Third. Whoever does a criminal thing freely, consents to sin, sins, and so is the cause of the criminal damage done to anyone through the criminal thing. But the counselor is an essential cause of whatever is done by the one who acts on his counsel, that is clear from 2 *Physics*. That person sins mortally, but those who counsel war are of this kind. Therefore, etc.

Psalm 56:5 supports the judgment just made. "Men! Even their teeth are bows and arrows, even their tongues a sharp sword." Augustine leans on this text, to prove that they are their brothers' killers who talk their brothers into doing evil. He says: "When you talk someone into a crime, do not think you have not murdered. You murder your brother if you talk him into a crime. So you may know you are a murderer, listen to the Psalmist: "Men! . . ." Augustine also says, "A dangerous deception it is to think the murderers are only those who do the murder and not also those whose counsel, deceit, and backing snuffed out the victims." And Augustine adds at the end of the chapter: "Let them also do penance for murder who counselled bloodshed, if they wish to save their souls."[148] So it is clear what guilt God lays on those who counsel the evil done.

THEREFORE THE GUILTY MUST MAKE RESTORATION

On peril of losing their souls, all who start wars of conversion, all who will in the future, all who assist in any way that we just said, all are bound to restore to the devastated pagan peoples whatever they took in war, permanent or perishable, and make up for whatever they destroyed. Make up totally.

---

[148] Gratian, causa 33, q. 3, i.e., "Tractatus de Penitentia," dist. 1, cap. 27 and cap. 23 [Friedberg, 1:1164, 1163].

Four proofs are required: One, all are bound to restitution; two, bound on peril of their souls; three, bound to total restitution, i.e., each one must restore everything; four, bound by all the damage done.

The first proof runs this way. It is unjust to take from one or many people what is theirs, or to damage them. Restitution is simply putting people back in possession or control of their own things. Restitution rights the balance of justice. It comes under commutative justice which consists in a certain equilibrium. Restitution then implies the return of something taken unjustly, so that the balance is back by the return of the thing, and justice is kept. So it follows that someone who took something unjustly from someone else must give it back to preserve justice.

It is true of them all who made or will make wars of conversion on pagan peoples, that they stole those peoples' goods great and small—chattel, territory, jurisdiction, rank, prestige, wife, child, freedom for self and family, etc., what we are wont to consider as goods needed for life. It is true that they did cruel damage, irreparable damage to those peoples. Then it follows that they are all bound to restore the goods and make up for the damage, if such can be done, so the balance of justice is kept—a thing returned for a thing taken. And the people, the victimized, the ruined, robbed people, restored to the possession and disposition of their chattel, territory, prestige and all else they had. And as a result, the justice due them is paid, the goods they owned restored.

Each one's own, we say, is what is essential to him or her, by the will of Divine Wisdom—i.e., a human being must have limbs, must have dominion over lesser animals. And God also submits to justice, giving to each his or her own, according to the requirements of nature and life-situation.[149]

And Cicero says in *De Officiis:*

> Much property is private due to long time occupation—settlers of once unowned land, or claimers, those who took over by war, by legal means, by a contract, by a deal, by luck, by any other like claim. If you grant this, then a moral person must act justly not only towards his personal property but towards others' property and the community's—i.e., he uses the communal as communal, the personal as personal. Whoever wants to take the communal as personal violates social justice.[150]

---

[149] S. Thomas teaches this in *Summa Theologiae,* Ia: q. 21, art. 1, ad 3m [*Opera,* 4:258–9]; q. 22, art. 4, corp. [*Opera,* 4:269]; and q. 19, art. 5, ad 3m [*Opera,* 4:240].

[150] Lib. 1, cap. 5 [sic: cap. 7, #21. Loeb ed., p. 22. The following par. is Las Casas' interpretation of Cicero's text, although the Ms wrongly closes quote there.].

Communal goods are somehow mine and yours. They are mine in that I can use them. They are yours in that I cannot use them as I use my own, assuming exclusive right to them. Whoever wants to usurp full rights to someone else's goods against that someone's will, without exchanging something of his own in payment, is going to violate social justice. If we have chattel we own by right or by law, no one can justly take it from us. And Aristotle says in 5 *Ethics* 4 that whoever tries to take something against the will of its owner and against the law is called unjust and must be forced by a judge to make restitution.[151]

It is true that territories, regions, kingdoms, ranks, jurisdictions, children, wives, chattel, and anything else we can count as a 'good' belong by right to pagans who never met us or harmed us, the ones we wage wars on, belong by right according to the needs of nature and conditions of life. It is true that these things belong to them by ordination of Divine Wisdom, and are personal goods privately held, and communal goods communally held. And it is true that those who start such wars, or have a hand in them in any way, usurp all these goods through violence and against their owners' will. They violate social justice. They must be forced to pay for what they took so justice may be served. They are therefore obliged to restitution.

Next, they are bound on peril of losing their souls. So that without restitution, without complete restoral, they cannot be saved. This we have to prove. There are six proofs.

First proof. It is impossible for someone to be saved without serving justice. That is clear from previous proofs and from St. Thomas.[152] So it follows, etc.

Second proof. Mortal sin must be quit; the soul is at stake. No one can stay a minute in mortal sin, as Ecclesiasticus 21:2 puts it: "Shun sin as you would a snake." It is not the only mortal sin to take and steal what belongs to someone else against his will, or do damage to him during the commission of the crime. It is a further mortal sin to keep the goods stolen against their owner's will, even for a moment. The keeping continues the damage done, furthers the injustice. So the criminal stays in mortal sin until he gives the stolen goods back and repairs what damage he can.

The reason why the robber does harm or an injustice to another, and therefore sins, is that the act of robbery is against the owner's will. If the robber keeps what he robbed after the fact—still against the owner's will—the damage continues, the injustice, the injury. As a

---

[151] [McKeon, 1007–10.]

[152] S. Thomas, *Summa Theologiae,* IIa IIae, q. 62, art. 2 corp. [*Opera,* 9:43].

result, the robber is still in mortal sin. But everyone is obliged to quit a state of mortal sin right away, and so right away a robber must restore the things he took and stole. To restore stolen goods is to cease sinning because the sin is the direct result of keeping the stolen goods against the owner's will.

Third proof. We are bound, on peril of losing our souls, by everything in God's commandments, as Matthew 19:17 says it: "If you wish to enter eternal life, keep the commandments." But God's command binds us to restore whatever we stole, as Exodus 20:15 says: "Do not steal." Every theft and all damage done a neighbor fall under that general prohibition.[153] But the retention of stolen goods harms the owner more than the theft, it stands to reason. To restore stolen property is a matter of saving one's soul.

Fourth proof. Take a man who makes a definite decision to steal. He is instantly guilty, worthy of eternal damnation, even if he later decides not to, or rejects the first decision, unless he placates God with heartfelt sorrow. The same is true on our topic. So also in the case of someone who incurs the obligation to restore property he took from someone else unjustly, violently—took it himself or through an agent and kept it—or harmed his neighbor in any way. Such a man is not free of the obligation unless he or his agent restores what must be restored —or otherwise receives a pardon freely given from the owner—and makes up for the damage that harmed the owner. If he skips the first— restitution—he cannot be saved, but is surely damned. Likewise if he skips the second—reparation—he will not be saved. So restitution is required on peril of losing the soul.

Fifth proof. Through the authoritative teaching of St. Paul—indeed of Christ!—in Romans 13:7 comes this: "Pay all of them their due, taxes to whom taxes are due, revenue to whom revenue is due, honor to whom honor is due, respect to whom respect is due." At the end he adds the negative precept: "Owe no one anything." That is, you sin against God if you retain contrary to another's will what you owe that other. Holy people teach the same.

And in Leviticus 19:13: "Do not keep your workers' wages until daybreak." St. Thomas says this passage applies to all other cases of restitution, the same issue is at work in them all.[154] The conclusion: Someone is in a constant state of mortal sin so long as he keeps an-

---

[153] Cf. Gratian, causa 14, q. 5, cap. 13 [Friedberg, 1:741]; and S. Thomas, *Summa Theologiae*, II[a] II[ae], q. 122, art. 6, 2[m] [*Opera*, 9:487].

[154] *Summa Theologiae*, II[a] II[ae], q. 62, art. 8, "Sed contra" [*Opera*, 9:59–60].

other's goods against the owner's will, and could give them back, but refuses, or doesn't really want to, though refusal is the worse of the two.

Sixth proof. Also from authority—Augustine to Macedonius—it is written: "If a stolen object, the cause of sin, can be returned and is not, penance for the sin is a fake, not real, and the sin is not forgiven until the stolen object is returned."[155] And: "You must make satisfaction by right, if you did culpable damage or caused injury or aided others to injure, or did the same but out of incompetence or carelessness. . . ."[156] And participants are ordered in appropriate terms to give back every single thing they took and kept through violence in an unjust war—the key word here being 'unjust.' And teachers of canon law say that the Church can compel, and directly, those who instigate an unjust war, and those who wage it, to restitution of those things they took and kept—because they got them by a rupture, a ruin of the peace, got them by sin.[157]

The second reason: Those who destroy the peace work against charity. They work against the cardinal precept of God. With good reason then God's Vicar takes cognizance of what they do.[158] There is a fine text that shows how breaking the peace comes under the judgment of a bishop or any ecclesiastical judge. It says:

> We order bishops to look only to God and to the salvation of their people, to put aside any laxness, to bend every effort, every suasion in common toward maintaining a firm peace, and to be deterred from it by nothing, love or hate. Whoever is found lax in the work of peace, does damage to his high office.[159]

Hostiensis says that judgment pertains to the Church as to whether a war is just or unjust when there is a condition of peace or treaty. The law further says that if a ruler injures a subject, the matter is to be brought to the bishop. Hostiensis also says that war is always presumed unjust, prima facie, on the part of the one who promotes it,

---

[155] Gratian, causa 14, q. 6, cap. 1 [Friedberg, 1:742–3].

[156] Gratian, causa 33, quaestio 3, i.e., "Tractatus de Penitentia," dist. 5, cap. 6 [Friedberg, 1:1241].

[157] *Decretals:* lib. 2, tit. 24, cap. 29 [Friedberg, 2:371–72]; also lib. 2, tit. 1, cap. 13 [Friedberg, 2:242–44], which clarifies the point. [We have omitted Las Casas' interpretation of this particular case.]

[158] As noted in *Decretals,* lib. 2, tit. 2, cap. 8 [Friedberg, 2:250]; and lib. 1, tit. 34, cap. 1 [Friedberg, 2:203].

[159] Gratian, dist. 90, cap. 11 [Friedberg, 1:315].

and that the burden of proof falls on the one who says the war is just, not on the one who says it is unjust, and there he puts his argument. Hostiensis says: "The booty of an unjust war must be given back."[160]

The third reason. We had to prove that participants in wars of conversion were bound to restitution, each and every one for the whole. This is clear from the maxim of the doctors of the Church, especially St. Thomas: "Whoever is the cause of unjust appropriation or damage is bound to restitution."[161] The participants, all and each, are causes or accomplices of the war we spoke of; and so, of unjust appropriation of whatever they took, and of the damage deriving from all the evils the pagans suffer, suffer unjustly. This is already proven. So each and every one is bound to restitution for the whole.

The minor premise is clearly proven, and the conclusion stands because the obligation to restitution follows on someone being the cause of the theft or the damage. In this instance, it affects those whose operations touched on all the unjust appropriations, all the damages done. They were the direct cause of the decision and the action in which all the goods were taken, all the damage inflicted, even though some were but partially involved. So their causality touched on all that happened. But causality of that kind—doing the ordering, doing the advising, doing the battling, doing things like these—touches on every good stolen, every evil inflicted. It is like a single decision, a single operation, even if individuals were partial causes by themselves. So each and every one is bound for the whole.

It is as if someone offends a ruler in such way that there is a just cause for war, then someone else offends the ruler in the same way, and a people is devastated due to both offenses: the offenders are equally bound to make good on all the harm done. That is why the law says:

> If two or more have stolen one log which a man by himself could not, we must call both guilty of the whole theft, even though one alone could not take it away. Thus we apply the law: Each one cannot be called guilty of part of the theft, but both of the whole theft, thus both are accountable for the whole.[162]

---

[160] See Hostiensis' commentary on the two decretals cited above in the statement of our sixth reason [notes 120 and 121], and also on the *Sext,* lib. 5, tit. 4, cap. 1 [Friedberg, 2:1080. Cf. Henricus Segusio, Cardinalis Hostiensis, *In secundum Decretalium librum commentaria,* Venice, 1581, fol. 136, and fol. 28.]. Here Hostiensis also cites the Authenticum, "Ut differentes iudices," section "Si contigerit," collatio 9 [i.e., Novella 86, cap. 4, Krueger, 3:421b] on the bishop's role of protecting the victim.

[161] *Summa Theologiae,* II* II**, q. 62, art. 7, corp. [*Opera,* 9:58].

[162] This is supported by various laws of the *Digest:* lib. 9, tit. 2, lex 51 [Krueger, 1:162b]; lib. 47, tit. 7, lex 6 [Krueger, 1:826b], and tit. 10, lex 34 [Krueger, 1:835b]; lib.

Likewise the law holds that if the group drops the log and the log crushes one of them, all are held responsible by the Aquileian law.[163] The laws just cited refer to the penalty all have to bear together. Nonetheless, in the forum of conscience, all must make restitution for the entirety if without them the crime would not have been done, even though they got none of the loot or did none of the harm themselves. If the crime would have been done anyway, then these others are no longer held totally responsible. We gave the reason earlier.

There is a fourth element in the corollary which must be explicated. The accomplices are responsible for all the damages: the hurts, the harms, the wounds, the deaths, the slaughters, dismemberments, robberies, lootings, losses of authority and status and liberty; the famine, the thirst, the exile, the expulsion, the flight, the ghost towns; the adulteries, debaucheries, rapes, missing wives, missing children; the damnation of the soul above all else (the invaders took away the chance to do penance in space and time). The accomplices are responsible for every other kind of wrack and ruin pagans undergo because of wars to convert them, beyond the ones we listed. They must do more than make restitution.

Though this point is clear from earlier proofs, nonetheless I want to prove it further. As evidence, consider first what Aristotle argues, and St. Thomas.[164] The imbalance that violates justice happens in two ways: one with respect to things external to a person, as when one keeps hold of another's property; the other, with respect to what one does, what one suffers, as when a person strikes another a violent blow.

Sometimes the two are separate, that is self-evident, sometimes together, as in the case of someone who does a violence which causes another harm and humiliation, e.g., he steals someone else's wife. In the light of this, righting the balance of justice means two things. Restoring the balance of external things is called restitution. Restoring the balance of what is done, what is suffered, is called satisfaction. There can sometimes be satisfaction distinct from any restitution, e.g., when someone apologizes to a neighbor for saying slanderous things about him. There can sometimes be restitution without satisfaction, the re-

---

47, tit. 2, lex 21, #9 [Krueger, 1:816b] [*N.B.* Here we unscramble the Latin text where the two quotations about the stolen tree are interrupted by the example of the ruler, perhaps through a copyist's error.]

[163] *Digest,* lib. 9, tit. 2, lex 11, #4 [Krueger, 1:157a].

[164] Thus Aristotle, 5 *Ethics* [McKeon, 1002-22]: and S. Thomas' commentary [*Opera,* 47:263-329]. Also S. Thomas on *IV Sentences,* dist. 15, q. 1, art. 5, qua 1. [*Opera,* Parma, 7-2:713].

turn of a loan. Sometimes there is need of both, e.g., when someone takes another's property violently.

Those who caused the wars we speak of did the two things. Through the war they waged they extracted from the New World pagans their property and whatever else they owned—household furnishings, to the smallest thing, purely physical things we would call them—then things far more precious to them: wife, child, kinfolk, authority, dignity, honor, men and women servants, every kind of freedom. They did all this through violence replete with massive injury, mockery, brutality, with damage beyond reckoning. They upset the balance of justice in the two ways, in external things and in what one does or suffers. They are therefore obliged to restitution, and beyond it to satisfaction, for the harm, the wounds, the humiliations, for the whole host of evils the pagans suffered.

Here we must repeat what we proved in the preceding section. The 'goods' required for life are proffered by nature and by law; they belong to someone by right, so parents, children, spouses, friends and such like are considered ours by right. To treat these possessions well or ill is to treat ourselves well or ill, as Aristotle says in 5 *Ethics*. He says further that whatever ill is inflicted on us to our harm or hurt, or inflicted on our possessions, is like unto a deal forced on us. Among the 'forced deals'—some without our knowledge, some with, and violent—Aristotle lists theft, incest, poisoning, cheating, fraud, ambush, perjury. All clandestine. He lists under 'violent' and 'coercive': brutality, bondage, imprisonment, enslavement, death, separation from parent or child, being cursed, being called names.

Through the power of the court, Aristotle says, the judge or the law should restore the balance of justice by correcting the offender, or condemning him, punishing him. For example, the man with the more, the man who harmed another, on his own or through an agent, who took what belonged to another, should have less through the condemnation, the punishment. In contrast, the injured party, the one with less, should have more through the punishment or satisfaction decreed; otherwise, the profit accrues to the criminal, the loss accrues to the victim.

At least that is the way the criminal and victim assess the profit and loss. Granted a murderer gets no real profit from a killing, but rather a terrible loss, he could be hung for it, yet he gets a good he values. He thinks to get for the killing more than a thousand ducats. The victim loses more than ducats. So the killer profits, the victim loses, as we understand it. Then Aristotle says that the balance between profit and loss is struck by a just correction, or a punishment which consists of correction. We appeal to a judge as often as a dispute arises. Appeal to a judge means appeal to law, because a judge ought to be the soul of law. People want a judge to balance things, to balance out disputes through punishment.

Since the goods needed for life belong to those who have them, since the conspirators in wars to convert do grave harm to those they attack, it is clear the latter must make compensation, make satisfaction. If a judge were to sit on the case, he would have to punish the guilty to restore the balance of justice.

Aristotle, in the place cited, provides a third proof in the following words.

> Whoever harms or hurts another unjustly, seems to take from that other a thing that then becomes the source of the harm, the hurt. To be harmed, to be hurt, comes down to a loss of what one ought to have of what one needs. And the one who does the harming has more—as we explained. So, to restore the balance of justice, the one who profits from victimizing a victim and has the more—the perpetrator of the harmful situation—is therefore bound to make restitution to the one who suffered, the victim of the harm, of everything that victim lost or suffered. All must make good on the humiliation the victim suffered. All unjust harmfulness is classified under "Harm Received," whatever the case. What has to be considered formally is the "harm" which is called "received"—whether it is done by arrest, arson, separation, or by any other action. Someone else is always harmed by these actions. That is true because one takes from an unwilling owner what belongs to him, even if not to give to someone else but to destroy it.[165]

Whoever injures another, therefore, is bound to satisfaction, not because he profited but because the other took some damage. That is the basis, the origin of the duty to make satisfaction and/or restitution, namely, that someone was unjustly harmed. This way the agent is classified under the name of injurer. As a result, he is bound to make satisfaction for every ounce of damage.

Whoever purposes to harm another is an injurer when the harm results from his activity, and is therefore bound to make satisfaction according to the norm of balance, i.e., total satisfaction. Example: If an agent does the damage by flattening someone's house, he is bound to make good to the victim, in comparable worth, the exact cost of the

---

[165] Aristotle, *Ethics,* lib. 5 [McKeon, 1006–12].

house. If the agent took the victim's life, or limb, or liberty, reputation, dignity, whatever, and there is no way to restore them in kind, the agent is bound to make restitution with money or with some honoring, according to the state in life of each person, the proportion to be decided by good people, i.e., prudent and learned. It suffices to make a restitution that is possible, not one that is not, as is clear in the case of honors due to God, to parents, so Aristotle says.[166]

Those who cause the wars of conversion afflict peaceful pagans with their wars, pagans who did them no harm. They afflict them grievously, outrageously in the crucial things of life—they take life and limb from men/women, young/old, great/small, prince/pauper—they take freedom, reducing multitudes to slavery, the very worst of all evils they can do them, by far, utterly worse than any other pain or suffering. They take the space and time the pagans need to do penance, to turn toward God. They do it by murdering the pagans while they are still unconverted and lacking faith and sacrament. So we can say they take salvation of soul away from these pagans. Perhaps, if the pagans had lived, some or all, they would have been saved, by the grace of God, in line with what Christ said: "Because if the wonders had been done in Tyre and Sidon, . . . they would have long since done penance in sackcloth and ashes." And: "If they had been done in Sodom, Sodom might still exist today." (Matthew 11:21, 23) Augustine concludes from these statements of Jesus, in *On the Gift of Perseverance:* "It is evident from the passages that some people have in their souls, as if by nature, a gift for understanding the divine. By it they are moved toward the faith if their minds pick up the right words or see the right signals."[167]

Tell me, what satisfaction will such damnable men make for the multitudes of souls who burn now in fiery torment forever, put there by the godless cruelty of their conquerors? How will they make up for the lesser evils—the overthrow of peoples, the emptying of places by the thousands, all the adulteries, all the kidnapings, all the rapes, all the violations of wives and daughters of the elders, pagans though they be, all the splittings-off of parents from sons and daughters, all the abase-

---

[166] 8 *Ethics* [McKeon, 1058–76]. Cf. S. Thomas, *Summa Theologiae,* II[a] II[ae], q. 62, art. 2, corp. and 1[m] and 2[m]; art 4, corp.; and art. 6, corp. [*Opera*, 9:42–43; 50; 53–54]. Also in his *IV Sentenciarum,* dist. 15, q. 1, art. 5, qua. 1, 2, 3, and 4, per totum [*Opera*, Parma, 7-2:713–15]. Also Petrus de Palude on dist. 15, q. 2, art. 3 [*Scriptum in quartum Sententiarum,* Venice, 1493, 68va–70vb. Two other commentators are omitted here since Las Casas cites them later.]. Finally, Adrian on *IV Sententiarum,* "De restitutione," at "Aggredior casus specialis" and passim. [Adrian VI, *Quaestiones de sacramentis in quartum Sententiarum,* Rome, 1522, "De Restit." at fol. 48rb-va, and passim to 52rb.]

[167] [*Catena Aurea*—S. Thomas, *Opera,* Parma 11:147b.]

ments of the natural rulers from status and dignity, all the enslavements, deprivations of freedom for so many free people, all the injuries, all the insults, infinite in number, by which they ruined those poor wretches?

Indeed experts say the more precious the thing that is taken wrongfully from someone, the more the taker is bound to satisfaction. Whence Scotus says that whoever murders someone is bound to accept the death penalty a judge would sentence him to for the murder. Or with the remainder of his life do something to honor God, like working to spread the faith or entering a religious order or doing some pious work.[168]

If the man murdered supported a wife, children, other people, the murderer must then support them for the length of time the murdered man would probably have lived. And Richard says, among other things, that if someone who sold another unjustly into slavery has not the wherewithal or power to buy him free, he is obliged to become a slave in the other's stead under the requirements of restitution/satisfaction, so the other can regain original freedom. The culprit is bound further to make satisfaction for all that the victim and the victim's wife, children, close relatives, suffered from the enslavement—even to asking the victim's forgiveness, humbly, for the offense, for the pain, for the damages, in accord with what was said earlier.[169]

It is utterly impossible for culprits in the previous cases, not to mention other cases, to make satisfaction. What will they do them, the wretched wagers of war to convert, the counselors who are principals along with the rest, one with the rest in sin, and obliged to satisfaction, the armed soldiery, the support people, the helping hands? They will not be able to make even the least satisfaction in their lifetime for what was done. Would to God they could be sorry for their hideous crimes before they die!

To frighten them back to their senses, and maybe God will then forgive them, I want to interject here some words of John Gerson— words I know are tailored to the culprits I described, more than to

---

[168] [See John Duns Scotus, *Quaestiones in quartum Sententiarum*—in *Opera Omnia,* Paris, 1894, 18:357–90. Here Scotus comments on Peter Lombard's problem: "Is someone who harms another in their very life, life of body or soul, bound to whatever restitution is possible to be truly penitent?" Scotus lists Richard of Middleton and Petrus de Palude on the same problem. Las Casas expands the list to include Adrian (note 165) and Gerson (note 169).]

[169] On *IV Sententiarum,* same dist. 15, art. 5, q. 2 and 3, see Ricardo [Richard of Middleton, *In quartum Sententiarum theologicarum Petri Lombardi,* Lyons, 1527, n-1ra-va, s.f.].

others, i.e., those who have harmed their neighbors anywhere and evidence proves it. In a sermon he wrote about "Repentance," for Holy Thursday, Gerson says: "There are four sins that stain so badly they can scarcely be cleansed. The first: The ruin of another's morality." Gerson says of this:

> Listen to Berengarius' dying words. "The Lord Jesus Christ will confront me this day, to award me heaven, as I hope, for my repentance, or hell, which I fear, for my ruin of others, those I could not bring back to the truth." And those who take demonic delight in leading others to damnation, especially the young, their own fate should horrify them. I am doubtful if such like could ever do sufficient penance. Their own damnation should have been enough for them. The second: To cause an unjust war, i.e., to order it, to fight it, to urge it, etc. The third: Improper representation or slander in which inheritances or reputations are lost. The fourth: Unjust bestowal of rank, through simony or other means.[170]

So whoever caused wars to convert, whatever way they caused them, we named many, are guilty of the sins we just cited—all our proofs show this. Therefore they are bound to make satisfaction, the kind described. They can never do it in this life. So they must fear the punishment that waits for them after they die.[171]

With these words I conclude my book *On the Only Way of Calling All People to a Living Faith.* I offer undying thanks to God Immortal Three and One Who gave me life, Who preserved it, Who graced it, Who supplied what it needed to come to its fruition. Amen.

TO GOD BE PRAISE.
TO THE LIVING, PEACE. TO THE DEAD, REPOSE.*
"When someone's ways please God, God makes even their enemies to be at peace with them" [Proverbs 16:7].

---

[170] [Jean Gerson, *Opera,* Paris, 1606, tom. 1, pars. 2a, 583, at C, D, E, and F.]

[171] [At this point, the scribe has inserted, probably from Las Casas' marginal note, a fourth proof of the general principle of restitution. It is *Decretals,* lib. 5, tit. 26, cap. 9—Friedberg, 2:880.]

* [To my sister Peggy, repose. 1991. To her husband Bobby, peace. 1975.]

BIOGRAPHICAL ADDENDA

ADDENDUM I:
LAS CASAS' ACCOUNT OF
HIS PROPHETIC CALL

INTRODUCTORY NOTE

Here we present the famous passage from Las Casas' own History
of the Indies *in which he relates the Cuban experiences that led him to
take up the cause of the Indians. It is important to read the text in toto
(A below), so as to avoid the false constructions that have come from
taking the central event out of context. These misinterpretations are
shocking: assertions that Las Casas was a conquistador and a heartless
encomendero, no better than the rest; that he underwent a Damascus
Road conversion, became penitent and made restitution by surrender-
ing his encomienda; that his return to Spain was connected with fac-
tional politics among the Spaniards on the islands and the return of
Diego Columbus.*

*Next we give the moving speech that "Micer Bartolomé" gave
before young King Charles, in which he describes his call (B below). We
conclude with a poignant extract from Las Casas' will in which he
professes his lifelong fidelity to his call from God (C below). Las Casas
never called himself a prophet, though in a 1546 sermon, in the cathedral of Mexico City, he told the viceroy and the Spaniards that they
wanted only to hear pleasant things from false prophets.*

*The definition of Las Casas as a prophet has taken hold in modern
scholarship. Starting with Marcel Bataillon's "Las Casas, un profeta?"*
(Revista de Occidente, *Madrid, no. 141, Dec 1974, 279–91), the
French school has adopted the idea. Compare Alain Milhou,
"Prophétisme . . . chez las Casas,"* Mélanges de la Bibliothèque Espagnole, *Paris (Madrid, 1982) 231–51; and André Saint-Lu's eloquent
preface to Philippe André-Vincent's* Bartolomé de las Casas, prophète
du nouveau monde, *Paris, 1980. Spaniards who agree include Carlos*

185

Soria, "Fray Bartolomé de las Casas, historiador, humanista, o pro-feta?" Ciencia Tomista, 101 (1974): 411–26. And especially Isacio Pérez Fernández in two analytical articles: "El perfil profético del Padre Las Casas," Studium, 15 (1975): 281–359; and "La fidelidad del Padre Las Casas a su carisma profético," Studium, 16 (1976): 65–109.

A. LAS CASAS' ACCOUNT OF THE ACTUAL EXPERIENCES
(From his *Historia de las Indias,* lib. 3, cap. 78 end,
and cap. 79; chapter breaks omitted, captions added.)

1. Seeing Conditions in Cuba

. . . We told how Diego Velásquez, in charge of Cuba for the admiral, marked out five places for settlement where all the Spaniards on the island were to live in groups. There was one already populated, Baracoa. The Indians who lived near each settlement were divided up and given to the Spaniards. Each Spaniard had an itch for gold and a narrow conscience. They had no thought that those natives were made of flesh and blood. They put them to work in mines and at other projects the Indians could accomplish as slave labor, put them to work so promptly, so pitilessly that in a few days' time many native deaths showed the brutality of Spanish treatment. The loss of people on Cuba was quicker, fiercer, during the early period than it was elsewhere. The explanation: the Spaniards roamed the island *pacifying* it. They took many Indians from the villages as servants for themselves. The Spaniards reaped but did not sow. As to the villagers, some fled; some, nervous and fearful, cared only to escape being killed as many another was killed. The fields were picked clean of food and abandoned.

Since greed fed the Spaniards, as I said, they cared nothing for sowing and reaping food; they cared only for reaping gold they had not sown, however they could, eating whatever scraps of food they could scrounge up. And they set men and women to work without food enough to live on, never mind work on, in the mines. It is a true story, one I told elsewhere, that a Spaniard recounted in my presence and in that of several others, as if he were telling a fine way of doing things. He had his allotted Indians raise so many thousand mound-rows. (That is how they grow [the root] cassava bread is made from.) He sent them every third day, or two on, two off, to the fields to eat whatever growth they found. With what they then had in their bellies he made them work another two or three days in the mines. He gave them not another bite to eat. Farm work means digging the whole day, a far harder job than tilling our vineyards and food gardens home in Spain. It means raising into mounds the earth they dig, three to four feet square, three to four hands high. And not with spades or hoes that are provided, but with pole-length, fire-hardened sticks.

Hunger, having nothing to eat, being put to hard labor, caused death among these peoples more quickly, more violently, than in any other place. The Spaniards took healthy men and women to do mine and other work. They left behind in the villages only the sick and the old, left no one to help them, care for them. So the sick and old died from anguish and age as well as from mortal hunger. I sometimes heard, back then when I traveled the island, as I would enter a village, voices calling from inside the huts. When I went in to find out what they wanted, they answered, "*Food!*" "*Food!*" There was not a man or a woman able to stand on two legs that they did not drag off to the mines. As for the new mothers with their small boy and girl children, their breasts dried: they had so little to eat, so much work, they had no milk left, the babies died. That was the cause of the deaths of seven thousand baby boys and girls in the space of three months. The event was described in a report to the Catholic king by a creditable person who had investigated it. Another event also occurred back then. An official of the king got three hundred Indians as his allotment. He was in such a hurry putting them to work in the mines and at the rest of his jobs that at the end of three months only a tenth of those Indians remained alive.

The crushing of Indians took this route and grew in ferocity each day. As greed grew and grew, so did the number of Indian dead. [While this was going on] Padre Bartolomé de las Casas (mentioned briefly above) was very busy looking after his own holdings. As the others did, he sent his allotted Indians to the mines to dig gold, to the fields to plant crops, profiting from his Indians as much as he could, though he was always careful to maintain them well in every way possible, and treat them kindly, and alleviate their hardships. But he took no more care than the others to recall that these were pagan peoples and that he had an obligation to teach them Christian doctrine and gather them into the bosom of the Church.

2. Hearing the call in Cuba

Diego Velásquez and the group of Spaniards with him left the port of Xagua to go and found a settlement of Spaniards in the province, where they established the town called Sancti Espiritus. Apart from Bartolomé de las Casas, there was not a single cleric or friar on the whole island, except for one in the town of Baracoa. The feast of Pentecost was coming up. So he agreed to leave his home on the Arimao River (accent on the penult) a league from Xagua where his holdings were and go say mass and preach for them on that feast. Las Casas looked over the previous sermons he had preached to them on that feast and his other sermons for that season. He began to meditate on some passages of Sacred Scripture. If my memory serves me, the first and most important was from Ecclesiasticus 34:18 ff.:

> Unclean is the offering sacrificed by an oppressor. [Such] mockeries of the unjust are not pleasing [to God]. The Lord is pleased only by those who keep to the way of truth and justice. The Most High does not accept the gifts of unjust people, He does not look well upon their offerings. Their sins will not be expiated by repeat-sacrifices. *The one whose sacrifice comes from the goods of the poor is like one who kills his neighbor. The one who sheds blood and the one who defrauds the laborer are kin and kind.*

He began to reflect on the misery, the forced labor the Indians had to undergo. He was helped in this by what he had heard and experienced on the island of Hispaniola, by what the Dominicans preached continually—no one could, in good conscience, hold the Indians in encomienda, and those friars would not confess and absolve any who so held them—a preaching Las Casas had refused to accept. One time he wanted to confess to a religious of St. Dominic who happened to be in the vicinity. Las Casas held Indians on that island of Hispaniola, as indifferent and blind about it as he was on the island of Cuba. The religious refused him confession. Las Casas asked him why. He gave the reason. Las Casas objected with frivolous arguments and empty explanations, seemingly sound, provoking the religious to respond, "Padre, I think the truth has many enemies and the lie has many friends." Then Las Casas offered him the respect due his dignity and reputation because the religious was a revered and learned man, much more so than the padre, but he took no heed of the confessor's counsel to let his Indians go. Yet it helped him greatly to recall his quarrel later, and also the confession he made to the religious, so as to think more about the road of ignorance and danger he was on, holding Indians as others did, confessing without scruple those who held or wanted to hold Indians, though he did not do so for long. But he had heard many confessions on that island of Hispaniola, from people who were in the same mortal sin.

He spent some days thinking about the situation, each day getting surer and surer from what he read concerning what was legal and what was actual, measuring the one by the other, until he came to the same truth by himself. Everything in these Indies that was done to the Indians was tyrannical and unjust. Everything he read to firm up his judgment he found favorable, and he used to say strongly that from the very moment he began to dispel the darkness of that ignorance, he never read a book in Latin or Spanish—a countless number over the span of forty-two years—where he didn't find some argument or authority to prove or support the justice of those Indian peoples, and to condemn the injustices done to them, the evils, the injuries.

3. Responding in Cuba

He then made a decision to preach his conclusion. But since his holding Indians meant holding a contradiction of his own preaching, he determined to give them up so as to be free to condemn allotments, the whole system of forced labor, as unjust and tyrannical, and to hand his Indians back to Governor Diego Velásquez. They were better off under the padre's control, to be sure. He had treated them with greater respect, would be even more respectful in the future. He knew that giving them up meant they would be handed over to someone who would brutalize them, work them to death, as someone did ultimately. Granted, he would give them a treatment as good as a father would give his children. Yet, since he would preach that no one could in good conscience hold Indians, he could never escape people mocking back at him, "You hold Indians nonetheless. Why not release them? You say holding them is tyranny!" So he decided to give them up completely.

To get a better understanding of all that happened, it would be right here to recall the close friendship the padre had with a certain Pedro de la Rentería, a prudent, deeply Christian man. We spoke of him earlier somewhat [saying that he was the only encomendero I remember who cared for the Indian soul]. They were not just friends, but partners also in the estate. They received together their allotments of natives. They had decided together that Pedro de la Rentería should go to the island of Jamaica where Pedro had a brother. The purpose: to bring back pigs to fatten and corn to plant, plus other things not found in Cuba since it was cleaned out, a fact already established. For the voyage they chartered a government ship for two thousand castellanos. So, since Pedro de la Rentería was away, and since the padre had decided to give up his Indians and go preach what he felt obliged to preach and thus enlighten those who were deep in the darkness of ignorance, he went on a day to Governor Diego Velásquez. He told him what he thought about his own situation, the situation of the governor, and of the rest of the Spaniards. He stated that no one in that situation could be saved, and he stated that he intended to preach this to escape the danger, and to do what his priesthood required. Thus he was determined to give back his Indians to the governor, to keep charge of them no longer. Therefore the governor should consider them available and should dispose of them as he wished. But the padre asked the favor that the business be kept secret, that the governor give the Indians to no one else until Rentería returned from the island of Jamaica where he was at the moment. The reason: the estate and the Indians they held in common might suffer harm if, before Rentería returned, the person to whom the governor gave the Indians might move in on them and the estate prematurely.

The governor was shocked at hearing such an unusual story. For one thing, that a cleric who was free to own things in the world should be of the opinion of the Dominican friars—they had first dared to think it and dared to make it known. For another, that the cleric had such a righteous scorn for temporal possessions that, having such a great aptitude for getting rich quickly, he should give it up. Especially since he had a growing reputation for being industrious: people saw him most zealous about his property and his mines, saw other acquisitive qualities in him. But the governor was mainly stunned, and answered him more out of consideration for what touched the padre in the temporal realm than for the danger in which the governor himself lived as top man in the tyranny perpetrated against the Indians on that island.

Padre, think of what you are doing. No need for scruples! It is God who wants to see you rich and prosperous. For that reason I do not allow the surrender you make of your Indians. I give you fifteen days to think it over so you can come to a better decision. After a fortnight you can come back and tell me what you will do.

The padre replied,

My Lord, I am most grateful that you want me to prosper, most grateful for all the other kindnesses your grace has done for me. But act, my Lord, as though the fortnight were over. Please God, if I ever repent of the decision I broached to you, if I ever want to hold

Indians again—and if you, for the love you have of me, should ever want to leave them with me or give them to me anew—if you accept my plea to have them, even if I wept blood, may God be the one to punish you severely, may God never forgive this sin. I ask your grace one favor, that this whole business be kept secret and that you do not allot the natives to anyone until Rentería returns, so his estate suffers no harm.

The governor promised. He kept his promise. From then on he had a far greater respect for the padre. And concerning his governance, he did many good things that touched on native matters and his own personal conduct, all due to the effect of the padre (as if he had seen him do miracles). The rest of the Spaniards on the island began to change their view of the padre from before, once they knew he had given up his natives. Such an action was considered then and always the consummate proof that could demonstrate sanctity. Such was and is the blindness of those who came out to the New World.

The padre made the secret public the following way. He was preaching on the feast day of the Assumption of Our Lady in that place where he was—[the town of Sancti Espiritus] mentioned earlier. He was explaining the contemplative and the active life, the theme of the gospel reading for the day, talking about the spiritual and corporal works of mercy. He had to make clear to his hearers their obligation to perform these works toward the native peoples they made use of so cruelly; he had to blame the merciless, negligent, mindless way they lived off those natives. For which it struck him as the right moment to reveal the secret agreement he had set up with the governor. And he said, "My Lord, I give you freedom to reveal to everyone whatever you wish concerning what we agreed on in secret—I take that freedom myself in order to reveal it to those here present." This said, he began to expose to them their own blindness, the injustices, the tyrannies, the cruelties they committed against such innocent, such gentle people. They could not save their souls, neither those who held Indians by allotment, nor the one who handed them out. They were bound by the obligation to make restitution. He himself, once he knew the danger of damnation in which he lived, had given up his Indians, had given up many other things connected with holding Indians. The congregation was stupefied, even fearful of what he said to them. Some felt compunction, others thought it a bad dream, hearing bizarre statements such as: No one could hold Indians in servitude without sinning. As if to say they could not make use of beasts of the field! Unbelievable.

B. LAS CASAS' SPEECH BEFORE YOUNG KING CHARLES
(From *Historia de las Indias,* lib. 3, end of cap. 148
and cap. 149; chapter breaks omitted, captions added.)

1. Closing statement by the Bishop of Darién:

> I saw that the territory was being lost. Its first governor was bad, its
> second much worse. But I saw that Your Majesty had entered that
> territory at just the right time. I decided to come and inform you of
> this out of duty to King and ruler. The hope of any remedy lies in
> you. As for the Indians, they are servile *by nature,* judging by the
> knowledge I have from the area I come from, and from what I saw on
> my journey in other areas. . . .

2. "Micer Bartolomé" responds from his own experience:

Monsignor de Xevres and the grand chancellor then rose, approached the king with the customary protocol to consult, then returned to their seats. The chancellor said to the padre: "Micer Bartolomé, His Majesty orders you to speak." Then the padre removed his biretta, made a profound bow, and spoke thusly:

> Supreme and mighty King and Ruler, I am one of the earliest to have
> gone out to the Indies. I have spent many years there. During those
> years, I have seen with my own eyes, not read in accounts that could
> be unreliable, I have felt, as if with my own hands, the cruelties
> committed there against those gentle, peaceful people, cruelties of a
> kind so great, so beastly, nothing like them was ever done in the past
> by harsh men or mindless barbarians. These cruelties had no rhyme
> or reason other than greed, the insatiable hunger and thirst for gold
> in our people.

> They did what they did in two ways. One, through unjust, cruel wars,
> against Indians, who live, with no offense to anyone, in peace, in
> their own homes, own lands. The people who died are without number, nations, races. Two, after they killed the native rulers and leading people, they put the Indians into servitude, parcelling them out
> to each other, by hundreds, by fifties, then sent them to the mines
> where, ultimately, due to unbelievable suffering at digging for gold,
> they all died. I see all those Indians doomed in these two ways wherever there are Spaniards. And one of those who helped in the tyranny was my very own father, though not anymore.

> It was the sight of all this that changed me. Not because I was a better
> Christian than someone else. It was because of an instinctive com-

passion, a grief I felt at seeing a people suffer awful oppression and injustice who deserved none of it. So I came back to the home country to inform the King, your grandfather, about the situation. I found His Highness in Placencia. I told him what I tell you now. He received me kindly, and promised reform when he got to Seville where he was headed. But he died en route. So neither my pleading nor his royal purpose brought any results. After his death, I made a presentation to the governors. They were the Cardinal of Spain, Don Fray Francisco Ximenez, and Adrian, who is now Cardinal of Tortosa. They set up, and well, everything necessary so the brutal affliction would stop and the Indians not perish. But the people assigned to carry out their provisions—to root out the evil and plant goodness and justice—were worthless. I took up the matter again, and after Your Majesty arrived, I explained it to you, and the situation would have been remedied if the first Grand Chancellor had not died in Zaragoza. I am at the same task again. And there are agents of the enemy of all virtue and goodness who, out of self-interest, would die to prevent reform. It is most important that Your Majesty understand the situation and order it remedied. Apart from how it affects your royal soul. No one of the regions you possess, nor all of them together, equal the least of those estates and goods anywhere overseas.

I know for sure that when I alert Your Majesty to that fact, I do Your Majesty one of the greatest services a loyal subject does any prince or lord in this world. I do not do it because I wish or want a reward for it or any distinction. For I do not do it to serve Your Majesty. What I say next is with all the respect and reverence which is due to such an exalted king and ruler. The fact is I would not go from here to that corner to serve Your Majesty—all due regard for the fidelity I owe as a subject—if I did not think and believe I was offering something great to God by doing so. But God is so jealous, so concerned for his own honor [creation]—it is to God alone that a creature owes honor and glory [moral behavior]—that I could not take one step in these matters, which I have laid upon my own shoulders, without causing, producing by it priceless goods and services for Your Majesty. And to reinforce what I have just said, I state, I affirm, that I renounce any reward or recompense Your Majesty could or would want to make me. If at any time, I, or someone for me, should ask for any reward, seek it directly or indirectly, Your Majesty should then not believe me in a thing I have said above. I should instead be thought a liar, a deceiver of my King and Lord.

But to move beyond this point, those Indian peoples, most powerful Lord, and the whole of the New World which is thick with throngs of them, are supremely capable of the Christian faith, of all virtue, of

civilized behavior, tractable to reason and revelation, and *by nature*
free peoples. They have native kings and lords who govern their
bodies politic. Compare what the reverend Bishop says, that the
Indians are *servile by nature,* with what the Philosopher says at the
beginning of his *Politics:* "Those who live by reason are the natural
lords and masters of others. Those lacking reason are natural servants." There is the difference of night and day between what the
Philosopher means and what the Bishop says. But even if what the
Bishop says is right, Aristotle was a pagan, and is now burning in
hell, so his teaching must be used only in such way as it fits with our
holy faith and the tradition of Christian religion. Our Christian religion is for all. It adapts itself to every people in the world. It accepts
all equally, it removes liberty from no one, sovereignty from no one,
puts no one in servitude under the ruse and rubric that they are not
free, they are *servile by nature,* as the reverend Bishop seems
to mean.

Therefore it is Your Majesty's role to root out, at the start of his
reign, from his kingdom, the tyranny—monstrous and horrible before God and the world—which causes such evil, such irreparable
harm, the damnation of a major part of the human race, [remove it]
so that the royal kingdom of Our Lord Jesus Christ, who died for
those Indian peoples, might grow through length of days.

C. EXTRACT FROM LAS CASAS' LAST WILL AND TESTAMENT
(From *Opúsculos* [*BAE,* 110], doc. 52, 539a–40a; captions and pars. added.)

The profession of faith. In the name of the Most Blessed Trinity,
Father and Son and Holy Spirit, one God and true. I, Bishop Fray
Bartolomé de las Casas, knowing that every believing Christian must
lay bare his soul at the time he comes to die, insofar as he can by the
grace of God, and knowing that many things can prevent this at the
hour of death: I wish to say solemnly before I see myself at that point
that I will live and die as I shall have lived, in the holy Catholic faith of
the Most Blessed Trinity, Father, Son, Holy Spirit, believing and holding, as indeed I do, all that the holy Church of Rome believes and
holds. I wish to live the rest of my life in that faith, right up to and
including death, and I want to die in that faith.

The call. And I testify that it was God in His goodness and mercy
who chose me as His minister—unworthy though I was—to act here at
home on behalf of all those people out in what we call the Indies, the
true possessors of those kingdoms, those territories. To act against the
unimaginable, unspeakable violence and evil and harm they have suf-

fered from our people, contrary to all reason, all justice, so as to restore them to the original liberty they were lawlessly deprived of, and get them free of death by violence, death they still suffer, they perish still the same way. Thousands of leagues of land were thusly depopulated; I witnessed a great deal of it. For almost fifty years I have done this work, in the court of the kings of Castile, back and forth between the Indies and Castile, Castile and the Indies, often, since 1514. I have done it for the sake of God alone, out of compassion at seeing the deaths of so many human beings, rational, civilized, unpretentious, gentle, simple human beings who were most apt for accepting our holy Catholic faith and its entire moral doctrine, human beings who already lived according to sound principles. As God is my witness, I had no other motive.

The prophecy. What I say next I hold as certain doctrine, I judge it certain, it is what I think the Holy Roman Church holds and values as a norm of belief for us. All that the Spaniards perpetrated against those [Indian] peoples, the robbery, the killing, the usurpation of property and jurisdiction, from kings and lords and lands and realms, the theft of things on a boundless scale and the horrible cruelties that went with that—all this was in violation of the holy and spotless law of Jesus Christ, in violation of the whole natural law, and a terrible blot on the name of Christ and the Christian faith. It was all an absolute impediment to faith, all a mortal damage to the souls and bodies of those innocent peoples. And I think that God shall have to pour out His fury and anger on Spain for these damnable, rotten, infamous deeds done so unjustly, so tyrannically, so barbarously to those people, against those people. For the whole of Spain has shared in the blood-soaked riches, some a little, some a lot, but all shared in goods that were ill-gotten, wickedly taken with violence and genocide—and all must pay unless Spain does a mighty penance. And I fear it will do so too late or not at all, because there is a blindness God permits to come over sinners great and small, but especially over those who drive us or are considered prudent and wise, who give the world orders—a blindness because of sins, about everything in general. But especially that recent blindness of understanding which for the last seventy years has proceeded to shock and scandalize and rob and kill those people overseas. A blindness that is not even today aware that such scandals to our faith, such defamations of it, such robbing and injustice and violence and slaughter and enslavement and usurpation of foreign rule and rulers, above all such devastation, such genocide of populations, have been sins, have been monumental injustices!

Bishop Fray Bartolomé de las Casas

ADDENDUM II:
LAS CASAS' PORTRAIT OF
PEDRO DE CÓRDOBA

INTRODUCTORY NOTE

Las Casas' account of the coming of Pedro de Córdoba and the first Dominicans to the New World is almost the sole source for the personal biography of the charismatic young vicar (A below). These were the friars who denounced Spanish conduct and the system in 1511, three years before Las Casas himself. Today, Córdoba would be called Las Casas' "spiritual father," though they were nearly the same age. Las Casas considered him a saint, as can be seen in the short passage that follows (B below).

Pedro de Córdoba and his followers on the islands and mainland are dubbed the "Antillean missionary current" in Daniel Ulloa's Los predicadores divididos *(Mexico City: El Colegio de México, 1977). Ulloa contrasts them with the ultra-reformist followers of Fray Domingo de Betanzos, who had defamed the Indians (Introduction above, note 37 and corresp. text), and who dominated and ultimately denatured the Dominican mission in New Spain. The Franciscans, too, were divided, with Las Casas finding strong allies among those who challenged conquistador brutality: Bishop Zumárraga, Fray Marcos de Niza, Fray Jacobo de Tastera. But their major missionary effort, lauded in Robert Ricard's* The Spiritual Conquest of Mexico *([Paris, 1933], Berkeley, 1966), approved Spanish dominion and the encomienda. Thus, Motolinía dismisses his own list of "ten plagues"—the horrors suffered by the Mexican Indians under the Spaniards—as God's punishment for prior pagan abominations!*

For a clear picture of conflicting missionary ideologies, see Paulino Castañeda Delgado, "Los métodos missionales en América: Evangelización pura o coacción?" Estudios sobre Fray Bartolomé de las Casas *(Seville, 1974), 123–89.*

A. PEDRO DE CÓRDOBA AND THE FIRST DOMINICANS
(From Las Casas, *Historia de las Indias,*
lib. 2, most of cap. 54, captions added.)

1. Córdoba's spiritual leadership

Fray Pedro de Córdoba [was] a man mature in virtue. God, Our Lord, gave him many gifts, vested him with graciousness in body and soul. He was a native of Córdoba, born of nobility and Christian. Physically tall, physically handsome. His judgment was superior, prudent, instinctively discreet, much at peace with itself. He was quite young when he entered the Order of St. Dominic. He was a student at Salamanca. It was there at St. Stephen's that he took the habit. He matured rapidly in the arts, philosophy, theology, and would have been summa cum laude if he had not gotten intense, prolonged headaches from severe practices of penance. The headaches caused him to cut back very much on his studies, to be satisfied with a modest command of the sacred sciences. Though he tempered his studies, he intensified the rigor of his penitential practices throughout the course of his life— every time the state of his health permitted it. He was a preacher, a devout and skilled one; that was among the many talents God gave him. He gave a remarkable, praiseworthy example to everyone, so inspiring were his practices of piety in the way of virtue on the quest for God. It seems certain that he departed from this life as clean of sin as on the day he was born. He was transferred from Salamanca, with other mature religious, to St. Thomas of Avila where fervor was flourishing at the time. . . .

Fray Domingo de Mendoza . . . sent the said Fray Pedro de Córdoba—twenty-eight years old then—as vicar in charge of two other friars, though they were older. He assigned also a lay brother to the group. These four members brought the Order of Preachers to Hispaniola. The lay brother later returned to Castile. That left the three— three whose lives began to permeate the place with their belief and their holiness. They were welcomed in by a good Christian who lived near town, Pedro de Lumbreras by name. He gave them a hut to live in at the edge of his place. There were no houses in those days, just small huts made of thatch. He gave them cazabi root to eat, a kind of bread poor in nourishment if eaten alone, not with meat or fish. They got but few eggs, and some fish, on rare occasions, if there was a catch. And cooked cabbage, without oil often, simply with *axi,* a pepper the natives use. There was an utter lack of Castilian products on that island. It was hard to get wheat bread or wine, even for mass. They slept on beds made of interlaced branches on notched poles covered with dry straw for a mattress. They dressed in a habit of coarse cloth and a cloak of untreated wool. Given this comfortable life and marvelous menu, they fasted seven months in a year with no break, as the Order required of them and still requires. They preached, they heard confessions with Godlike strength. They had to.

Every Spaniard on that island had perverted the Christian practices, especially the fasts and abstinences required by the Church. The Spaniards ate meat on the Sabbath, even on Fridays, even for the whole of Lent. Their slaughterhouses were going all the time, unashamedly, even religiously, as they are for Easter time. The friars through their preaching, and more through their severe penance and abstinence, brought the Spaniards to an awareness of their behavior, to give up their gluttony during the seasons and days established by the Church. There was a kindred grand corruption in money matters and usury. Yet the friars stopped it, made many give back the money. Other notable effects worthy of Christianity and the Order of St. Dominic followed their providential arrival.

2. *Córdoba's missionary leadership*

At the time they came ashore in the port city of Santo Domingo, the Admiral Columbus had gone, along with his wife, Doña Maria de Toledo, to visit the town of Concepción de la Vega. They were staying on there. So Fray Pedro de Córdoba, the holy man, went to tell the two of his arrival, on foot, without pomp, eating roots for bread, taking for drink cold water from the many arroyos. He slept on the ground in the open fields and in the hills with a cloak for his bedding. Thirty leagues' hard journey. The admiral received him, as did Doña Maria, his wife, with great kindness and favor. They bowed to him as anyone would on seeing him for the first time. His appearance, for all his twenty-eight years, was venerable and saintly and peaceful and ascetic.

He came on Saturday, I think. On the Sunday which fell in the Octave of All Saints, he preached a sermon on the glories in paradise God prepared for His elect, preached with intensity and eagerness a sermon that was lofty, heavenly. I heard it and thought myself lucky to do so. He urged his audience, all of them, that at the end of their served meals they should send off to church the Indians they kept to do the household work. So the congregation sent them, men, women, great and small. Córdoba, seated on a stool with a crucifix in his hand, using some interpreters, preached. He began with the creation of the world, narrating its history up to the point where Christ was put on the cross.

It was a sermon eminently worth hearing, and remembering, very fruitful for the Indians—they had never to that point heard someone like him or such doctrine. He was the first ever to preach to them or to other island natives in the many years since the Spaniards came. Most Indians died without hearing the faith preached. The Spaniards as well could draw much profit from that sermon. If what he said was preached in any quantity to the Indians, there would have been a much greater harvest of native souls than there was. God would have been better known, better loved, much less offended. Finally, having paid his due respects to the admiral, having completed his business in a few days' time, he returned to Santo Domingo. He left behind with all those who heard or saw him vivid impressions of his love and his piety.

Then, if I remember rightly, the force behind this first mission, Fray Domingo de Mendoza, came in one of the newly arrived ships bringing a solid group of sturdy friars. They were all outstanding religious. They had offered to come knowingly and willingly. They knew for certain they would bear great burdens on the island. They would eat no bread, drink no wine, have no meat, they would not travel on horseback, not dress in linen or wool, not sleep on sheepskin mattresses. They would have to put up with the menu and discipline of the Order. And even that much would often be lacking. And this was the prospect that moved them to suffer for the sake of God—eagerly and joyfully. As a result only stalwart religious came out.

Once there, in that town, among that people, Fray Domingo de Mendoza and his brethren were impressed beyond words by Fray Pedro de Córdoba and by those with him. Since they were all now in number over twelve or fifteen as I recall, they agreed unanimously, and with a will to do good, to add certain rules and regulations to the established constitutions of the Order—and whoever keeps the existing ones does a good deal already—so as to live a greater austerity. They had in mind that when they kept the new rules they surely kept the old constitution, the one put in place by the saintly founders of the Order, kept it inviolably alive and effective. I recall that they decided on one policy among others: they would not beg for bread, nor wine, nor oil, while they were healthy. If such food was sent unasked, they would eat it and thank God. For the sick, one could beg from door to door. So it fell out that on Easter day they had nothing to eat except some boiled cabbage, no oil, garnished only with *axi* and salt. They kept to this life of austerity for many years, at least for the whole time the saintly priest Fray Pedro de Córdoba lived. They did great works of penance. The religious spirit waxed mightily in their practice of obedience and poverty. The pristine period of St. Dominic was brought to life again there.

Fray Pedro de Córdoba's reputation for holiness grew so much that the king of Portugal wrote asking the king of Spain or the officials of the Order to send him Dominican friars from the Indies, either to reform Portugal or to fill out the ranks of the Order in India or anywhere else.

There was a command that each Sunday and feast day of obligation a friar should preach to the Indians after dinnertime, just as the servant of God, Pedro de Córdoba, had begun it in the church at Concepción de la Vega. I, who am writing this, took on that task at one time.

B. PEDRO DE CÓRDOBA'S IMPRESSION ON FERDINAND
(From Las Casas, *Historia de las Indias,*
lib. 3, cap. 17, near the beginning.)

The vicar [of the Dominicans], padre Fray Pedro de Córdoba, reached Spain and went to court. . . . He spoke at length to the king, giving him a full account of the facts and the reasons, and what had moved them to preach [against Spaniards holding Indians in encomienda]. . . . The king gave him a most respectful hearing. Fray Pedro was, in his person, a very impressive man. There was an aura of holiness about him, so anyone at all who saw him or spoke with him or heard him speak knew God lived in him. He had the inward grace and outward manner of sanctity. The king conceived a great esteem for him and treated him as one does a holy man. And the king was right to do so.

ADDENDUM III:
LAS CASAS' CONDEMNATION OF AFRICAN SLAVERY

INTRODUCTORY NOTE

This final Addendum contains three passages from Las Casas' History of the Indies on the importation of African slaves into the New World. The first two—his original suggestion, and his later repentance (A.1 & 2, below)—are favorites of those who falsely charge him with responsibility. The third is an unfamiliar passage (B, below)—Las Casas' lengthy and impassioned condemnation of the cruel and lawless Guinea slave trade, citing the same scriptural text he used for the account of his prophetic call.

The unfounded charge, started in the eighteenth century, has been knocked down partially in the nineteenth and twentieth. See Manuel Josef Quintana's 1833 biography, App. 7; Wagner-Parish (1967) 40–41, and 246–47 with notes 7–8; and André-Vincent, "Las Casas et la traite des noirs," App. 2 of his 1980 biography. Isacio Pérez' recent volume, Bartolomé de las Casas ¿contra los negros? (1991), attempts a full refutation, by reviewing the course of the calumny, the requests and licenses to bring black slaves to the islands, and possible stages in Fray Bartolomé's discoveries about the Guinea traffic.

Finally, a forthcoming article by Parish will supply evidence that the actual story is almost the opposite of the slander. Early on, Las Casas did repeat a suggestion made by friars, laymen, and officials, to bring over a few Christianized black slaves from Spain, duty free. But the suggestion was not followed. Independently, an exclusive license was 'bought' by a courtier and resold to Genoese merchants at an exorbitant price, to ship four thousand blacks from Africa. And this monopoly deliberately blocked all but a trickle of slaves for a decade and more, until the gold was gone and most of the Indians wiped out

*on the islands and coasts of the Caribbean. Then high prices for blacks
yielded a ten-fold profit! It was the sugar industry, the new bonanza,
that brought large shipments of African slaves to the deserted West
Indies. And it was Bartolomé de las Casas who discovered in 1552 that
the Portugese (with Papal blessing) had used Europe's defensive war
against Islam to cloak a lucrative trade in innocent blacks captured on
the Guinea coast.* Far from promoting the traffic, Las Casas was the
only person in his century to denounce black African slavery.

A. LAS CASAS CONFESSES AND REPENTS HIS ERROR
(From his *Historia de las Indias,* lib. 3, caps.
102, 129; captions added.)

1. His early involvement

. . . Some Spaniards on the island contacted the cleric Las Casas.
They saw his purpose, saw that the religious of St. Dominic would not
absolve those who held Indians unless they gave them up. If he could
get them a license from the king so they could import from Castile a
dozen blacks, they would free their Indians. The cleric agreed and
requested in his reports that the favor should be done the Spanish
settlers on the islands, and they each should be given a license to bring
in from Spain about a dozen black slaves. The settlers could thus continue to work the land, consequently they would free their Indians.
When the cleric Las Casas first gave that advice—to grant the license to
bring black slaves to the islands—he was not aware of the unjust ways
in which the Portuguese captured and made slaves of blacks. But after
he found out, he would not have proposed it for all the world, because
blacks were enslaved unjustly, tyrannically, right from the start, exactly
as the Indians had been.

2. His judgment on himself and on the Spaniards

. . . Before sugar mills were invented, some settlers, who had some
wealth they had gotten from the sweat and blood of the Indians,
wanted a license to buy black slaves back in Castile. The settlers saw
they were killing off the Indians. But they still had some. So they promised the cleric Bartolomé de las Casas that if he succeeded in getting
them the license to import a dozen blacks to the island, they would
allow the Indians they held to be set free. With this promise in mind,
the cleric Las Casas got the king to allow the Spaniards of the islands to

bring in some black slaves from Castile so the Indians could then be set free. As we said earlier, Las Casas was in favor with the king who had recently come to power, and watch over the new territories had been put in Las Casas' hands. The council, with the accord of the authorities in Seville, decided that a license should be given to import four thousand black slaves, for starters, to the four islands: Hispaniola, San Juan, Cuba, Jamaica. Sure enough a Spaniard from the Indies who was then at court found out about the decision, and slipped the information to the governor of Bresa—a Flemish gentleman who had come with the king and was of his inner circle—so he could request the franchise. He requested it, he got it, he sold it to the Genoese for twenty-five thousand ducats. The Genoese were shrewd and set a thousand conditions. One was that for eight years no further license be given out to bring black slaves to the Indies. The Genoese then sold individual licenses for individual blacks at eight ducats apiece minimum. Thus, the permission the cleric Las Casas had gotten so the Spaniards could get help in working the land, so as to free their Indians, was turned into a profit-making scheme. It proved to be a great setback to the well-being and liberation of the Indians. The cleric, many years later, regretted the advice he gave the king on this matter—he judged himself culpable through inadvertence—when he saw proven that the enslavement of blacks was every bit as unjust as that of the Indians. It was not, in any case, a good solution he had proposed, that blacks be brought in so Indians could be freed. And this even though he thought that the blacks had been justly enslaved. He was not certain that his ignorance and his good intentions would excuse him before the judgment of God.

There were at that time only ten or twelve blacks on the island; they belonged to the king, they had been brought in to construct a fortress which overlooked the river mouth. But once the license was given and implemented, others followed and frequently, so eventually thirty thousand blacks were brought to the island [Hispaniola], and I reckon 100,000 to the Indies as a whole. But the traffic did not help or free the Indians. And the cleric Las Casas could not exert further influence—the king was away, the council got new members every day, and were ignorant of law, law they were obliged to know, I have said this often throughout my *History*. As the sugar mills increased daily in number, the need to put blacks to work in them also increased; the water-powered ones needed at least eighty, the mechanical ones thirty to forty, so that the profit to the king increased. Something else followed from this situation. The Portuguese had made a career in much of the past of raiding Guinea and enslaving blacks, absolutely unjustly. When they saw we had such a need of blacks and they sold for high prices, the Portuguese speeded up their slave raiding—they are still in a hurry. They took slaves in every evil and wicked way they could. And blacks, when they saw the Portuguese so eager on the hunt for slaves, they themselves used unjust wars and other lawless means to steal and sell to the Portuguese. And we are the cause of all the sins the one and the other commit, in addition to what we commit in buying them.

B. LAS CASAS' CONDEMNATION OF THE AFRICAN SLAVE TRADE
(From his *Historia de las Indias,* lib. 1, cap. 24;
captions added.)

Capturing the Innocent

I want to cite here one stark story from among the many offenses, grave evils, gruesome injustices, the shocking damages done by the Portuguese in their discoveries during that period of time, done against the natives of those lands—Moor or Indian or black or Arab—innocent of anything against the Portuguese. The year was 1444. The story is from Juan de Barros, lib. 1, cap. 8, 1st decade, and from Gómez Eanes de Zurara, lib. 1, caps. 18–24. Gómez gives the fuller version.

Some rich and important people of the city of Lagos in Portugal pressed the Infante to give them a license to go to the discovered territory, and they would give him in return a certain share of the profits they made. The Infante complied. So they armed six caravels. The Infante appointed as captain of the fleet a man named Lanzarote who had been in his service. They left Portugal, they reached an island we now call Las Garzas, on the eve of Corpus Christi, where they killed many natives who were at their evening rest. From Las Garzas they went on to attack an island called Nar; it was nearby and well populated. On Corpus Christi Day (good day, good deeds!), at sunup, they attacked the natives who were still in bed and off guard. The war cry was, "Santiago, St. George, Portugal, Portugal!" The natives were terror stricken by the attack, so large, so sudden, so wicked. Parents abandoned children, husbands abandoned wives; some mothers hid their offspring out in the grasses, the thickets. Everyone ran aghast, out of their heads.

A Portuguese chronicler says this: "Finally, Our Lord God, who rewards every good deed, saw to it that those who took this risk for his service should win the victory over their enemies and receive profit and praise for their labors and costs. They captured and held 155 natives. They killed many another who put up a fight. Many another drowned escaping." Can there be a more senseless description than this one? To serve God, the chronicler says, they killed, they sent to hell so many infidels, they left that whole island in shock and hatred of the name Christian and filled with grief and bitterness.

There were only thirty Portuguese, and not enough shackles to hold all those peaceful people. So the Portuguese left some men with part of the captives, took another part back to the ships. They were jubilant on arrival, then returned in their boats to pick up those left. You see how peaceful, how unwarlike the natives were, if thirty Portuguese from far away can capture 150 of them abed and asleep in their huts.

The ships went to another nearby island, called Tider, to make another haul, but they were spotted first; the Portuguese found it empty, the natives had fled to the mainland, a matter of eight leagues' distance. The Portuguese tortured a Moor, or whatever they were, so as to find out where more people could be located. They kept on from island to island for two days, then in raids they made on the mainland they took into captivity a further forty-five natives. On their return trip to Portugal, they took en route fifteen fishermen and one woman. In all they captured on their slave raids 216 human beings, people who had never harmed them, who owed them nothing, people who were weaponless, who lived at peace in their own places. When the ships returned to Portugal, Lanzarote was received by the Infante with great ceremony. He personally named Lanzarote a knight and heaped honors on him.

The next day, Captain Lanzarote spoke to the Infante:

> Lord, Your Highness well knows you are due a fifth of these captives we brought back, a fifth of all else we got from our foray in that land where you sent us in the service of God and in your own. Due to the length of the voyage and the time it took to sail it, the men are exhausted, and more so due to the fret and fear they themselves had to live with, so far from home, making captives, not knowing how things would come out. And many are sick and quite worn down. Given all this, I suggest it would be a good idea for you to order that the ships be unloaded tomorrow and the haul be brought to a field outside of town where a five-way split can be made of the slaves. And Your Highness can come and choose what will please and satisfy you most.

The Infante answered that it was a good idea.

The next day morning, Captain Lanzarote ordered the masters of the caravels to empty them and bring the captives to the field. But before they divided them, they chose out a Moor, the best of the lot, as an offering to the Church of the place, the city of Lagos, where the raiders all lived, and where they made port. The Infante was in residence there at the time. They chose out another Moor to send to San Vicente del Cabo where, the story goes, the slave lived later very religiously. The raiders wanted to give God his share after the bloodshed, the unjust and wicked enslavement of those innocent people, as if God were some wicked, malevolent tyrant they could please and He would approve the viciousness of those who made the offering. Those awful men did not know the scriptural passage: "God does not approve those who harm their neighbors sinfully, then offer God a sacrifice from their ill-gotten goods. Such sacrifice is instead like honoring and serving a father by hacking his son to pieces as he looks on" (Ecclesiasticus 34). The fact that the Moor they gave to San Vicente del Cabo, or that many others, or all, grew holy later does not excuse those who seized them, nor do they gain remission of their sins by such a gift as they made. The holiness was not their doing, it was due entirely to the infinite generosity of God who chose to draw such a priceless good out of such damnable evils. It is a gospel truth and Catholic law that one cannot commit even the smallest venial sin in order to draw the greatest good one can imagine from it. How much less commit the greatest of mortal sins.

Back to the theme. I want to include here, and word for word, no addition, no subtraction, what Gómez Eanes writes in his account—I mentioned him earlier—about the pack of people Lanzarote took captive. I think Gómez was there, an eyewitness. He says in exclamation,

> Oh, heavenly Father, You rule the infinite host of Your holy city without effort, Your divine excellence is so, and You keep in order the orbits of the higher globes in their nine circles, and You make the aeons short or long according as You please. I beg You that my tears should not count against me. Their being human has a hold on me, not their beliefs. So I weep from sorrow over their suffering. If brute beasts with their brute feelings can recognize the suffering of their own kind by the instinct of nature, what can you expect my human nature to do seeing before me that stricken group, as I remind myself they are all by generation children of Adam?

> Next day, it was 8 August, early because it was hot, the crews began to work their boats, unload their captives and take them ashore as ordered. The captives, when gathered in the field, were a strange sight to see. Some among them were nearly white, handsome, slim; others were darker, seemed like mulattos; others black, like Ethio-

pians, gross in face and body—it appeared to people that they saw a reverse image of the world. What heart, hard as it might be, would not feel pity stir at the sight of such a group? Some had their faces down, wet with tears; some looked at the others and were groaning with grief; some looked to high heaven, fixing their look on it, shouting aloud up to it, as if asking the Father of Nature for help; others beat their cheeks with their palms, or threw themselves flat on the ground; others made lamentation in a song-like manner after the custom of their homeland. And though the words of their language could not be understood by us, their sorrow was understood indeed. A sorrow that increased when those in charge of dividing them came and started to split them one from another to make even groups. To do this it became necessary to take children from parents, wives from husbands, brothers from sisters. For kin and kindred no rule was kept, each captive landed where luck would have it. Oh mighty Fortune, you wheel back and forth over the things of this world as you please! Would that someone could place before the eyes of those pitiful people some knowledge of the good to come in future centuries so they could have some consolation in the midst of their great suffering! And you, who work this partition, respect and pity such misery, see how they cling together, you can scarcely pry them apart. Who could make the separation without violence? Things were such that those who were put in one partition—children who saw their parents in another—got up and ran over to them; mothers gripped their other children in their arms and huddled with them on the ground, heedless of the lashes on their own flesh, so the children would not be torn from them. So the partition took a lot of trouble.

It was difficult enough with just the captives, but the field was also full of people, from the city itself and from the surrounding areas. People had quit work that day, work they had to do for a living, just to see something new; and what with some deploring what they saw going on, and some approving, they made such a hubbub that they rattled the ones in charge of the partition. The Infante was there, mounted on a powerful horse, accompanied by his people, giving away his goods like a man who does not want to be rich himself. He gave away in a short time the 46 souls that fell to his fifth. His principal wealth was in good conscience, and the salvation of those souls pleased him mightily, they would otherwise be lost.

His judgment was not an empty one, for, as we said already, soon as the slaves learned the language, they readily became Christian. And I who write the history in this volume saw, in the city of Lagos, lads and lasses, the children, the grandchildren of those slaves, born here —and they such good and true Christians, it's as if they were Chris-

tians forever back, the offspring of those who were the first baptized.
And though the grief of those being split up was indeed great at the
moment—especially after the split had been made, and each owner
had carried off his share, and some sold theirs, who were then taken
to other parts of the country, so the story goes that a father remained
in Lagos, a mother was taken to Lisbon, children elsewhere—though
the grief was acute at the start, the damage was at the beginning.
Later, after it all, everything would change to joy and happiness, for
they received the Christian faith, they gave birth to Christian children, and many later got back their freedom.

This is the way, to the letter, the incident was put by the Portuguese historian Gómez Eanes. He seems little less foolish than the
Infante, unable to see that neither the Infante's good intention, nor the
good results that later followed, excused the sins of violence, the deaths,
the damnation of those who perished without faith or sacrament, the
enslavement of the survivors. Nor did intention or results make up for
the monumental injustice. What love, affection, esteem, reverence,
would they have, could they have for the faith, for Christian religion, so
as to convert to it, those who wept as they did, who grieved, who raised
their eyes, their hands to heaven, who saw themselves, against the law
of nature, against all human reason, stripped of their liberty, of their
wives and children, of their homeland, of their peace? Even the historian himself, and the people who stood around, wept with compassion
over the sorry affair, especially when they saw the separation of children from parents, of mothers and fathers from children. It is obvious,
the error, the self-deception of those people back then. Please God it
did not last, it does not still last. It is from his exclamation, so I think,
that the historian shows the event to be the horror that it is, though
later he seems to soft-soap it, to blur it with the mercy and goodness of
God. If anything good did come of it later, it all came from God. What
came from the Infante and the raiders he sent out was brutality, theft,
tyranny—nothing more.

TEXTUAL APPENDICES

APPENDIX I:
THREE VERSIONS OF *THE ONLY WAY*

INTRODUCTORY NOTE

From the Preface and the Introduction, the reader already knows that there were three versions of The Only Way. *Mainly this has been shown by the* external evidence *of moments of Las Casas' life when he wrote these versions, each longer than its predecessor, for specific purposes. These moments were unknown previously because whole sections of his biography were garbled and shadowy, notably his years as a friar before returning to court, and his final years in Spain. The principal early account had serious gaps and flaws; and modern scholars added documents and details to known episodes, without unscrambling the story or supplying the large missing pieces. Our Introduction does just that, from new discoveries in* Las Casas en México, The Untold Story, *and elsewhere, to reveal the full context of* The Only Way *at last.*

This first textual Appendix highlights several other kinds of evidence: vague and precise ancient accounts of the first writing and first use of The Only Way, *its long and short versions, its final form; revealing passages in the work* itself, *and in other writings by Las Casas, that indicate how* The Only Way *was written and rewritten on different occasions; and, most persuasive, actual manuscripts of* The Only Way, *not just the huge surviving Oaxaca fragment, but two much shorter versions from earlier periods. All this evidence—external, internal, contemporary, and manuscript—is fitted together here for a full corroboration and description of the three versions of* The Only Way.

A. THE FIRST VERSION—DATING, SOURCE OF *SUBLIMIS DEUS*

1. Wrong dates: Remesal, unfounded conjectures. When and where did Las Casas write the Latin work "De unico modo"? Specifically, when did he write the first version? His earliest major biographer, Fray Antonio de Remesal, gives the only external clue: Las Casas had this treatise with him in Guatemala at the start of 1537, having written it "a few years before" (había algunos años); he preached his ideas from it, was laughed at by the conquistadors, and signed a contract with Governor Alonso de Maldonado, which allowed him to demonstrate these principles in the unconquered "Land of War" (Remesal, *Historia* of 1619, lib. 3, caps. 9–10).

The contract was indeed signed on May 2, 1537, but Remesal's account of Las Casas' previous decade is wildly confused—he has Fray Bartolomé spend three prior years in Central America and visit Mexico City six years before, all demonstrably false. On this wrong basis, several noted scholars conjectured that *The Only Way* was written in Guatemala, and one even speculated that a couple of bishops in Mexico City had urged Las Casas to write the work! In fact, Fray Bartolomé had already preached such ideas in Nicaragua and been yanked from the pulpit in 1536; and his two stays in that province and his two visits to Mexico City had occupied about a year and a half (mid-1535 through 1536) crowded with activity. There was *no* Central American interlude when he could have written *The Only Way*, and he had no reason to do so. "A few years before" points clearly to his years as a friar on Hispaniola, from his entering the Dominican Order in 1522 to his leaving the island in late 1534, and there is now full consensus on this obvious conclusion. (See Pérez, "Sobre la fecha y el lugar," 127–30.)

But those twelve Hispaniola years—when, as Fray Bartolomé himself wrote, "it seems he slept"—remain almost blank if one removes Remesal's errors (cf. Wagner-Parish, 76–82). So more unfounded conjectures have attempted to pinpoint the first writing of the treatise on the island. Most ingenious is Pérez' notion that Las Casas wrote "De unico modo" in 1522–1526, as a work of theological reflection during his obligatory course of study as a new Dominican—another impossibility. With such a thesis, he would have been a candidate for the degree of lector, and might well have been assigned to teach at the House of Studies, which would become the University of Santo Domingo during the next decade. Further, the treatise's ideas about predestination and mission theory are a non sequitur for his situation. Las Casas had never been a missionary, and with the island natives almost gone, Antilles Dominicans could only work as missionaries in Middle or South America. However, Pérez was right about the academic and scholastic character of the surviving MS—it is no student essay, but the work of a retired bishop and honorary professor in the Dominican College at the University of Valladolid years later. (See App. I.C.)

One other conjecture deserves mention. André Saint-Lu suggests that Las Casas wrote "De unico modo" as prior at Puerto de Plata, since his 1531 letter from there to the Council of the Indies mentions some similar ideas (*La Vera Paz*, 31, 34–35, 554). But these similarities are brief—God wants all people saved, cruel governors are bad evangelists and should be replaced. More space is given to the Bull of Donation being solely for conversion; a scheme for *forts with one hundred or fifty soldiers each,* to protect bishops and friars converting the Indians; and restitution by the Spaniards. Reinterpreting the papal donation is new, but protection recalls the Pearl Coast tragedy, and forts and restitution are old proposals. Besides, Prior Bartolomé was busy building a monastery, starting to write history, sending impassioned memorials to court (one produced the antislavery law of 1530), and preaching subversive sermons that got him recalled to Santo Domingo and silenced for two years! In the Puerto de Plata outpost, he lacked any motivation or well-stocked library for writing the treatise, and faint similarities hardly count. From 1519 to 1522, Las Casas had publicly advocated and personally tried to carry out ideas *identical* to the doctrine of *The Only Way.*

2. Correct date: sources, occasion and means. This raises key questions that must be answered in context. What were the *prior sources* of Bartolomé de las Casas' peaceful conversion ideas—and *when and why* did he originally write them in *The Only Way?* As shown in the first section of the Introduction, the sources were his own experiences: his "peaceful reduction" of most of Cuba as a white shaman baptizing Indian children; his declaration to a royal junta about Indian capacity and Christianity's appeal and welcome for all nations of the world, without conquest or subjugation; his failed attempt as a cleric-colonist to protect Pedro de Córdoba's peaceful conversion experiment on the Pearl Coast; and Cardinal Adrian's decisive oration on converting the Indians "by the way of love and gentleness instituted by Christ himself," which swayed the assembled councils to vote that "the cleric Las Casas should have charge of the conversion" of that region. And lastly, his second success at peaceful reduction and conversion, namely his two visits to Chief Enriquillo, the Indian guerrilla, which had cemented a shaky peace treaty: the month-long stay when Fray Bartolomé married the couples and baptized the children; the return visit, when

Fray Bartolomé brought Enriquillo to the capital and persuaded him to come out of hiding and settle with his followers! (See Introduction above, Sections 1 and 2.)

A single crucial occasion—Betanzos' shocking defamation of the Indians and the resulting revocation in 1534 of the antislavery law that Fray Bartolomé had promoted—coalesced all these ideas and led Las Casas to compose the first version of *The Only Way*. Betanzos had pronounced the Indians incapable of the faith, and asserted that all laws to protect them were useless since God had condemned them to extinction for their bestial sins! In his answering treatise, Las Casas wrote that Providence had predestined salvation for the elect of *all* peoples, *including the Indians;* that the Indians had *full capacity* for the faith and for self-government; and that evangelization must be by the one and only way, gentle and humane, that Christ Himself had established, and not by wars of conquest that brought death, torture, and brutal exploitation.

So Bartolomé de las Casas wrote his first book, *The Only Way*, in 1534, during his enforced idleness at the Dominican House of Studies in the city of Santo Domingo, where he could use the best library on the island of Hispaniola. Pérez thinks that this first book had to precede Las Casas' 1527 start on his *History of the Indies;* but that monumental work occupied him off and on for the next forty years, until shortly before his death, and is not a reference point. *External evidence* (the need, opportunity, and means to answer the defamation) and *internal evidence* (the contents of the tract which provide an exact answer) fit together perfectly in 1534.

3. Confirmation: short version, results. Furthermore, there is cumulative data on an original version of *The Only Way* far shorter than the incomplete late version that has survived. Agustín Dávila Padilla, a Dominican chronicler earlier than Remesal, briefly mentions two Las Casas' texts "on the promulgation of the Gospel": a short Spanish version, and a longer one in Latin with "the arguments and well-supported reasons" (*Historia de la fundación y discurso de la Provincia de Santiago de México,* Madrid, 1596, lib. 1, cap. 99). A Spanish text is questionable; but Las Casas regularly *expanded* his shorter writings (the *Anti-Slavery Tract,* the *Eighth Reform* amid sixteen, the *Rules for Confessors, Thirty Propositions,* the *Defense* against Sepúlveda, and the written text of the *Decimation*). And an inventory of his MS works handed over to the Spanish government after his death includes a description of "a handwritten book of 73 leaves, vellum bound," bearing on its cover the Latin words "De unico vocationis modo omnium

gentium ad veram religionem" (*DIE,* 8:557). But the surviving fragment of 220 leaves contains only the central portion, with a draft of the
last portion (App. I.C, sect. 1); so this vellum-bound book was a much
shorter text. And its cover bears a further legend, suggesting a dedication to the second version (App. I.B, sect. 2). Therefore the first version
would have been shorter still.

Finally, this short first version of *The Only Way* left a clear train of
influence in the New World and the Old. A newly identified MS confirms that Las Casas had the treatise with him at the Mexican ecclesiastical conferences of 1536: a holograph opinion by Bishop Zumárraga
(but preserved in Las Casas' papers), with a central set of "Six Truths"
in Latin by Fray Bartolomé on the illegality of conquest and slavery,
and "the only way" to convert the Indians! As told in the Introduction,
the resulting resolution and a copy of the treatise, carried to Rome by
Bernardino Minaya, became, point by point, the great papal encyclical
of 1537, *Sublimis Deus.* That same year, Las Casas successfully
launched his own peaceful conversion experiment in Guatemala, while
his new friend, Fray Jacobo de Tastera, failed at a similar attempt in
Yucatan. (*N.B.* The usual date of 1534 for Tastera's experiment is
based on a misprint; the correct date was 1537.) Concurrently, Minaya
seems to have stopped off twice at the University of Salamanca—en
route to Rome with the treatise, and on his return with *Sublimis Deus.*
The results were historic. A noted Dominican professor, Fray Francisco de Vitoria, in an aside to his prepared talk "On Temperance,"
rejected the current pretexts for conquering and enslaving the Indians;
and then, in his famous first public lecture "On the Indies," Vitoria
denied the right of conquest and formulated beneficial grounds for the
Spanish presence in the New World. (See *Las Casas en México,* App.
1. Zumárraga's opinion; and Postscript of Introduction above, note 90
and corresp. par. of text on Las Casas and Vitoria's *four* dicta on the
Indians.)

B. SECOND VERSION—DONE IN MEXICO, PRELUDE TO NEW LAWS

1. Mexican additions. Following the first version, there is now
ample evidence that Las Casas wrote a second or expanded version of
"De unico modo" in New Spain (modern Mexico) in 1539—mainly to
add dramatic new "proof" of his doctrine and a powerful dedication to
Emperor Charles V. The reader is familiar with the *external* events
from the Introduction; here, we add contemporary data, and *internal*
testimony from the work itself and another book by Las Casas.

Dávila Padilla (1596, *loc. cit.*) mentions a longer version of the treatise, with added arguments and authorities, presumably from canon law which Las Casas was "studying" [researching] at the time. The most important of these added "proof texts"—the papal encyclical *Sublimis Deus* and its related brief, supporting Las Casas' doctrine and his interpretation of the Bull of Donation—reached him in Mexico City in 1538. An entire section of the surviving manuscript is devoted to the two papal decrees: cap. 5, sect. 36. Another section, tacked on at the end, was likewise written after his stay in Mexico City: cap. 7, sect. 6, in which Fray Bartolomé entreats his fellow friars *not* to use whips, chains, or confinement to correct the sins of Indian neophytes, despite the bishop's permission. (See Hanke's 1942 Introduction [Pte. III, cap. 3 of his *Lucha*], note 41, on Bishop Zumárraga's involvement.)

In addition to these two sections, we can infer Las Casas' "Mexican" expansion of the opening portion of the treatise, on Indian capacity—fitting his freshly gathered material on the Aztec and Inca empires into Aristotelian requirements for polity: cities, laws, rulers, nobles, soldiers, merchants, farmers, artisans. (Doubtless inspired by his friend Tastera's major letter on these points, written to answer Betanzos' defamation—*Cartas de Indias,* Madrid, 1877, 1:62–66.) The surviving MS cannot confirm this, since its capacity portion (caps. 1–4) was removed during Las Casas' last period and incorporated in his huge new *Defense of the Indian Civilizations.* But visible evidence of its former location remains in plain sight: Cap. 263 of this *Defense (Apologética historia)* summarizes how the Indians qualify on all eight points, and in a final three-page peroration, insists that the Indians therefore have *full capacity for the faith*—a correct conclusion for *The Only Way,* but quite unrelated to the new volume.

When and where did Las Casas make these "Mexican" additions: the papal decrees of 1537, his plea against brutal punishment of Indian converts, and the eight [Aristotelian] requirements for Indian civilizations? Noticing some of them, previous studies favored Mexico City, but new information, detailing Las Casas' activities and whereabouts at the time, points farther south.

2. Memorials, dedication, results. In Oaxaca in 1539, Bartolomé de las Casas spent four months drafting and writing the memorials he planned to present at court. He was going back to Spain at last as a Dominican Missions Recruiter with a variety of errands. He would make the crossing with the Franciscan Missions Recruiter, Fray Jacobo de Tastera, and Bishop Zumárraga had written a joint recommendation for them. But both Fray Bartolomé and Fray Jacobo also intended to stay over and work for legislation on behalf of the Indians.

To that end, Las Casas prepared two documents to reach the conscience of the king, the absent Emperor Charles V; Tastera could carry them personally to the Low Countries. One was a brief sketch of the tale of atrocities during the conquest, *The Decimation of the Indies,* that Las Casas was preparing for an oral presentation illustrated with notarized documents—Las Casas had packloads of these documents with him on the way to Oaxaca, and Tastera did apparently present the emperor a horrifying tale (*Las Casas en México,* App. 16.D, no. 6; *DIE,* 13:427). The other document was, almost certainly, the second version of *The Only Way,* with a dedication to the emperor in his role of Charles I, king of Spain. For the handwritten book of seventy-three leaves, cited above, bore this total legend on its vellum cover:

"De cura habenda regibus Hispaniarum circa orbem Indiarum, et [*sic:* sc.], De unico vocationis modo omnium gentium ad veram religionem"

The apparent dual title has mystified scholars, but one need only suppose an obvious misreading. Change *et* (and) to the abbreviation *sc.,* almost identical in a script of the period, to read *scilicet* (namely, *viz.,* i.e.) and the expanded title makes instant sense:

"How the Kings of Spain Must Care for the [New] World of the Indies: *viz.,* [by] The Only Way to Draw All People to a Living Faith"

With *Sublimis Deus* in hand, Las Casas' dedication could tell the king forcefully that the papal Bull of Donation granted the Indies to Spain for *conversion,* not conquest and exploitation, and beg him to reform the system.

The emperor *was* moved, and did return to Spain and name an Imperial Reform Commission. And the three memorials that Las Casas had composed at Oaxaca in 1539—the bloodcurdling *Decimation of the Indians* (which would transfix its hearers), the second version of *The Only Way* (presented as the royal duty), and the "Sixteen Remedies for the Plagues [of Forced Labor and Slavery] Destroying the Indies" (supplemented by his lobbying and legislative work at court)—led to the promulgation in 1542–1543 of Charles V's famous New Laws for the government of the Indies and the "good treatment and preservation" of the Indians.

C. THIRD VERSION—MUTILATED BULWARK, CLASSROOM TEXT

1. MS description, dating, context. Again, the reader is familiar
with the third version of *The Only Way,* written in Spain after Las
Casas resigned his bishopric. Today, it is the best known of the three,
from the sole surviving manuscript copy, which was found coinciden-
tally in Oaxaca in the last century (cf. App. III.A, sect. 2). This MS
begins with Cap. 5 of Part One, and lacks Part Two on "Restitution"
which Las Casas himself cites repeatedly in his other late works (See
esp. *Historia,* Lib. 3, last sentence of Cap. 153 on restitution. For documentary evidence on Part Two and its contents, and for his other
citations, see below, third and fourth pars. of this section.) But its for-
mal heading implies that the removal of Caps. 1–4 was deliberate:

CHAPTER FIVE
of the first book [of the work] entitled "The Only Way to Draw
All People to a Living Faith," by Fray Bartolomé de las Casas of the
Order of Preachers, former Bishop of the Royal City of Chiapa in the
New World of the Indies.

Also, although the MS is incomplete by definition, containing only
Chapters 5, 6, and 7 of Part One, its length and appearance are impressive: 220 leaves [440 pages] in a noncursive sixteenth-century italic
calligraphy, with a contemporary binding of embossed sheepskin and
paper pasteboards. And in its subject matter, this large "fragment"
constitutes a complete treatise.

Moreover, the fullest contemporary description, by the indispensable Fray Antonio de Remesal, fits it closely. Remesal had a MS copy
of "De unico modo" himself, and his summary corresponds almost
exactly to the Oaxaca manuscript, except for one notable variation. His
recap of the first four chapters is nearly identical to the recap that
begins the MS. He describes Chapter 5 with thirty-six long sections,
and Chapter 6 with eight, the same number as in the Oaxaca MS. He
transcribes three paragraphs of the Latin text, and the identical paragraphs appear in the MS with a single variant word (cf. Millares Carlo's
1942 Preface, note 11).

However, for the last portion of the book—on unjust wars and
restitution—Remesal summarizes "four kinds of infidels," of whom
the blameless fourth kind (including the Indians) cannot be justly attacked by Christians. This passage is *not* in the surviving MS, but a
cross-reference indicates that it appeared in the earlier truncated
Chapter 3; and the rest of Remesal's corresponding material is in a

Chapter 7 which he does not mention. Apparently then, the Oaxaca MS was a penultimate draft of the third version, and its Chapter 7 (with six sections) plus the earlier Chapter 3 would become Part Two on "Restitution."

There is ample further evidence—an ancient imprint and unpublished MSs—that this separation and rearrangement actually occurred. A later seventeenth-century summary of *The Only Way*, by Bishop Peña of Quito, also contains the "four kinds of infidels," with different details (App. II.B and Introductory Note, last par.). And in the eighteenth century a tireless archivist, Juan Bautista Muñoz, described an untitled Las Casas manuscript of 109 folios that exactly corresponds to Remesal's two-part description of the finale—i.e., the lost Part Two of *The Only Way*. (See App. 3.A, third and fourth pars. of sect. 2. Las Casas' own references to both the former Cap. 3 and Lib. 2 include these same topics—cf. Pérez 1978, note 51 with Barreda, *Ideología y pastoral missionera,* Cap. 2 at pp. 34–41.)

So Remesal, writing in the first decades of the seventeenth century, was undoubtedly summarizing the final text. For the chronicler says he has seen *four* copies of the work in the *selfsame* [*scribal*] *handwriting:* his own, two others in Mexico and Guatemala, and another in the College [of San Gregorio], where we know Las Casas lived and wrote from 1552 to 1559. (Cf. App. III.A, sect. 1 for these four copies, and still others of the final version.)

And of course, it was at San Gregorio that Las Casas himself mutilated *The Only Way,* removing the four opening chapters on Indian capacity for use in his promised second rebuttal to the defamer Sepúlveda. To build up that vast *Defense of the Indian Civilizations,* Fray Bartolomé also added data received from friars in the Indies, theoretical chapters on the Aristotelian categories, and, for purposes of comparison, ancient history to the point of unreadability. (See Introduction above, Section 3.)

2. Scholastic stuffing, date, results. Something similar befell *The Only Way* in its last stage. This was the period of Las Casas' big academic writings for a dual purpose: to block the forces of revocation and reaction, and to train a new generation at the great Spanish universities. So in the fifties, he added section after section of Aristotelian psychology (fifteen sections on the mind and will!) to the prime peaceful-conversion portion of *The Only Way.* He also stuffed in whole sections of patristics, and in the last portion, solid pages of Roman and canon law citations, to buttress his daring conclusions on restitution.

One such accretion is most useful, since it confirms the dating of this third version of *The Only Way:* apocryphal stories of the apostles carrying out Christ's mandate for peaceful conversion. These are drawn from the spurious *Historia Apostolica,* then considered authentic and attributed to Abdyas of Babylon (a personage in the "Acts" of Simon and Judas)—a work first published by Wolfgang Lazius of Basle, Switzerland, in 1551.

Today, these endless "authorities" seem dull and unconvincing, yet Remesal voices the admiration they elicited in that era. Only a few modern scholars have appreciated Las Casas' erudition: See Millares Carlo on the works cited in *Del único modo*—1942 Preface, notes 19–27, and corresponding text; also *De unico modo,* 1990 edition, Indices of Las Casas cits., 599–626! But Bartolomé de las Casas' academic method, truncating and stuffing the third version of "De unico modo," along with ideas borrowed from the treatise itself for other "academic" works, did bear permanent fruit in the classrooms and at court. Spanish canonists for the rest of the century adopted his views on the papal donation for *conversion, not conquest.* Sale of the Peruvian Indians was blocked. And many reform laws, which he had inspired and strengthened, remained in place to assure the survival, if not the welfare and freedom, of the remaining Indians (Introduction, Section 3 and Postscript).

3. Titles and Summary. Las Casas gave this third version its own distinctive title, as he had with the previous two. The earliest title was a simpler description, and the second began with the Dedication to the emperor. The final text bore the title by which the work is known today—an expansion of the heading to a tract then attributed to St. Ambrose, about salvation being offered to all peoples: *De vocatione omnium gentium* (Migne, *PL,* 51:639–722, and cf. 17:1167, for the attribution to St. Ambrose). The "proofs" from this *tractatulus*—that all peoples are called and none are so defective as to be incapable—apparently occupied the first two (lost) chapters of *The Only Way;* the third (lost) chapter was originally Las Casas' little treatise on the kinds of infidels; and the fourth (lost) chapter was his detailed exposition of Indian capacity.

To summarize, we list the three versions of *The Only Way,* their titles, lengths, places and dates of composition, and purposes:

First
"De unico trahendi modo universas gentes ad veram religionem"—

"The Only Way to Draw All People to A Living Faith." (Cited thus once, in *Historia de las Indias,* lib. 3, near beginning of cap. 11.) Shortest. Written at Santo Domingo, Hispaniola, 1534. To answer Betanzos' defamation of Indians, revocation of 1530 antislavery law.

Second
"De cura habenda regibus Hispaniarum circa orbem Indiarum, et [*sic:* sc.] De unico vocationis modo omnium gentium ad veram religionem"—"How the Kings of Spain Must Care for the World of the Indies: *viz.,* [by] The Only Way of Calling All People to a Living Faith," 73 fols. Written at Oaxaca (Mexico, near the Guatemalan border), 1539. To move the king's conscience on Las Casas' return to court.

Third
"†De unico vocationis modo omnium gentium ad veram religionem†"—"The Only Way of Calling All People to a Living Faith." Surviving MS of 220 fols; caps. 5, 6, 7 of Part One. (Also another MS of 109 fols. in his papers, corresponding to cap. 3 of Part One, cf. App. III.A, sect. 2. Lost MS.) A penultimate draft. Final version slightly longer, with cap. 3 and seven sections shifted to form Part Two. Written at College of San Gregorio, University of Valladolid, between 1552 and 1559. A powerful late academic writing.

* . . . * = Our title.
† . . . † = Las Casas' usual title.

APPENDIX II:
THE PUBLISHED SEVENTEENTH-CENTURY SUMMARIES

INTRODUCTORY NOTE

The surviving manuscript of The Only Way *contains just the central portion, or basic thesis, plus an attached conclusion; the first portion was removed by Las Casas himself. We know the form and contents of the entire work from the extensive summary by Fray Antonio de Remesal, whose* History *appeared in 1620, a half-century after Las Casas' death. This precious source is given in full here (A below).*

Remesal owned a MS copy of the final version of De unico modo, *and his summary corresponds almost exactly to the Oaxaca manuscript, with only two differences. His recap of the missing early chapters is fuller, because the pages of the corresponding recap in the Oaxaca MS are badly deteriorated. And his full picture of the closing portion—on unjust wars—suggests a final separation and summarizes a section on "the four kinds of infidels" missing from the surviving MS.*

Also, we include a much briefer summary (B below), first published a hundred years after Las Casas' death, in Alonso de la Peña Montenegro's Handbook for parish priests of Indians, *a steady seller of the colonial period. (Cf. App. III.A, sect. 1.) Apart from its wide circulation, his summary has several noteworthy features. He, too, summarizes the "four kinds of infidels," but with other details. And he inserts rebuttals and a discussion from Juan de Solórzano Pereira's* De iure indiarum, *Madrid, 1629—showing that* The Only Way *was a subject of controversy in the seventeenth century.*

A. THE REMESAL SUMMARY
(From Fray Antonio de Remesal, O.P., *Historia de la provincia de San Vicente de Chyapa y Guatemala de la*

Orden de nuestro glorioso padre Sancto Domingo, Madrid,
1619 [1620], lib. 3, cap. 9, no. 1. Captions added.)

Humanity of the Indians

It was some years ago now that Padre Fray Bartolomé de las Casas
wrote a book entitled *The Only Way.* In it he showed first how the
chosen people were to be called and gathered in from all the people of
the earth, from every race, as a result of the deeds and the example of
Christ Our Lord, the Head of the Church. Thus no nation in the entire
world was wholly excluded, bereft of divine mercy, the grace of it, the
gift of it. Some, from each nation, be they few or many, were predestined for eternal life. This truth must be understood therefore of the
nations, the peoples of the New World; it must be believed and affirmed of them.

Next he proved that divine predestination is not blocked by sin,
however great, or grievous, or gruesome, however guilty of sin a people
in general or a person in particular may be, and however much people
or persons are bent on continuing to sin. And predestination is not
blocked if people are lax or lazy or vain or weak or crafty or inconstant
or savage or cruel. It is unthinkable that an entire group of people, or
race, or city, or town should be so deficient that they cannot grasp the
gospel, even though, among the peoples of the world some may be
quicker than others to understand. To prove this, [Las Casas] brings in
many authorities, many arguments from reason and revelation.

Next he offered proof that one had to conclude the following:
among the peoples of the Indies there were not only various levels of
intelligence, as in the rest of the world, but also there was an ability
among them to govern human life, and it was a better ability than in
the rest of the world. If it was sometimes lacking, the lack was minimal,
and so rare out there in the Indies it was of no account. He proved his
point by appeal to causality, the remote and the proximate, the condi-
tional, the accidental. He proved it from what was observable, i.e., the
fostering influence of the heavenly bodies creating a calm and pleasant
climate throughout the area where the Indians live, the balance and
proportion of their bodily makeup, the healthfulness of their diet.
These were all listed under remote explanations.

Next his proof dealt with the proximate, the natural causes: the
balancing forces of personality, the right ordering of their inward
powers and faculties, the facility to synthesize sense experience, to
imagine, to dream, to remember, to judge. Next his proof dealt with
accidental causes: moderation in food and drink, restraint, control of

bodily desire. They had no need to be anxious about day-to-day things, or about shifting, changing states of soul, those that produce sorrow, grief and such like. [He proved their intelligence also] through the amazing, ingenious things they made by hand, classifiable under mechanical arts. And about their skill in the liberal arts, he says, up to now they have achieved the same high level.

The Only Way

After the long treatment of Indian capacity, Las Casas begins writing his description of the natural, normal, single and standard way that those chosen beforehand by God are to receive their call to faith in Jesus Christ Our Lord and the Christian religion. The call starts the process toward the fulfillment of predestination. When he has stated that the call must be considered as basic to what he is about to say, he sets out the following conclusion:

One way, one way only, of teaching a living faith, to everyone, everywhere, always, was set by Divine Providence, the way that wins the mind with reasons, that wins the will with gentleness. It has to fit all people on earth, no distinction made for sect, for error, even for evil.

True Evangelization

He proves his point in a very scholarly way—in thirty-six ample sections which come to four hundred pages in tiny script—by presenting the thinking, the practice of the fathers of the faith, some from the Old, some from the New Testament. Then presenting the wish and will of Christ Our Redeemer, and the manner of preaching the gospel He prescribed for His apostles. Then the way the holy apostles carried that out. Then the suasive authority of the holy doctors, the teachers of the Church. Then the ancient way of holy Church itself under the guidance of the Holy Spirit. Then a series of decrees from supreme pontiffs who ruled the Church at different times.

False Evangelization

Then, in a further eight sections, in the same elegant and effective and packed style, he goes on to show the contradiction involved in persuading the mind to the things of our holy faith by way of war and conquest, subjecting by force of arms those who are to be converted. In the process he describes the fruits of war in utterly apt terms. I think I should not translate them. [Left in Latin], the style of the book can be known, and the effectiveness of its author. [Here we omit four Latin paragraphs.]

Four Kinds of Infidels

Las Casas said there are four different kinds of infidels. The first kind are those who live in a Christian population and are subjects of Christian kings, i.e., Indians, and Moors who have long lived in Castile and are called *Mudejar Moors.* Since this kind live under the authority and jurisdiction of Christian kings they are subjects de jure and de facto, and thus are required to obey just laws imposed on them, to live according to those laws, as does every subject who lives under the jurisdiction of a prince or potentate.

The second kind of infidels are those who seize the land and lordship of Christians lawlessly by force, by violence. As the Turks have done, the Moors in Africa, the Holy Land, Hungary, in other regions and realms that one time were Christian. In this second, specific kind are found the Turks who fight against Christendom with all their might, killing, capturing those who belong to Christ. We see it every day. Their prime purpose is to block, to destroy the faith, the name of Christ, then to spread their wicked sect. These are properly so called enemies of the faith and Christendom. They are by all legality subject to the Church due to the damage, the harm they have done to the Christian people. Thought not subject in actual fact, they are so powerful.

The Church has four legal rights for making war against them. Firstly, *the right of recovery,* to recover the realms, the territory, they captured unjustly. Secondly, *the right of self-defense.* It is a right for even a private person to defend himself. Thirdly, *the right of punishment.* Any prince [whose land was seized] can make war in self-defense and recover what was captured from him. But he can go further and punish those who caused him damage. Fourthly, *the right of liberation,* to free Christians taken into captivity.

The third kind of infidel is the heretic, the apostate. Both are legally subject to the Church and the supreme pontiff and prelates spiritual. The legal basis is the solemn vow they made when taking holy baptism. In that vow, the one baptized states a promise to believe in God, three and one, and to keep to the faith of Jesus Christ. On that ground, the Church can justly punish them, can deprive them ipso jure and ipso facto of all temporal or spiritual goods, of their estates, their honors, their positions, can deprive them of royal or imperial title and authority, can apply many other penalties which civil and ecclesiastical law give over heretics and make them incapable of any jurisdiction. As a consequence, the kingdoms of heretics can be called kingless, and since it is like something without an authority over it, the pope can and has given such vacant realms to some Christian king who then takes them over and keeps them as his own.

The fourth distinct kind of infidel is the kind that controls no captured territory that was Christian at one time, who did not strip the Church of it by force, who never did the Church harm or hurt or any evil, who does not now intend to do so. This kind of infidel is not, nor was in centuries past, subject to Christian rule, was never a member of the Church de jure or de facto, not in any way at all. There are many nations of the world free in all these matters. Especially where one finds pagan, Gentile peoples whose lands are distant from Christian ones, lands they lived in long before others came. In sum, all those nations who do not and have never harmed Christendom. Christendom has no rights over such nations. (Cf. St. Paul in *1 Corinthians 5:* "We have no right to judge those who are outside us.") Christians instead must love such infidels as themselves, must try through teaching and good example to draw them, gain them for Christ [Gratian, "De Poenitentia," cap. "Charitas"—a garbled citation, *non sit.*]. Next, this kind of infidel has his own realms, lords, kings, authorities, the greater and the less, judges, magistrates, territories within which he can use his power legitimately, can use it freely.

Wars of Conquistadors Unjust

Given the above analysis, Las Casas draws the following conclusions as to the source, the root of all the bad will, the hatred, the horror that is a constant in the souls of the Spaniards, called conquistadors, in the Indies.

It is lawless, unjust, wicked, tyrannical, the war the conquistadors make on this fourth kind of infidel, with the putative purpose of the war being to subject people to the rule of Christians, so that way they are opened to receive the faith of Christ and Christian religion, or made to give up those impediments to belief that might exist. Padre Bartolomé de las Casas proves in two lengthy sections what kind of war that really is. Then he draws some corollaries, some conclusions from his proof, using argument, authority—divine and human—and cogent example, corollaries required by the truth he has established. He proves them the same way he proved his main point.

B. THE "ITINERARIO" SUMMARY
(From Alonso de la Peña Montenegro, bishop of Quito,
Itinerario para parochos de Indios, Madrid, 1668,
lib. 2, tract. 8, sect. 5. Captions added.)

Can the Church, can Christian princes in its name, use force to make infidels accept the faith?

The Only Way

The holy bishop of Chiapa, Don Fray Bartolomé de las Casas, dealt with this question in a scholarly way in an entire book he named *The Only Way of Calling. . . .* The book argues that under the impulse of Christ, the Head of the Church, the predestined are to be called together from every nation, every tribe on earth, so that no nation in the whole world should be excluded from, should be deprived of such a great gift of grace, the mercy of God. Then one must understand this as true of the tribes and nations of the New World, one must believe and affirm this. Christ, in the fullness of mercy, called them.

Rebuttal

Let painters portray the God of love however they want, now with crown, now without, now with mouth open, now mouth closed, now with golden arrows, now with lead ones, now with fire, now with rays. We still find in Luke 14 the most living portrait of Christ, the lover of souls anxiously in search of them. He is portrayed in the likeness of a human king who readied a great supper (a metaphor for the Church), invited many guests to it, and at the hour of eating sent his servants out (a metaphor for the prophets, the apostles, the masters, the preachers, the teachers, like Origen, Chrysostom, St. Jerome, St. Gregory, and Bede). St. Ambrose says that means Jews, Gentiles, heretics. The call to them was, "Everything is now ready." That meant that on God's part all was prepared, a creature had only to desire it to have eternal life. The Church was ready, the faith, sacraments, grace, God present on the altar table beckoning, summoning in the bread and wine become His Body and Blood, "Everything is now ready." But some of the invited excused themselves disrespectfully, some gave gross excuses. The king was angered. He ordered them excluded as unworthy. He ordered the poor invited, "Bring in the poor, the weak, the lame." The servants then reported, "We have done what you commanded, Lord, but there are still empty places." So the king said, "Go out through the squares, the streets, the sections of the city and compel them to come in until every place is taken." That is how great God's desire is that we come to His supper, His wedding feast: He orders people hauled in by force, dragged in, that is what the word compel means.

Four Kinds of Infidels

To understand this "compel," one must turn to the interpretations the Doctors of the Church provide on the subject. They differentiate between four kinds of infidels.

First kind, those who are vassals and thereby subjects of Christian princes, e.g., Jews and Moors who have lived long in Castile. They who are subjects of the Catholic kings are obliged to obey just laws imposed on them, and live in accord with those laws, the way any subject must obey those of the prince under whom he or she lives.

Second kind, those who hold land and rule taken against the law from Christians, by force, by violence. Such are Turks, the Moors in Africa and the Holy Land. Against them the Church has the right to make war, the right of recovery, in order to regain the territories Turks and Moors had seized and alienated unjustly. Next, there is the right of defense, and that is evident since even an individual is allowed such. There are further rights, the right to pursue and punish. Any prince is permitted war in self-defense and war to recover lost territory. He is also permitted to punish those who commit injustice against him, who do him harm.

Third kind of infidel, heretics, apostates. They are subjects of the Church, the supreme pontiff, and other prelates spiritual. The basis is the solemn vow these infidels made when taking holy baptism, a vow every baptized person makes, plus the promise to believe in God, three and one, and to hold to the faith of Christ. On this basis, the Church can punish them justly, depriving them ipso facto of all their temporal and spiritual goods, of their station, honors, dignities, and there are many other penalties which civil and ecclesiastical law apply to heretics. As a result the kingdoms of heretics can be declared vacant, as places that have no head. The pope can grant such places to Christian kings, for their occupancy, their possession as their own.

Fourth kind, different from the others, infidels who do not hold captured territory that one time was of the Church, who did not take territory from the Church, nor ever did harm to it at any time, nor injury, nor evil, who do not intend to do so now. Furthermore, they are not now subjects of Christian rule, nor were they so in the past, nor under any member of the Church, de jure or de facto, in any way. There are many such like nations in the world free of all these attributes. Especially if they are pagan Gentiles who hold territories far separate from those of the Christians, ones they occupied first before others, like the distant provinces of Dorado which stretch for more than eight hundred leagues as the crow flies and is populated by countless pagan Indians who have done no evil to any Christian prince, who have never even thought of Christians. And therefore all those nations who have not offended Christian rule or Christian religion have no relationship to Christendom. As St. Paul says, "It is not for us to judge those outside us." Instead, Christians are obliged to the love of them God commands, seeking them out, drawing them to the Church by teaching and good example without taking from them the land they live on or their liberty, and using no force to make them accept the faith.

Wars Against Fourth Kind Unjust

This is the teaching of Don Fray Bartolomé de las Casas. He draws the following conclusion to the entire work he wrote entitled *The Only Way of Calling.* . . . War made against infidels of this latter kind is lawless, unjust, perverse, tyrannical, war made so that through it such infidels may be subjected to the rule of Christians and that way be set up to accept the faith and Christian religion. Pope St. Gregory speaks against such war, forbids it in *Epist.* lib. 1, no. 9, #1, where he says, "It is a new and bizarre teaching that exacts faith by torture since Christ ordered His apostles to say [peace] first, wherever they went . . . 'your peace will return to you.' " And Gregory is cited again on this in cap. "Quid autem," 45 [Gratian, Dist. 45, cap. 1, Friedberg, 1:160]. Faith must not be induced by blows, by violence, by force, but rather by invitation, by kindness, by gentleness, by meekness, by good example, by peace, just as Christ commanded His apostles to do it when He made them caretakers of the entire world. The prophet King David said it clearly in Psalm 53, "I will offer to You freely, I will confess Your name, O Lord, how good it is!" Freely, willingly, spontaneously, with pleasure, with desire you are to offer victims on your altars, and abundant holocausts. That is never done well which is not done willingly and with desire. Thus no one must be forced to do things.

The preceding is confirmed by the customary practice of the Church. The Church has never wanted the Gentiles to come in dragged, forced. Clement III expressed it in cap. 9, "Sicut," *De Iudais*

[*Decretals,* lib. 5, tit. 6, cap. 9, Friedberg, 2:774], where he says: "We declare that no one should force unwilling Jews to baptism, or Jews refusing it." He gives the reason: "We do not think they have real faith in Christ who do not accept the baptism of Christians willingly, who are forced to it against their will." They are not really Christian who, without the will and wish for it, are force-baptized. God does not want conscript soldiers in his Church, God wants the willing, to whom He can then trust the battle.

The reason which strikes me as the strongest is found in the words which St. Dorotheus [of Gaza] said in *Doctrina,* no. 10 [*PG,* 88:1723–34]: "Our elders have taught that whatever the soul does against its will cannot last long." That which is done by force is violent and constraining, and it soon fails. Like a rock thrown up in the air. The force that comes from the hand that threw it is soon lost and the rock drops back to earth. God frees us, the saint says, from the state in which a man does not want to do anything, in which he must be obliged to do what he does! He will stay at it a very short time, will obey but briefly, will quickly quit his task. For that reason Julius III drew up a document, dated the ninth of June, 1551. It begins "Cum sicut accepimus." He forbids, under pain of suspension and a thousand ducat fine, anyone to baptize the children of Jews without their parents' consent. The baptism could be null in the opinion of some theologians. And besides, God wants willing sacrifices, offerings, in His Church, not forced ones, violent ones.

This is the opinion of St. Thomas in [*Summa Theologiae*], 2ª 2ᵃᵉ, q. 10. art. 8. An opinion most doctors follow. Solórzano cites them when dealing with this question in *De Iure Indiarum,* vol. 1, lib. 2, cap. 17 entire. There he proves the point by citing many authors, texts, arguments. I refer the reader there so he can benefit from the lucid expositions.

The Opposite View

We have now to respond to the arguments of the many people who hold the opposite view. They say no one can, by force of arms, make those accept the faith who are Gentiles and not subject to the jurisdiction, the power of the Church or Christian princes. Solórzano cites the many authors he finds—see *De Iure Indiarum,* vol. 1, lib. 2, cap. 18. They are of the opinion that religion, the Christian faith, must be accepted freely, spontaneously, as argued above, but this can be understood only of those who have the power to reason, those who have the capacity to weigh the truth, the precepts of God and nature. But the Indians are raw and barbaric, they do not reason, they have no mind to distinguish between good and evil, it is a waste of time to try to convince them with argument and lengthy teaching. So they assert, "One can use the rod, beating, on these barbarians for a time, one should, so they learn first what human is, then after, they will let in the light of gospel truth when it is preached to them."

The well-known Fray Luis de León based this view on the parable Christ Our Lord told in Luke, 14:16–23. He treats the matter, this great doctor, in his commentary on Abdyas [of Babylon], cap. ultimate, p. 661, where he says that those invited, those the king ordered his servants to drag into the banquet by force—*compelle entrare*—must be understood to mean the Indians. That is, the conversion of the New World, whose inhabitants live in forests and fields, they are beastly and cruel. And since God knows they are such wild people, and must hold commandments and culture of little worth, God allows violence to be used against them, so they will be open to faith. See St. Thomas, in *De signis ecclesiae Dei,* lib. 4, caps. 7, 8, and 9, Fray Thomas de Jesus, *De procuranda omnium gentium salute,* lib. 4., part. 1, cap. 1 [Antwerp, 1613], and Fray Juan de Torquemada, *Monarchia Indiana,* lib. 16, cap. 4. And St. Augustine gives the same impression in *Epist. 50,* "Ad Bonifacium." In it he gathers together the calls of the parable and says, "In those who are drawn first gently, obedience happens; in those who are forced, obedience is made to happen."

But here, as with the other texts and authorities Solórzano adduces, there is a reply, that force of arms can be used only *secondarily, indirectly,* to make infidels accept the faith, in a just war, intimidating them, that is what the parable proves. The other interpretation of obliging them unconditionally by force, by violence, is repugnant to the sacrament, so much so that the sacrament is null when someone accepts it out of fear, against their own will, and the one who applies the force is an accomplice in sacrilege. The doctors are in agreement on this, as in the canon "Majores," at "Item quaeritur," *De baptismo* [*Decretals,* lib. 3, tit. 42, cap. 3, Friedberg, 2:646, passage beginning "Item vero quaeritur"]. There the case is presented about Gentiles seeking of their own free wills to become Christians. They ought not to be admitted to baptism right away, but must be made to wait for a time and be instructed first in the obligations of the law of Jesus Christ which they wish to profess. "So they do not facilely revert to what they

spat out," as Antonio Ricciullo puts it in Tractatus *De iure personarum
extra ecclesiae gremium* [Rome, 1622], lib. 2, cap. 31. Others say this
also. For whoever makes a quick decision can quickly change purpose
and turn back to the filth of infidelity when they discover with time
that the obligations of Christians are greater than they first thought.

APPENDIX III:
FAME, LOSS, AND RECOVERY;
OUR RESTORATION

INTRODUCTORY NOTE

Here, we piece together for the first time the saga of the final MS of The Only Way *(A below): A direct witness reveals that Las Casas had many scribal copies made; apart from the printed tracts, he normally used this older method to distribute his works. Indirect testimony confirms that in the sixteenth and seventeenth centuries there were MS copies of "De unico modo" on both sides of the Atlantic, and the treatise was widely read by missionaries and discussed in publications on history and pastoral care. But for the eighteenth century, we have traced only a single MS of the last portion in Spain; and we find that in the political chaos of the nineteenth century all MS copies disappeared in Spain and Spanish America, and it became a "lost work." The rest is known. In 1886 a surviving MS was found in Oaxaca, and in 1942 it was at last published in Mexico as* Del único modo.

This Oaxaca MS is almost identical to the final [messed-up] academic version. So we conclude by explaining how we revised and arranged it, on the strength of all our evidence, into an earlier, more powerful version (B below). The process involved identifying and removing late scholastic additions that break the argument; supplying missing sections from summaries in Las Casas' other writings; and approximating the original form and size. A complete Chart, with the "Oaxaca MS" and "Our Restoration" in parallel columns, shows minutely how we rebuilt a readable text—verified by stylistic variations in the Latin of "De unico modo."

A. FINAL MS: DIFFUSION AND LOSS;
RECOVERY AND PUBLICATION

1. A widely read manuscript work. "De unico modo" was widely read and circulated in Las Casas' own lifetime and the following century, in the New World and the Old. But always in MS copies and mainly in monasteries. He himself had "printed in type" (en molde impreso) in 1552 only eight polemical tracts—small and large pamphlets for distribution at court and in the colonies. But he left instructions that his great *History of the Indies* should *not* appear in print until forty years after 1560—i.e., in 1600 (Pérez, *Inventario,* no. 296). All the rest of his writings were intentionally in manuscript and circulated in that form. He himself had handwritten copies of many made at San Gregorio, and presented them to royal councilors, the king, even the pope—and sent them overseas to correspondents in England and America.

After all, Las Casas was born in 1484, so in his youth most books were still reproduced by hand for private, monastic, and university libraries. Books were not only published in these two fashions, but they were usually in two different languages, the "vulgar" or common tongue for the large public, and Latin for the educated or a specialized group. His own Latin works are invariably those dealing with "subversive" subjects, specifically the powers and duties of kings. So *The Only Way* in all its versions, was a subversive Latin work intended for a select audience.

We have direct and indirect evidence of manuscript copies of "De unico modo" in Spain, New Spain, and South America, starting with Fray Antonio de Remesal's descriptive list of Las Casas' MS and printed works:

> [Then there is the] book, mentioned above, which he called *De unico vocationis modo.* It seems he had many copies made of it because I have seen four of them: the one that's in the College [of San Gregorio], the one I have, another in New Spain, and another in the possession of Licenciado Antonio Prieto de Villegas, priest of Mazaltenango on the Guatemalan coast, and all in the very same handwriting.
>
> (*Historia de Chyapa y Guatemala,* lib. 7, cap. 16, no. 5)

Other sources bear him out. Alonso de la Peña Montenegro, seventeenth-century bishop of Quito, Ecuador, also used a MS copy of the final version for the summary in his *Handbook* (cf. App. II above, last par. of Introductory Note)—thereby attesting to the diffusion of the work in South America. This *Itinerario para parochos de Indios* had seven editions between 1668 and 1771, done by different publishers in Madrid and Antwerp, so his chapter on Las Casas' "only way" was in circulation for more than a century. And of course, the final MS was copied and recopied, and passed from hand to hand, especially in Mexico City. For a seventeenth-century Franciscan friar there had been no need to explain his proposal that the missions of Alta California should be founded "according to the principles of Las Casas in *The Only Way*" (MS from Archivo General de México, on microfilm in the Bancroft Library).

2. *Its disappearance and recovery.* During the eighteenth century, however, the picture changed. We have traced but a single copy in 1784, from letters of Juan Bautista Muñoz, official historian of the Indies, to the Secretary for Indies Affairs. Muñoz—who had set up the Archives of the Indies in Seville and was scouring Spain for more documents—asked for *five volumes* of manuscript works by Las Casas, already in the Secretariat Library, as well as remaining Las Casas MS volumes left in San Gregorio. In two dovetailing accounts of an *untitled* Latin MS of 109 leaves, Muñoz clearly describes the *concluding portion* of "De unico modo," lib. I, for his notes correspond exactly to Remesal's and Peña's summaries of the ending, and to a reconstruction of the truncated Cap. 3!

Thus, from Muñoz' duplicating requests of January 18 and 20, here are the more detailed statements from each:

A treatise by Fray Bartolomé de las Casas, distinguishing various kinds of infidels—the term includes all those [who are far away *crossed out*] who do not hold the true faith of the Catholic church. (a) In it he tries to prove that it is not legal to subjugate them by force of arms, nor to compel them to accept Christianity. (This [argument] begins with [fol.] 81 and the heading: Corollarium incidentale 2^m.) (b)

      (a) RAH, Colección Muñoz, t. 119, fols. 127v–128.
      (b) AHN, Diversos, Docs. de Indias, num. 489.

Similarly, Remesal tells how Las Casas classifies the "four kinds of infidels," with the Indians as the fourth and blameless kind, and claims it is lawless and wicked for conquistadors to make war on them and subjugate them, allegedly so they will accept Christianity. And how Las Casas proves in two long sections what sort of war this really is, and draws some corollaries (App. II.A above). And Chapter Three of the surviving text begins with the "four kinds of infidels," explains that the Indians are the blameless kind, and ends with a declaration that wars to make them accept Christianity are unjust and illegal (Pérez, "Sobre la fecha y el lugar," note 51 on cross-references to Cap. 3 in the Oaxaca

MS). And Chapter Seven, on restitution, has indeed two long sections on the injustice of such wars, and the corollaries.

But Muñoz' letters are the last clue. He did receive the five Las Casas volumes, and a number are still in his collection, yet this treatise —Part Two of *De unico modo* (see above, App. I.C, sect. 1)—vanished without a trace. It was apparently *not* among his papers willed to the crown upon his death in 1799, nor among the works on the Indies transferred from the Secretariat Library to the Palace Library. Since twenty-two volumes out of 134 in the Muñoz Collection also vanished, all these MSS may have been carried off or scattered in the upheavals after the Napoleonic invasion of Spain. All MS copies of "De unico modo" in the New World also disappeared, perhaps with the anticlerical dismantling of monasteries during the Wars of Independence in the nineteenth century. By 1881, the Mexican historian Joaquín García Icazbalceta called *The Only Way* a lost work, and the bibliographer Robert Streit deemed its disappearance "a monumental loss for mission theory" (Hanke, 1942 Introduction, notes 1 and 3, and corresp. text).

Then in 1886, another Mexican savant, Nicolás León, discovered a surviving manuscript in the library of the State of Oaxaca. (See the annotated reprint of his announcement, *Noticia y descripción de un códice de ilmo. D. Fr. Bartolomé de las Casas,* Mexico City, 1967; also above, App. I.C, sect. 1, for a description of the MS.) Seals branded on the edges of the pages show that this codex had once belonged to the Library of the Oaxaca Dominicans. It may have been brought back to America in 1573 along with other writings from the end of Bishop Las Casas' life by his executor, Fray Alonso de la Vera Cruz, the most learned Augustinian in New Spain (cf. Wagner-Parish, ch. 19, notes 4, 13, 18 and corresp. text).

So we should thank Alonso de la Vera Cruz, Nicolás León, and Lewis Hanke, dean of modern Lascasistas, for saving *The Only Way* from oblivion. For at Hanke's initiative, this sole MS was brought to Mexico City and photocopied at the Museo Nacional; and later, the Ministry of Public Education helped arrange a bilingual (Latin and Spanish) first edition of the entire text by the Fondo de Cultura Económica in 1942, with an Introduction by Hanke. (See Preface above, 1st par. of note 3 and corresp. text.) In 1966, the manuscript was shown in an exhibition honoring the fourth centennial of Las Casas' death; and in 1975, the Fondo issued a paperback reprint of *Del único modo,* but without the annotated Latin text or the full Index.

Finally in 1990, a second complete edition of the Oaxaca MS appeared in Madrid as volume 2 of Las Casas' *Obras completas: De unico vocationis modo,* edited by Paulino Castañeda Delgado and Antonio García del Moral. The Latin text has copious footnotes to citations, all itemized in twenty-eight pages of Indices, and a graceful Spanish translation with thirty small-print pages of theological endnotes. Introductions are by Barreda, from studies by himself and Pérez (cf. Preface, note 2); Castañeda, on contemporary theory about evangelization by force; and García, on Las Casas' scholasticism and cogent thesis. The whole 633-page volume emphasizes the academic character of the work.

B. OUR RESTORATION: METHODOLOGY, CHART

1. Method: cutting, adding, arranging, captions. As mentioned in the Preface and explained in Appendix I.C, this surviving text is the truncated, stuffed, reorganized third version of a forceful and readable work. The opening chapters on Indian capacity have been lopped off for use elsewhere, warping the argument. The main central thesis, on peaceful conversion, is interrupted with masses of "proof" material, much of it incomprehensible or boring today. The concluding portion (in this penultimate draft) begins with a reference to the missing Cap. 3; and its last sections, on restitution, are not separate as in the final text. Apart from two meaningless captions, there are no headings of any kind in the 440 MS pages, nothing but chapter and section numbers.

Restoring *The Only Way* to its former sense and strength was imperative, and our efforts followed clear guidelines. Easiest was removal of the stuffing, especially the Aristotelian psychology—fifteen chapters on the mind and will, where the strong opening statement on the "one and only way instituted by Christ" is followed by an interval of deadly boredom. Much of the patristics was also easily eliminated. But one shining section from Chrysostom on the "ideal missionary" was emphatically retained: the passage may have been annotated by the saintly Fray Pedro de Córdoba himself as a model, since it gives a perfect portrait of Las Casas' mentor! Classical authors were dispensed with; and so were the apocryphal "Testament of the Twelve Patriarchs" and most of the apocryphal anecdotes on the apostles from Abdyas of Babylon. Brief citations of canon and Roman laws and their principal commentators were retained; but solid pages of legal references were removed without regret from the conclusion on restitution.

More difficult decisions were required to restore a suitable prologue on the capacity of the Indians. No attempt was made to rebuild in toto the four opening chapters on Indian qualifications, which Las Casas himself had removed. Rather, we chose entire pieces from his

other writings, dealing precisely with the points in the deteriorated
pages of the opening recapitulation in the Oaxaca manuscript—and
the parallel points of Remesal's intact and fuller recapitulation that
follows it verbatim. Most useful was Las Casas' own summary of Indian capacity from cap. 263 of his *Apologética Historia (Defense of
Indian Civilizations)*, a summary that was evidently once part of "De
unico modo." (See above, App. I.B, sect. 1, penultimate par.) But perhaps most interesting was Las Casas' own description of the Indians as
the blameless "fourth kind of infidel"—we took it from a late work,
containing a section on the four kinds of infidels, obviously written in
1538–1539, as it speaks of this fourth kind in connection with a *new*
papal bull, *Sublimis Deus* [1537] (*Opúsculos* [BAE 110], "Principio
II," 487b ff., esp. 489a–91a). The paragraph we chose corresponds
closely to the Zumárraga-Las Casas "Six Truths" presented in 1536,
which also insists on the innocence of the Indians as the "fourth kind of
infidel."

Lastly, we arranged the result so as to approximate the logical,
original form—primarily with simple captions. The missing opening
chapters had been restored briefly as a "Prologue," so we incompletely
restored the closing portion on restitution, by separating or moving out
the corresponding sections and labeling them "Epilogue." Again, we
sensibly divided the main central portion into its two clear parts: "True
Evangelization" as laid out in Chapter Five; "False Evangelization" as
laid out in Chapters Six and Seven. (Throughout, we placed Las Casas'
own summaries at the close of each division, instead of as a recapitulation at the start of the next; and we divided the sections by subject, not
into mere numbered section-lengths for several copyists, as in the MS.)
This obvious structure was completed by three minor internal shifts: a
gentle, Christological description was moved from the horrors-of-war
division to "True Evangelization." Likewise, the papal brief *Pastorale
officium* (condemning the enslavement or despoiling of Indians) was
taken from "True Evangelization," and the warning against harsh missionary methods was taken from the end of the manuscript, and both
were appropriately placed in the "False Evangelization" division.

Finally, in place of the absolutely meaningless table of contents of
the "Oaxaca fragment"—almost nothing but numbers—we inserted
[without brackets] clear headings that enable the reader to see at a
glance the dynamics of Las Casas' brilliant and moving treatise.

2. Chart explaining restored text. The following chart, with "Oaxaca MS" and "Our Restoration" in parallel columns, explains each
step of the process. As further validation of our revisions, Sullivan

found that they corresponded to stylistic variations in Las Casas' Latin, already noted by Millares Carlo (1942 Preface, penultimate par.): "passages of undoubted eloquence," *retained;* passages "loaded with the common jargon and stock phrases" [of argumentation], *removed.* Also the *length* of our "new restored version" comes closer to the powerful central version of *The Only Way*—a complete seventy-three-leaf text —than to the huge, truncated surviving MS of 220 leaves.

OAXACA MS	OUR RESTORATION
(Author and Title:)	*(Author and Title:)*
"**CHAPTER FIVE** of the first book [of the work] entitled 'The Only Way to Draw All People to a Living Faith,' by Fray Bartolomé de las Casas of the Order of Preachers, former Bishop of the Royal City of Chiapa in the New World of the Indies."	**Bartolomé de las Casas—** **THE ONLY WAY** **TO DRAW ALL PEOPLE TO A LIVING FAITH,** p. 59.
	PROLOGUE: HUMANITY OF THE INDIANS, pp. 63–67.
Four-paragraph summary of removed Chapters 1–4. (*Inadequate. Pages deteriorated, too fragmentary to use.*)	(*Filled in here on the basis of more complete summary by Remesal—see Appendix II.A— using brief corresponding extracts from* Apologética historia sumaria, Apologia [vs. Sepúlveda], "De unico modo" MS fragment. *and* Doce dudas —cf. Ed.'s notes 1–9.*)

**PART ONE. TRUE
EVANGELIZATION**

Section 1. Conclusion.
Statement of thesis.

**The Only Way:
Winning the Mind and Will,** pp.
68–69. (*Identical to MS*)

Syllogistic proof of thesis.
(*Scholastic method, classroom
material.*)

(*Omitted*)

Sections 2–14.
Aristotelian psychology,
apocryphal sacred history from
Abdyas of Babylon, etc.
(*Classroom addition.*)

(*Omitted*)

Sections 15–16, 17, 19.
Christ establishes only way! If not
accepted, depart. Risen Christ
still commands it.

By the Way of Christ, pp. 69–84.
(*Identical to MS*)

Section 18.
Patristic confirmation of above.
(*An interruption.*)

(*Omitted*)

Sections 20–21.
Apostles imitate Christ's way.
Data from Scripture, patristics.

By the Example of the Apostles,
pp. 84–94.

Sections 22–23.
Individual apostles, from
Scripture and Abdyas of Bablyon.

(*Omitted*)

**CHAPTER SIX
Sections 7–8.**
Christ's deeds for His
kingdom, a model for earthly
kings. (*Shifted from war
section to peace section, except
last two-page contradiction.*)

**Christ's Kingdom of Compassion
and Peace,** pp. 94–103.
(*Identical to MS; but part of sect.
8 is moved to between sects. 7
and 8.*)

Sections 24, 25.
Five traits of the ideal
missionary; more on fifth trait.
(*Drawn from Chrysostom, but
also a portrait of Fray Pedro de
Córdoba.*)

The Ideal Missionary, pp.
103–112.
(*Identical to MS*)

Sections 26–33.
Extensive quotations from the
fathers, examples from the saints,
and pious customs of the
Church. (*Classroom style.*)

(*Omitted*)

Section 34.
Minor Church decrees, *Sublimis
Deus,* and *Pastorale officium.*

**Papal Endorsement of Peaceful
Conversion,** pp. 112–116.
(*Only minor decrees and*
Sublimis Deus *identical to MS.*
Pastorale officium *shifted to end
of Part Two.*)

Sections 35–36.
Summary of entire Chapter Five.

(*Omitted; a shorter summary of
Part One substituted, identical to
first two paragraphs of Chapter
Six.*)

CHAPTER SIX

**PART TWO: FALSE
EVANGELIZATION**

Section 1.
The contrary way, the horrors of
war, creates aversion of mind
and will.

**The Opposite Way: Violating the
Mind and Will,** pp. 117–121.
(*Identical to MS, except
recapitulation.*)

Section 2.
Conquest and torture shatter
mind, will, and all human
feelings.

**Wars of Conversion Contradict
Human Way,** pp. 121–124
(*Identical to MS*)

Section 3.
Perpetration of such horrors contradicts Christ's life and teachings.

Wars Contradict Way of Christ, pp. 124–128.
(*Identical to MS plus two pages on contradiction, from end of sect. 8.*)

Sections 4–5.
Warriors are missionaries of evil.

Wars Contradict Way of Missioner, pp. 128–143.
(*Identical to MS*)

Section 6.
Christian conquest to convert is worse than Moorish conquest to convert.

Ways Contradict Way of Christian, pp. 143–151.
(*Identical to MS*)

Sections 7–8.

(*Shifted to Part One, center.*)

CHAPTER SEVEN
Section 6.
Missionaries sin gravely who use whips, chains, or prison to punish Indians for sins before or after conversion. (*Misplaced in Oaxaca MS at close of Chapter Seven, section is shifted here for sense and symmetry.*)

The Brutal Missionary, pp. 151–156.
(*Identical to MS; now contrasts with The Ideal Missionary. N.B. Final paragraph of this section rightly ends Epilogue below.*)

CHAPTER FIVE
Section 34.
Only the brief *Pastorale officium*. (*Shifted from earlier section where it followed Sublimis Deus.*)

Papal Condemnation of Armed Oppression, pp. 156–157.
(*Identical to MS. This brief is put here for symmetry in the restoration. See explanation preceding this chart.*)

CHAPTER SEVEN

EPILOGUE:
RESTORATION
OF THE INDIANS

Lead-in paragraph announcing conclusion and corollary requirements.

Restitution Required from All, because:
(*Caption substitutes for lead-in paragraph.*)

Section 1. First Conclusion and Section 2 up to first corollary. Conclusion in four parts, each supported by references to previous chapters, or citations of Scripture, patristics, or law.

Wars for Conversion Are Mindless and Unjust, pp. 158–164. (*Identical to MS*)

Rest of Section 2–Section 3. The first corollary.

Wars for Conversion Are Mortal Sin, pp. 164–171. (*Identical to MS*)

Sections 4–5. The second corollary.

Therefore the Guilty Must Make Restoration. pp. 171–182. (*Identical to MS*)

Section 6. Only last paragraph. (*Entire section is now next to last in Part Two.*)

Concluding paragraph of treatise. (*Identical to MS*)

BIBLIOGRAPHY

I. MANUSCRIPTS OF "THE ONLY WAY"

Casas, Bartolomé de las. "De cura habenda regibus Hispaniarum circa orbem Indiarum, et [*sic:* sc.] De unico vocationis modo omnium gentium ad veram religionem" ("How the Kings of Spain Must Care for the World of the Indies: *viz.,* [by] The Only Way of Calling All People to a Living Faith"), 73 fols. Lost MS of second version. Cf. App. I.C, final summary; App. I.B, sect. 2.

——. "De unico trahendi modo universas gentes ad veram religionem" ("The Only Way to Draw All People to a Living Faith"). Lost MS of first version. See App. I.C, final summary; App. I.A, sect. 3.

——. "De unico vocationis modo omnium gentium ad veram religionem" ("The Only Way of Calling All People to a Living Faith"), 220 fols. Surviving MS of final version, penultimate draft of Part One, caps. 5, 6 and 7. A scribal copy preserved in the Biblioteca Pública del Estado de Oaxaca (call no. $A^8 Z^8 A2^8 D2^8 E2^6$). Cf. App. 1.C, sect. 1 and final summary. Printed entire, 1st edition (from a photocopy in the Museo Nacional, Mexico City) in Bartolomé de las Casas, *Del único modo,* see below, *II. Las Casas' Writings.*

——. "De unico vocationis modo omnium gentium ad veram religionem," 220 fols. Surviving MS same as foregoing. Printed entire, 2nd edition (from a microfilm of the photocopy in the Biblioteca Pública del Estado de México, D.F., call no. Registro 1384, Estante 22, Cajón 152, Orden 18) in Bartolomé de las Casas, *De unico vocationis modo,* vol. 2 of his *Obras Completas,* see below, *II. Las Casas' Writings.*

————. "De unico vocationis modo omnium gentium ad veram religionem," 109 fols. Lost MS of cap. 3, from penultimate draft of final version of Part One. Cf. App. III.A, sect. 2; and App. I.C, sect. 1, penultimate par. See below, Muñoz.

Herrera, Antonio de. *Libros y papeles que dejó escritos Fr. Bartolomé de las Casas, Obispo de Chiapa, y que se hallaron en el colegio de San Gregorio de Valladolid.* Holograph MS signed. *DIE*, 8 (1846): 557–59, printed from the original MS then in the possession of Don Pedro Sainz de Baranda. In this inventory of Las Casas' papers, Herrera describes the MS of the second version of *De único modo,* see above, Bartolomé de las Casas, "De cura habenda regibus Hispaniarum. . . ." (This MS concludes with Hererra's request for the papers and the delivery documents.)

León, Nicolás. *Noticia y descripción de un códice de Ilmo. D. Fr. Bartolomé de las Casas,* ed. by Andrés Henestrosa. Mexico: Técnica Gráfica, 1976. Annotated reprint of his 1889 notice in *Anales del Museo Michoacano,* 2:177–79. This is León's announcement of the discovery of the extant MS of *De unico modo.*

Muñoz, Juan Bautista. "Razón de los manuscritos del Obispo Don Fr. Bartolomé de las Casas que en 5 tom. fol. se hallan en la Secretaria del Despacho Universal de Indias." Holograph MS, signed, Madrid, Jan. 18, 1784. In Real Academia de la Historia (RAH), Madrid, Colección Muñoz, vol. 119, fols. 127–128v. For Tom. 3, he describes an untitled 109 fol. tract that corresponds exactly to the missing cap. 3. of *De unico modo,* final version, penultimate draft.

————. "Razón de los Manuscritos del Obispo Don Fr. Bartolomé de las Casas, que en 5 tom. fol . . ." Holograph ms. signed. Archivo Histórico Nacional (AHN), Madrid, Sección de Diversos, Documentos de Indias, no. 489. Two fols., s.n. The same heading as the MS above, but different descriptions, followed by a request to Don Juan de Gálvez for these papers. This second description of Tom. 3 contributes additional details of the MS fragment of *The Only Way* which corresponds to cap. 3.

II. LAS CASAS' WRITINGS

Casas, Bartolomé de las. *Apologética Historia Sumaria quanto a las cualidades, dispusición, descripción, cielo y suelo destas tierras, y condiciones naturales, policías, repúblicas, manera de vivir e costumbres de las gentes destas Indias Occidentales y Meridionales cuyo imperio soberano pertenece a los Reyes de Castilla* (*Defense of the Indian Civilizations*), Ed. by Edmundo O'Gorman. 2 vols. Mexico City: Universidad Nacional Autónoma de México, Instituto de Investigaciones Históricas, 1967.

————. *Apologia* [*adversus Sepúlvedam*]. In Juan Ginés de Sepúlveda/ Fray Bartolomé de las Casas, *Apologia,* ed., introd., and Spanish trans. by Angel Losada, appending full facsimiles of Latin texts. Madrid: Editora Nacional, 1975.

————. *Del único modo de atraer a todos los pueblos a la verdadera religion.* Introduction by Lewis U. Hanke, Preface and transcription of Latin text by Agustín Millares Carlo, Spanish trans. by Antenógenes Santamaría, notes on citations, and index. Mexico City: Fondo de Cultura Económica, 1942; reprint without Latin text or index, as the Fondo's Colección Popular, no. 137, 1975.

————. *De l'unique manière d'evangéliser le monde entier.* Preface and French translation of the central thesis of the work by Marianne Mahn-Lot from the Spanish of the foregoing edition. Paris: Cerf, 1990.

————. *De regia potestate o derecho de autodeterminación.* Crit. ed. by Luciano Pereña, José Manuel Pérez-Prendes, Vidal Abril, and Joaquín Azcarraga; Latin text, Spanish trans. (*Corpus Hispanorum de Pace,* vol. 8.) Madrid: Consejo Superior de Investigaciones Científicas, 1969.

————. *De unico vocationis modo.* vol. 2 of Las Casas' *Obras completas.* Ed. by Paulino Castañeda Delgado and Antonio García del Moral. Introds. by both eds. and Jesús Angel Barreda, transcription of Latin text, with Spanish translation facing, discursive notes, bibliography, indices of citations. Madrid: Alianza Editorial, 1990.

————. *Diario del primer y tercer viaje de Cristóbal Colón.* vol. 14 of Las Casas *Obras completas.* Critical ed. by Consuelo Varela includes: full introduction; new transcriptions with apparatus criticus and notes; and appendices. Madrid: Alianza Editorial, 1989.

————. *Historia de las Indias.* Introduction by Lewis Hanke, transcription and index by Agustín Millares Carlo. 3 vols. Mexico City: Fondo de Cultura Económica, 1951.

————. "La exención o la damnación!" Spanish trans. and 1st and critical ed. of his "De exemptione sive damnatione." In Parish with Weidman, *Las Casas en México.* See below *IV. Modern Studies.*

————. *Las Casas' Life of Columbus.* Trans. by Francis Patrick Sullivan, introduction by Rolena Adorno. Berkeley: University of California Press, 1992 (in preparation).

————. *Las Casas' Tracts for the Indians.* Vol. 1. *For New Laws.* Trans. by Francis Patrick Sullivan, introduction by Helen Rand Parish. Kansas City: Sheed & Ward, 1992 (in press).

————. *Los tesoros del Perú.* Latin text of *De Thesauris qui reperiuntur in sepulcris Indiorum* (*The Treasures in the Inca Tombs*). Ed. by Angel Losada with a Spanish trans. Madrid: Consejo Superior de Investigaciones Científicas, 1958. [Chapter 36, missing from this text, is printed in Las Casas' *De Regia Potestate,* Appendix 12.]

————. *Opúsculos, cartas y memoriales.* Ed. by Juan Pérez de Tudela Bueso, vol. 5 of Las Casas' *Obras escogidas* (Biblioteca de Autores Españoles, vol. 110). Madrid: Ediciones Atlas, 1958. Includes *Entre los remedios* (*Twenty Reasons*), doc. 11; *Brevísima relación de la destruición de las Indias* (*Decimation of the Indians*), doc. 14; *Tratado sobre los indios que se han hecho esclavos* (*Against Enslavement of Indians*), doc. 28; "Carta al maestro fray Bartolomé Carranza de Miranda," doc. 37; *Tratado de las doce dudas* (*Twelve Doubts on the Conquest of Peru*), doc. 50.

————. *Tratados.* Preface by Lewis Hanke, Introduction by Manuel Giménez Fernández, transcription by Juan Pérez de Tudela Bueso, and trans. of Latin material by Agustín Millares Carlo and Rafael Moreno, 2 vols. Mexico City & Buenos Aires: Fondo de Cultura Económica, 1965. With complete facing facsimiles of the eight tracts Las Casas himself had printed in Seville in 1552–1553.

Colón, Cristóbal [Christopher Columbus]. *Libro copiador.* See below, *IV. Modern Studies:* Rumeu de Armas. *Libro copiador.*

III. ANCIENT WRITERS; DOCUMENT COLLECTIONS

Abdyas of Babylon [pseudonym]. *Historia apostolica,* Basle: Wolfgang Lazius, 1551.

Cepeda, Gabriel de. *Historia de la milagrosa y venerabile imagen de Nuestra Señora de Atocha, patrona de Madrid: discúrrese sobre su antiguedad origen y prodigios,* etc. Madrid: Imprenta Real, 1670.

Dávila Padilla, Agustín. *Historia de la fundación y discurso de la Provincia de Santiago de México de la Orden de Predicadores, por las vidas de sus varones insignes y casos notables de Nueva España.* Madrid: Pedro Madrigal, 1596.

DIE: Colección de documentos inéditos para la historia de España. Madrid: Impr. de M. Ginesta. Vol. 8, 1846; vol. 13, 1848.

DII: Colección de documentos inéditos, relativos al descubrimiento, conquista y organización de las antíguas possessiones españolas de América y Oceanía, sacados de los archivos del reino, y muy especialmente del de Indias (Documentos inéditos de Indias). Madrid: Impr. de Manuel B. de Quirós, vol. 1, 1864.

Konetzke, Richard, comp., *Colección de documentos para la historia de la formación social de hispanoamérica 1493–1810.* Vol. 1, 1493–1592. Madrid: Consejo Superior de Investicaciones Cientificas, 1953.

López de Gómara, Francisco. *Hispania Victrix: Primera y segunda parte de la Historia General de Indias.* Biblioteca de Autores Española, 22 (1852): 155–355.

Parecer de Yucay: "Copia de carta . . . donde se trata el verdadero y legítimo dominio de los Reyes de España sobre el Perú, y se impugna la opinión del Padre Fr. Bartolomé de las Casas." *DIE* 13 (1848) 425–69. Recent critical ed.: "Anónimo de Yucay (1571): Dominio de los Yngas en el Perú del que Su Magestad tiene en dichos reinos." Introduction and transcription by Josyane Chinese from MS no. 9442, Biblioteca Nacional, Madrid. *Historia y Cultura* (Organo del Museo Nacional de Historia, Lima) 4 (1970): 97–152.

Peña Montenegro, Alonso de la. *Itinerario para parochos de Indios.* Madrid: Joseph Fernández de Buendía, 1668.

Remesal, Antonio de. *Historia de la Provincia de San Vicente de Chyapa y Guatemala de la Orden de Sancto Domingo,* Madrid: Francisco de Angulo, 1619 [1620].

Solórzano Pereira, Juan de. *De Indiarum iure,* Madrid: Tipografía de Francisco Martínez, 1629.

IV. MODERN STUDIES

André-Vincent, Philippe. *Bartolomé de las Casas, prophète du nouveau monde.* Foreword by André Saint-Lu. Paris: Tallandier, 1980.

Barreda, Jesús Angel. *Ideología y pastoral misionera en Bartolomé de las Casas, O.P.* Madrid: Instituto Pontificio de Teología, 1981.

Bataillon, Marcel. "Las Casas, un profeta?" *Revista de Occidente,* 47, no. 141 (Madrid, Dec. 1974): 279–91.

———. "La Vera Paz." In his *Etudes sur Bartolomé de las Casas.* Paris (1965): 137–202.

———. "Zumárraga, reformador del clero seglar: una carta inédita del primer obispo de México." *Historia méxicana* 3 (Mexico City, 1953): 1–10.

Batllori, Miguel. "Las ideas de las Casas en la Italia del siglo XVII: Turin y Venecia como centros de difusión." *Estudios sobre Fray Bartolomé de las Casas.* Seville (1974): 303–17.

Cantù, Francesca. "Per un rinnovamento della coscienza pastorale del cinquecento: il vescovo Bartolomé de las Casas ed il problema indiano." Extract from *Annuario del Istituto Storico Italiano per* l'età moderna e cotemporanea (vols. 25–26, 1973–74), Rome, 1976.

Carande, Ramón Thobar. Carlos V y sus banqueros. 2 vols. Madrid: Sociedad de Estudios y Publicaciones, 1965, 1967.

Castañeda Delgado, Paulino. "Los métodos missionales en América: Evangelización pura o coacción?" In Estudios sobre Fray Bartolomé de las Casas. Seville: Universidad de Sevilla, 1974, 123–89.

Dussel, Enrique. "Lascasian Perspectives from Medellín and Puebla." Unpublished paper given at the Quincentennial Symposium, "Las Casas Lives Today," Berkeley, Jan. 22, 1985.

Giménez Fernández, Manuel. Bartolomé de las Casas: vol. I. Delegado de Cisneros para la reformación de las Indias, 1516–1517; vol. II. Capellán de S.M. Carlos I, poblador de Cumaná, 1517–1523. Seville: Escuela de Estudios Hispanoamericanos, 1953–1960, 2nd ed., 1984.

———. "La juventud en Sevilla de Bartolomé de las Casas, 1474 [sic]-1502." Miscelánea de estudios dedicados al Doctor Fernando Ortiz. Havana, 1956, 2:670–717.

Goldwert, Marvin. "La lucha por la perpetuidad de las encomiendas en el Perú virreinal." Revista histórica. Peru, 22 (1955–1956): 36–60, and 23 (1957–1958): 207–45.

Gómez Canedo, Lino. "Bartolomé de las Casas y sus amigos franciscanos." In Libro Jubilar de Emetrio S. Santovenia. Havana, 1957: 75–84.

Gutiérrez, Gustavo. Dios o el oro en las Indias (siglo XVI). Lima: Instituto Bartolomé de las Casas y Centro de Estudios y Publicaciones (CEP), 1989.

Hanke, Lewis. La lucha por la justicia en la conquista de América. Buenos Aires: Editorial Sudaméricana, 1949.

Hanke, Lewis, and Manuel Giménez Fernández. Bartolomé de las Casas, 1474 [sic]-1566: Bibliografia crítica y cuerpo de materiales para el estudio de su vida, escritos, actuacion, y polé micas que *suscitaron durante quatro siglos.* Santiago de Chile: Fondo Histórico y Biliográfico José Toribio Medina, 1954.

Heschel, Abraham. *The Prophets.* New York: Harper & Row, 1962.

Keen, Benjamin. "Approaches to Las Casas, 1535–1970." Introduction to Juan Friede and Benjamin Keen, *Bartolomé de las Casas in History: Toward an Understanding of the Man and his Work.* DeKalb: Northern Illinois University Press, 1971: 3–63.

Larios Ramos, Antonio. "Evangelisación y combate por la justicia. Colloquio de Toulouse (25–28 Oct. 1984) sobre Bartolomé de las Casas," *Communio* 18 (1985): 127–52. Papers on themes related to Las Casas' *Only Way* were presented by Philippe André-Vincent, Niceto Blazquez, Lorenzo Galmes, Marianne Mahn-Lot, Raymond Marcus, Alian Milhou, and Monique Mustapha.

Lohmann Villena, Guillermo. "La restitución por conquistadores y encomenderos: un aspecto de la incidencia lascasiana en el Perú." In *Anuario de estudios Américanos* 23, Seville, 1966: 21–89.

Losada, Angel. "La doctrina de Las Casas y su impacto en la Illustración francesa: Voltaire, Rousseau . . ." In *En el Quinto Centenario de Bartolomé de las Casas.* Madrid: Ediciones Cultura Hispánica, Instituto de cooperación Iberoaméricanas, 1986.

Milhou, Alain. "Prophétisme et critique du système seigneurial et des valeurs aristocratiques chez Las Casas." *Mélanges de la Bibliothèque Espagnole, Paris, 1977–1978.* Madrid: Ministero de Asuntos Exteriores, 1982.

Neal, Marie Augusta. *The Just Demands of the Poor: Essays in Socio-theology.* New York: Paulist Press, 1987.

Otte, Enrique. "La flota de Diego Colón: españoles y genoveses en el comercio transatlántico de 1509." *Revista de Indias* 24 (1964): 475–503.

———. *Las perlas del Caribe.* Caracas: Fundación John Boulton, 1977.

———. "Los Jerónimos y el tráfico humano en el Caribe: una rectificación." *Anuario de Estudios Américanos* 32 (1975): 187–204.

Parish, Helen Rand. *Las Casas as a Bishop: A new interpretation based on his holograph petition in the Hans P. Kraus Collection of Hispanic American Manuscripts in the Library of Congress.* Washington: Library of Congress, 1980.

———. *Las Casas: The Untold Story.* Berkeley: University of California Press, 1992 (in preparation).

———. *The Royal File on the administration of the Indians.* Washington: Library of Congress, 1992 (in press).

See Wagner, Henry R. and Helen Rand Parish.

Parish, Helen Rand, with Harold E. Weidman. "The Correct Birthdate of Bartolomé de las Casas." *Hispanic American Historical Review* 56 (1976): 385–403.

———. *Las Casas en México: Historia y obra desconocidas.* Mexico City: Fondo de Cultura Económica, 1992 (in press).

Pennington, Kenneth. "Bartolomé de las Casas and the Tradition of Medieval Law." *Church History* 39 (1970): 147–61.

Pérez Fernández, Isacio. *Bartolomé de las Casas ¿contra los negros? (Revisión de una leyenda.)* Madrid: Editorial Mundo Negro, and Mexico City: Ediciones Esquila, 1991.

———. *Cronología documentada de los viajes, estancias y actuaciones de Fray Bartolomé de las Casas.* Bayamón. Puerto Rico: Centro de Estudios de los Dominicos del Caríbe (CEDOC). Universidad Central de Bayamon, 1984.

———. "El perfil profético del Padre Las Casas." *Studium* 15 (Madrid, 1975): 281–359.

———. *Inventario documentado de los escritos de Fray Bartolomé de las Casas.* Revised by Helen Rand Parish. Bayamón, Puerto Rico: Centro de Estudios de los Dominicos del Caríbe (CEDOC), 1981.

————. "La fidelidad del Padre Las Casas a su carisma profético." *Studium* 16 (Madrid, 1976): 65–109.

————. "Sobre la fecha y el lugar de redacción del 'primer libro' de Fray Bartolomé de las Casas: 'De único vocationis modo omnium gentium ad veram religionem.' " *Ciencia Tomista* 105 (1978): 125–43.

Quintana, Manuel Josef. *Fray Bartolomé de las Casas.* In *Vidas de españoles célebres.* Madrid: Imprenta de D. M. de Burgos, 3 (1833): 255–510.

Ramos, Demetrio. "El P. Córdoba y las Casas en el plan de conquista pacifica de Tierra Firme." *Boletin Americanista* 1 (Madrid, 1959): 175–210.

Ricard, Robert. *The Spiritual Conquest of Mexico* [Paris, 1933], trans. by Lesley Byrd Simpson. Berkeley: University of California Press, 1966.

Rodríguez Valencia, Vicente. "Isabel la Católica y la libertad de los indios de América: Devolución de los esclavos." *Anthologica Annua* 24–25, Rome, 1977–78.

Rubio, Vicente. "Una carta inédita de Fray Pedro de Córdoba, O.P." *Communio* 1 (Seville, 1980): 411–25.

Ruiz, Enrique. "Bartolomé de las Casas y la justicia en las Indias—De único vocationis modo omnium gentium ad veram religionem." *Ciencia Tomista* 101 (1974): 351–410.

Rumeu de Armas, Antonio. *Hernando Colón, historiador del descubrimiento de América.* Madrid: Instituto de Cultura Hispánica, 1973.

————. *Libro copiador de Cristóbal Colón: Correspondencia inédita con los Reyes Católicos sobre los viajes a America.* vol. 1. Estudio historico-critico y edicion. (Colección Tabula Americae, vol. 8.) Madrid: Ministerio de Cultura; Testimonio, Compañia Editorial, 1989.

Saint-Lu, André. *La Vera Paz, esprit evangélique et colonisation.* Paris: Centre de Recherches Hispaniques, 1968.

Serrano y Sanz, Manuel. *Origenes de la dominación española en América.* Vol. 1 (Nueva Biblioteca de Autores Españoles, vol. 25). Madrid, 1918.

Soria, Carlos. "Fray Bartolomé de las Casas, historiador, humanista, o profeta?" *Ciencia Tomista* 101 (1974): 411–26.

Tellechea Idigoras, José Ignacio. "Bartolomé de las Casas y Bartolomé Carranza de Miranda." *Scriptorium Victoriense* 6 (1959): 7–34.

Ulloa, Daniel. *Los predicadores divididos.* Mexico City: El Colegio de México, 1977.

Varela, Consuelo. See above, *II. Las Casas' Writings:* Casas, Bartolomé de las. *Diario del primer y tercer viaje.*

Wagner, Henry R. and Helen Rand Parish. *The Life and Writings of Bartolomé de las Casas.* Albuquerque: University of New Mexico Press, 1967.

Zavala, Silvio. *La encomienda indiana,* 2nd ed. Mexico City: Editorial Porrúa, 1973.

INDEX*

---

* Las Casas' cits. are indicated by asterisks. See below, *Only Way, The:* **Proof texts,**
for a complete chart.